Easy-to-Follow Indian Vegetarian Cookbook for Beginners:

250 Healthy and Tasty Recipes from India. Indian Vegetarian Food.

by

Noah White

Copyright © [Noah White]

All rights reserved. No part of this guide may be reproduced in any form without permission in writing from the publisher except in the case of brief quotations embodied in critical articles or reviews.

Table of Contents

Introduction 12

Chapter 1 Breakfast 16

Broken Wheat Upma 16

Coconut Dosa 16

North Indian Vegetable Pulao 17

Bread Upma 18

Vermicelli Upma 18

Semolina Dosa 19

Oats Dosa 20

Potato Paratha 21

Cottage Cheese Paratha 21

No Yeast Appam 22

Pongal Breakfast 23

Poori Bhaji 24

Fenugreek Leaves Paratha 24

Spinach Paratha 25

Rice Batter Dosa 26

Masala Dosa 26

Finger Millet Dosa 28

Set Dosa 28

Mysore Masala Dosa 29

Wheat Dosa 30

Cheese Dosa 31

Butter Roast Dosa 32

Yogurt Dosa 32

Idli-South Indian Style 33

Instant Semolina Idli 33

Chapter 2 Snacks 35

Vegetable Pancake 35

Crispy Vegetable Pakoras 35

Spinach Pakora 36

Spicy Corn Salad 37

Vegetable Samosa 37

Roasted Caramelized Fox Nuts 38

Cauliflower Fritters 38

Coconut Fudge 39

Indian Savory Crackers 40

Corn Fritters 40

Spicy Snack 41

Potato Patty 41

Masala Vada 42

Gram Flour Dhokla 43

Vegetable Cutlet 44

Mushroom Cutlet 45

Cottage Cheese Cutlet 46

Vegetable Kabab 46

Crispy Cauliflower Manchurian 47

Black Gram Fritters 48

Dry Chili Paneer 49

Easy Cottage Cheese Tikka in a Pan 50

Instant Semolina Dhokla 51

Cauliflower Manchurian Dry 52

Spinach Kabab 53

Chapter 3 Salads 55

Vegetable Salad 55

Tropical Fruit Salad 55

Sprout Salad 56

Corn Salad 56

Potato Salad 57

Avocado Salad 58

Yellow Lentil & Split Chickpeas Salad 58

Onion, Tomato & Cucumber Salad 59

Chery Tomato Salad 59

Carrot Salad 60

Bean Sprout & Bell Pepper Salad 60

Beetroot and Carrot Salad 61

Chickpea Salad 62

Fruit & Vegetable Salad 62

Potato Herb Salad 63

Cucumber Salad 63

Mango Salad 64

Watermelon and Mint Salad 64

Onion Ring Salad 65

Potato and Pomegranate Salad 65

Roasted Mushroom and Bell Pepper Salad 66

Spinach and Paneer Cheese Salad 66

Tomato and Lettuce Salad 66

Tomato Basil and Feta Cheese Salad 67

Cabbage Salad 67

Chapter 4 Stew/Soups 69

White Pumpkin Stew 69

Sambar 69

Red Lentils and Clarified Butter Soup 70

Green Gram Soup 71

Carrot Soup 71

Tomato Soup 72

Vegetable Soup 72

Corn Soup 73

Spinach Soup 74

Mushroom Soup 74

Broccoli Soup 75

Hot and Sour Soup 76

Pumpkin Soup 76

Lemon Coriander Soup 77

Creamy Corn Veg Soup 78

Vegetable Stew 78

Vegetable Stew South Indian Style 79

Malabar Vegetable Stew 79

Mughal Vegetable Stew 80

Panjabi Kadhi 81

Dal Makhani 81

Split Chickpeas Stew 82

Spiced Red Lentil Stew 83

Spring Onion Soup 83

Chapter 5 Main Meals 85

Vegan Cheesy Flatbread 85

Carrot Chickpea Curry 85

Rice and Butter Cauliflower 86

Rice and Cauliflower Lentil Curry 87

Vegetable Biriyani with Baked Tofu 87

Garlic Naan 89

Palak Paneer 89

Potato and Cauliflower Spice Mix 90

Black Chickpeas with Potato 90

Ghee Rice 91

Mint Rice 92

Rice Flour Bread 93

Tomato Broth 93

Bell Pepper Rice 94

Spicy Veg Pulao 95

Vegetable Pulao 96

Indian Vegetable Roll 97

Biriyani Rice 98

Mango Rice 98

Spinach Paratha 99

Mix Vegetable Paratha 100

Corn Pulao 100

Sweet Corn Fried Rice 101
Poori 102
Coconut Milk Pulao 102
Paneer Pulao 103
Skillet Pulao 104
Green Peas Pulao 105
Carrot Pulao 106
Black Eyed Peas Pulao 106
Coconut Rice 107
Mint Rice 108
Cabbage Rice 109
Fenugreek Leaves Rice 110
Potato-Fenugreek Leaves Paratha 110
Potato Rice 111
Yogurt Rice 112
Sweet Rice Pulao 112
South Indian Sour Cream Rice 113
Split Chickpeas Pulao 114
Lemon Millet 115
Pineapple Fried Rice 116
Curry Leaves Rice 116
Carrot Rice 117
Lentil Khichdi 118
Khichdi with Tapioca Pearls 119
Kashmiri Pulao 119
Beetroot Rice 120
Cabbage Paratha 121
Coconut Milk Rice 122

Chapter 6 Rice & Grains 123
Jeera (Cumin) Rice 123
Yogurt Rice 123
Lemon Rice 124

Onion Rice 124

Garlic Rice 125

Tomato Rice 126

Lentil Rice (Khichdi) 126

Veg Spicy Khichdi 127

Oats Lentil Khichdi 128

Rasam Rice 129

Eggplant Rice 130

Veg Biriyani 130

Vegetable Fried Rice 132

Peanut Rice 133

Red Kidney Beans rice 134

Collard Green Lemon Rice 135

Mixed Vegetable Rice 135

Saffron Rice 136

Masala Rice 137

Bell Pepper Rice 138

Steamed Rice 139

Clarified Butter Rice with Shallots 139

Mushroom Biriyani 140

Plain Biriyani 141

Tamarind Rice 142

Chapter 7 Pasta & Noodles 144

Masala Pasta 144

Indian Style Macaroni 145

White Sauce Pasta 145

Pasta Salad with Vegetables 146

Creamy Mushroom Veg Pasta 147

Cheese Pasta with Vegetables 147

Garlic Spaghetti Pasta 148

Whole Wheat Spaghetti Pasta with Vegetables 149

Spring Onion and Bell Pepper Pasta 150

Chickpea Pasta 150

Herb Pasta 152

Veg Hakka Noodles 152

Noodles with Vegetables 153

Tangy Bell Pepper Noodles 154

Quick Masala Noodles 155

Broccoli and Baby Corn Noodles 155

Noodle Basket with Veg Stir Fry 156

Veg Thai Pad, Indian Style Noodles 157

Baked Noodles with Spinach and Yogurt 158

Crispy Fried Noodles 159

Indian Rice Noodles 159

Chapati Masala Noodles 160

Garlic Noodles 160

Hakka Mushroom and Rice Noodles 161

Chapter 8 Beans, Soy, Legumes 163

Black-Eyed Beans Sabzi 163

Black-Eyed Mixed Vegetable Salad..163

Soy Kurma 164

Mashed Green Gram Masala 164

French Beans and Carrot Soup 165

South Indian Soy Curry 166

Vegan Red Kidney Beans Curry 167

Black-Eyed Beans and Sprouted Green Gram Salad 167

Soybean Sindh Style Curry 168

Soy Chunks Curry...168

Butter Beans Masala Curry 169

Instant Pot Lentils Fry 170

Goan Dry Peas Curry 171

Yellow Cucumber and Lentils 172

Beans Masala Dry Fry 173

Potato Beans...173

Sautéed Green Beans 174

Beans Patolli Vapid 174

Beans Thoran 175

Ghar Ki Bhaji 176

Mixed Kathol 176

Instant Pot Lentil Bafla 177

Spinach and Lentil Gravy 178

Indian Mixed Beans Curry 179

Instant Pot Green Coriander and Chickpeas Masala 180

Chapter 9 Drinks 182

Lemonade 182

Cumin Drink 182

Lassie 183

Buttermilk 183

Rooh Afza 184

Cardamom Saffron Drinks 184

Mango Drinks 184

Lemon Squash 185

Vetiver Syrup 185

Jackfruit Milkshake 186

Chapter 10 Desserts 187

Burfi with Chickpea Flour 187

Dairy Free Rasmalai 187

Chickpea Flour Ladoo 188

Cheese Cake 189

Creamy Rice Dessert 190

Vermicelli Dessert 190

Tapioca Pearls Dessert 191

Whole Wheat Vermicelli Dessert 191

Milk Dessert 192

Badam Milk Dessert 192

Split Green Gram Coconut Milk Dessert 193

Classic Creamy Pudding 193
Split Chickpea Dessert 194
Lotus Seed Pudding 194
Carrot Halwa 195
Conclusion 196

Introduction

Recipes are the most critical factors which determine the quality of the food. The right method with the exact quantity of ingredients even takes the dish to a different level. The main intention behind this e-cookbook is to familiarize you with Asian vegetarian recipes, focused mainly on Indian vegetarian dishes.

I remember one of my friends incidentally asked me while in college to name the dishes I love to make. When I think about the answer, I gave then, I feel quite bizarre now. I said that I didn't like to cook at all. Being an individual who was always frightened of burns and frying pans to organizing the whole kitchen; we all have all since grown and have found ourselves to be confident with food in the kitchen. The flaws one makes while cooking dishes helps us to learn and develop a discipline with ingredients The hints and tips I pass on in this book, will help you to avoid the mistakes I made.

Most of us might have a vague memory of burning our fingers while cooking. Ruining a dish is also a part of the learning process. I regard myself as someone who had a challenging time to prepare food for survival and later I have made this into a hobby which has since become a passion. Now I love cooking, which I think is not an easy task, but not a difficult task either. In this e-cookbook, I express my love for cooking through some delightful recipes. If you are a beginner or want to experiment with cooking Indian cuisine, this cookbook will be helpful for you.

India is a land of spices. The exceptionally flavorsome and luscious Indian foods have consistently fascinated foreigners over the years. One of several things which excite me about India is their delicious flavors. I eagerly await to have Indian food every time whenever I plan a trip to the country. Professional visits often confined me from exploring a lot; however, I never miss a chance to try different cuisines during my several visits.

If you visit an Indian restaurant or household, the first thing that greets you is the fragrance of spices and masala. The people are amiable, and they show their love through tasty food. It doesn't matter where you are; whether it is streets or restaurants, the ambiance is vibrant with the pleasant smell of the masalas.

The food in a region is also a part of its culture that is followed by the people from centuries and handed down precisely to the other generations as well. Food is a symbol of the country's culture and heritage, but the taste and recipes vary locally.

Asia dominates with about 90% of the total rice production in the world. As anticipated, Asians are more sensitive towards rice food. No wonder most Asians couldn't make it through the day without having rice for at least one of their meals. Rice is an essential ingredient in Asia; for Indians, it is somewhat part of their daily life, different types and varieties of raw rice are the specialty of the country.

Especially in South Asian countries, a dining table without rice is very uncommon. In India, the situation is not different, but more likely, it varies depending on the states. While the southern part of the country is more likely to have rice items for their three meals, wheat flour and other grains are essential for the Northern, Eastern, Western and middle parts of the country. Some locations cannot live without wheat flour as well.

Indian dishes are mostly famous for extra spicy recipes; the spicy masala mixes and spluttering of mustard seeds in the hot oil pan are sometimes overwhelming for outsiders. For seasoning, south Indian dishes use coconut oil, clarified butter, mustard oil, sesame oil, etc. But in the northern part of India, clarified butter, sesame oil, and mustard oil are used.

In south Indian dishes, curry leaves (botanical name: Murraya koenigii) play a significant role in adding to the sumptuous taste of the food. At the same time, in north India, cilantro leaves and mint leaves are trendy, and the northern Indian dishes use these ingredients to enhance the taste of the food. However, you can find a crossover of usage of spices in the north and south Indian dishes. Among the Asian recipes, Indian cuisines are widely accepted and loved all over the world.

In India every state has thousands of unique dishes, and the dishes never compromise on quality. Whether it is East, West, South, or North, every state in India has different tastes and styles of food making. Indian masalas have also gained wide popularity over the years. Most of the dishes contain the three mandatory masalas; chili, coriander, and turmeric powder.

Indian desserts are one of my favorites. The meals are not complete without a dessert/sweet wind up course. It could be 'mithais' or 'payasam' depending on which part of the country you are visiting. If you are in the northern part of the country, it would be mithais, and if you are in the southern part of the country, it would be payasam, both are sweet and delicious. It is a must, especially during the celebrations and festivals, they serve these at the end of the main meal.

Home snacks are one of the specialties in Indian cuisines. Rather than eating instant packed snacks, Indians have grown up eating home-made snacks. The snack items even differ in each state. In the e-book, you can find 25 snacks of drawn from different states of India.

Indian dishes are a mixture of fried and boiled, and both steps are commonly used in a single dish. Adding masalas and spices to a hot pan filled with oil would be the first step of most of the recipes. Clarified butter and vegetable oils are used lavishly to keep the aroma and deliciousness of food. The love for fried and boiled food can be found in many sections of the recipes. Whether it is fried or boiled, one plus point about Indian vegetarian recipes is that the recipes comprise of fully cooked or half-cooked meals. Except for salads, you cannot find recipes using raw vegetables. Within salads, these have been rinsed thoroughly, scrubbed, peeled or de-seeded as per the nature of the ingredients.

In this cookbook, I present different types of vegetable recipes with a total of 250 recipes, which include breakfast, main meals, rice & grains, snacks, salads, soup & stews, pasta & noodles and beans, legumes & soy, drinks, and desserts. Each series typically has 25 recipes, but the main meals contain 50 recipes, and we focus on ten different types of drinks and 15 varieties of recipes on desserts.

All recipes include the total cooking time, and the number or people the recipe serves, which will let you choose and plan the recipe you can make for the day. For diet conscious people, they can select their choice food matching to the dietary requirements by reading through the nutritional values. You may find some of the recipes require overnight soaking, and some recipes need extended hours of cooking. But making some changes to the cooking style can reduce the cooking time, as there are always mechanisms to reduce the cooking time.

In the ingredient section, each ingredient shows the number of units or measurements required to use for the cooking. Similarly, moving to the cooking instruction, it refers to the start and end.

The step-by-step instructions are easy to follow, and even a person who does not know much about cooking will find them easy to follow.

Instead of traditional cooking vessels like clay and ceramic pots for cooking, I have introduced saucepans, non-stick pans, pressure cooker, Instant Pot, non-stick skillet, microwave oven, blender mixer, and a dry grinder to ease up the cooking process. I know you will find it a challenging experience using a mortar pestle, which is practically impossible to use in a modern kitchen.

The recipes are also viable to cook by using an Instant Pot and Slow Cooker. People who want to use an Instant Pot for pressure cooking can use it by checking through the user's manuals. An Instant Pot offers excellent features for sautéing the ingredients and can quickly change the cooking mode to pressure cooking. It is a versatile and multipurpose cooking appliance that can be used for many vegetarian dishes. The book makes things easy for cooking traditional Asian style food, which focuses on Indian cuisine by using modern kitchen appliances.

Almost all spices referred to in the book are available in most of the EU and US markets. So, you won't have problems in collecting Indian spices and other cooking ingredients. The vegetables described in the book are also commonly available in almost all groceries.

Breakfast is undoubtedly the important and first meal in a day one should not avoid. We have a collection of 25 breakfast recipes to start your day pleasantly, ranging from dosas, aloo paratha, veg pulao, and so on in south Indian and north Indian style.

The main meal collection includes a total of 50 recipes to quench your appetite covering veg biryani with baked tofu, rice flour roti, cheesy vegan flatbread, garlic naan, etc.

Recipes on vegetable stews & soups, which add extra delight to your main meals, include white pumpkin stew, carrot soup, corn soup, mushroom soup, etc.

Different types of south and north Indian snack recipes such as vegetable pakoras, masala vada, cottage cheese cutlets are also the specialty of the cookbook in the snack section.

Indians are particular about every grain available; they try everything possible with the grain products. Rice, corn, barley, and wheat are some of the daily and most used grains in India. You can see different varieties of rice items in India; rather than simply boiling the plain rice, they love to experiment with other ingredients. Some of such rice recipes you can see in the cookbook which includes jeera rice, onion rice, lemon rice, yogurt rice, tomato rice, etc.

Noodles are Asian in origin, whereas pasta is likely to have the lineage of noodles, despite its Italian ancestry. The book has recipes with delightful noodles and pasta, including garlic noodles, Hakka mushroom & rice noodles, whole wheat pasta, masala pasta, etc.

Beans, legumes & soy are inevitable ingredients of Asian vegetarian foods. In this e-cookbook, I made a conscious effort to bring the best recipes using beans, legumes & soy, such as chickpea beans sabzi, South Indian soy curry, vegan red kidney bean curry, Goan dry peas curry, etc.

After eating all the delicious dishes, let's conclude the meal with some refreshing drinks and desserts like lemonade, lassie, buttermilk, mango drink, jackfruit milkshake, rice kheer, yogurt missmal, moong dal payasam, and badam kheer, etc.

Cottage cheese, cauliflower, mushroom, and soy are some of the vegetarian specialty foods in India. Sometimes those dishes are used as a substitute for non-veg dishes, whether it is for an occasion or celebration. The delicious flavor of vegetarian specialties surpasses the imagination of non-vegetarian foods.

Some of the recipes are very long but most contain a wealth of various spices. These spices are essential to enhance the taste of the food and keep it unique. Sometimes you may be shocked by seeing 15 to 20 ingredients. Yet, those ingredients are the reason for having a mouthwatering aroma and delicious taste. So, make it a point to collect all the ingredients before you start experimenting. It is okay, even if you are short of some of the ingredients you can still certainly have a unique vegetarian food with what the ingredients that you have available to you; but wherever possible make sure to have all the main ingredients before cooking.

Good food indeed slays. An excellent proper recipe makes an ordinary dish exceptional. I need not say that the quantity of the ingredients and how and when we add them while making a dish plays a crucial role in determining the overall quality of the dish.

Anyone could be a good cook if you have the right ingredients and follow the right recipe. Many consider cooking to be a natural talent. Cooking is indeed an art that is not easily accomplished by everyone. From my experience, I can say that anyone can master the technique, and regular practice can make you an expert in cooking. Every day is a learning process; similarly, every cooking process will let you learn something new and also let you correct the past mistakes.

This cookbook is for food lovers who are keen to try Asian or Indian recipes. Here in this e-cookbook, you may find that delicious dish you have tried in one of your trips to Asia or India that remains in your heart as a delightful memory. I have tried my best and did enough research to choose the best recipes.

Make yourself familiar with the most appreciated Asian and Indian recipes. Try the recipes at home and treat your family and friends with delicious continental dishes. I hope this e-cookbook with its very detailed cooking descriptions is helpful for you to get to know the Indian cuisine better.

Thank you for buying this book.

Chapter 1 Breakfast

Broken Wheat Upma

Cooking Time: 8 minutes |Serves: 15 |Per Serving: Calories 122, Carbs 22g, Fat 2.9g, Protein 4g

Ingredients:
- Broken wheat - ½ cup
- Onion – 1 large, finely chopped.
- Mixed vegetables – 1 cup
- Green peas, boiled – 1 tbsp.
- Green chilies – 2, finely chopped.
- Ginger, grated – 1 tbsp.
- Water – 4 cups

For tempering:
- Clarified butter – 2 tsps.
- Mustard seeds – 1 tsp.
- Split black lentils – 1 tsp.
- Split chickpeas – 1 tsp.
- Curry leaves – 1 twig

For garnishing:
- Cilantro leaves, coarsely chopped – 2 tbsps.
- Coconut, fresh grated – 1 tsp.

Directions:
Soak the broken wheat for 6 hours or overnight. In a large pan, pour clarified butter and bring the heat to medium-low. When the butter becomes hot, add mustard seeds until they splutter. Then add black lentils, split chickpeas, curry leaves, grated ginger, finely chopped chilies and sauté continuously for 2-3 minutes, until the aroma starts to release. At this point, add chopped onion, salt, and sauté for 3 minutes until it becomes tender and golden brown. Adding salt with onion will help to cook the onion faster. Add 4 cups of water and bring to a rolling boil. Reduce the heat to low and add soaked broken wheat gradually by stirring continuously. Cook until the water evaporates thoroughly. Garnish with cilantro leaves, grated coconut and serve hot.

Coconut Dosa

Cooking Time: 15 minutes |Serves: 12 |Per Serving: Calories 133, Carbs 18.8g, Fat 5.2g, Protein 2.7g

Ingredients:
- Raw rice – 1 cup
- Coconut, grated - ⅓ cup
- Split black gram – 3 tbsps.
- Salt - ½ tsp.

- Water - 1¼ cups.
- Oil – 2 tbsps, for spreading on the pan.

Directions:
Soak the rice and split black gram for 6 hours or overnight. After soaking, drain the rice, black gram, and put in a wet grinder jar. Add salt, grated coconut, 1¼ cup of water and grind to make a smooth thin batter. If the batter is too thick, add little water. Make sure it is not watery. Keep the batter covered for 30 minutes.

Now place a cast iron pan on the stove and set the heat to medium-high. When the pan becomes hot, spread some oil on the pan. Stir the batter and scoop a ladle full of batter and pour it on the center of the pan. Spread it circularly outward with a spoon or using the same ladle to make a round dosa. Then, cover the pan and cook for 2 minutes. When the base of the dosa becomes crispy, flip it and cook for 1 minute. Check the heat, and if it is too high, reduce to medium-low. Continue the same process for making the dosa. Serve hot with chutney or sambar.

North Indian Vegetable Pulao

Cooking Time: 25 minutes |Serves: 2 |Per Serving: Calories 445, Carbs 66g, Fat 16.9g, Protein 9g

Ingredients:
- Basmati rice - ½ cup
- Onion – 1 medium size, finely chopped
- Tomato – 1 medium size, finely chopped.
- Green peas, fresh - ¼ cup
- French beans – 3 tbsps, finely chopped.
- Carrot - ¼ cup, finely chopped.
- Bay leaf – 1
- Cinnamon – 1 inch
- Cloves – 2
- Garam masala powder - ¼ tsp.
- Turmeric powder - ⅛ tsp.
- Red chili powder - ½ tsp.
- Cilantro leaves, coarsely chopped – 2 tbsps.
- Oil – 2 tbsps.
- Clarified butter – 1 tsp.
- Water – 1 cup
- Salt - ½ tsp.

Directions:
Rinse and soak the rice for about 20 minutes. After the soaking period, drain it and keep ready to use it. In a 2-liter pressure cooker heat oil and clarified butter at medium-low temperature. Put bay leaf, cinnamon, clove, and sauté until the aroma emanates for about 1 minute. Add chopped onion and stir fry for about 2 minutes until it becomes tender and brown. Now add the carrot, French beans, green peas, tomato, and sauté for about 3 minutes. Add the drained rice, turmeric powder, garam masala, chili powder, salt and stir for about 3 minutes. Pour 1 cup of water and

combine gently. Close the cooker and pressure cook for 2 whistles at a medium-low heat. After the 2nd whistle, turn off the stove. Let the pressure settle naturally, and after that, open the lid. Fluff the rice and keep as it is for 1 minute. Garnish the vegetable pulao with chopped cilantro leaves and serve.

Bread Upma

Cooking Time: 20 minutes | Serves: 3| Per Serving: Calories 263, Carbs 33g, Fat 11.7g, Protein 7g

Ingredients:
- Brown bread slices – 6, chopped into cubes
- Oil – 2 tbsps.
- Mustard seeds – 1 tsp.
- Cumin seeds - ½ tsp.
- Onions, chopped - ⅓ cup.
- Green chili – 1, thinly chopped
- Ginger, minced – 1 tsp.
- Curry leaves – 1 twig
- Tomatoes, chopped - ½ cup.
- Turmeric powder - ¼ tsp.
- Red chili powder - ½ tsp.
- Hing - ⅛ tsp.
- Salt - ½ tsp.

Directions:
Cut the bread slices into cubes and keep it ready. Add 2 tablespoons of oil to the pan and select the cooking mode to medium-low heat. Put the mustard seeds in when the oil becomes hot and let it crackle. Add cumin seeds, and after sizzling, put in the chopped onion and sauté it for about 3 to 4 minutes at medium-low heat until it turns golden brown. Stir in green chili, ginger and curry leaves to the pan and sauté for about 2 minutes until the raw smell of ginger disappears. To this, add the finely chopped tomatoes and sauté until it becomes tender. Sprinkle the red chili powder, turmeric powder, hing and mix them well. Add salt and combine well. Continue sautéing and let the tomato cook well, and oil starts to release from the mixture, and the mixture becomes completely dry. Finally, add the bread cubes. Reduce the heat to low and stir fry the bread cubes for about 5 minutes until they become crispy from the edges. Garnish it with coriander leaves and serve hot!

Vermicelli Upma

Cooking Time: 15 minutes | Serves: 3| Per Serving: Calories 263, Carbs 47g, Fat 7.9g, Protein 3g

Ingredients:
- Vermicelli - 1 cup. Broken
- Onions - ½ cup. Finely chopped
- Ginger - ½ tsp, Minced
- Green chili - 1. Chopped
- Chopped Curry leaves – 1 twig

- Dry red chili - 1. Broken
- Clarified butter - 2 tbsps.
- Mustard seeds - ½ tsp.
- Cumin seeds - ½ tsp.
- Black gram - 1 tsp.
- Hing- ⅛.
- Water - 2 cups.
- Sugar - ½ tsp.
- Salt - ¾ tsp.
- Cilantro leaves - 2 tbsps. Chopped
- Cashew nuts - 20. Roasted

Directions:
Roast vermicelli in a hot pan, stirring continuously under medium-low heat until it becomes a golden color. Do not let it burn. Keep the roasted vermicelli aside in a separate bowl and add clarified butter to the pan by keeping the heat at a medium-low setting. When the butter becomes hot, add mustard seeds and let them crackle. Once they start to splutter, add the cumin seeds and let them sizzle. Then, add black gram, red chili, and fry for half a minute. Now add the roasted cashews. Add the chopped onions. sauté until they turns translucent and brown. Add the chopped green chili, ginger, curry leaves, hing, and stir fry at medium-high heat for 2 or 3 minutes until they produce the aroma. Add water, salt, sugar, and stir well. Add the roasted vermicelli to it when the water starts to a rolling boil and let it cook well. Reduce the heat and keep stirring until the water evaporates entirely. Garnish it with coriander leaves and serve with coconut chutney.

Semolina Dosa

Cooking Time: 25 minutes | Serves: 12| Per Serving: Calories 93, Carbs 15g, Fat 2g, Protein 1g

Ingredients:
- Fine semolina - ½ cup. Unroasted.
- Rice flour - ½ cup.
- All-purpose flour - ¼ cup.
- Onions, chopped - ⅓ cup.
- Green chilies – 2 chopped.
- Ginger - ½ inch minced.
- Crushed black pepper - ½ tsp.
- Cumin seeds - ½ tsp.
- Curry leaves – 10 chopped.
- Salt - ¾ tsp.
- Water - 2.5 cups.
- Clarified butter - 2 tsps.

Directions:
Combine semolina, rice flour, and all-purpose flour in a bowl. Add the onions, ginger, green chilies, black pepper, cumin seeds, curry leaves, and salt as required, to the flour mixture. Mix it thoroughly. Add water in the required quantity and whisk well to get a thin consistency batter

without any lumps. Leave the batter aside for 20 to 30 minutes. Spread clarified butter evenly on a cast iron pan and bring to a medium-low heat. Mix the batter well and pour a ladle full of batter at the center of the pan and spread outward in a circular motion slowly with a spoon. Let the dosa cook and fry well. Sprinkle a bit of butter on the top and sides and spread it evenly. Cook till the dosa is crisp. Fold and serve the semolina dosa with chutney or sambar. In case you are using a non-stick dosa pan, do not spread oil/clarified butter on the pan for making the dosa.

Oats Dosa

Cooking Time: 25 minutes | Serves: 8 | Per Serving: Calories 91, Carbs 12g, Fat 3g, Protein 2g

Ingredients:
- Oats - ½ cup.
- Semolina – ¼ cup.
- Rice flour – ¼ cup.
- Yogurt – ½ cup.
- Water – 1 cup.
- Onions, thinly chopped – ¼ cup.
- Ginger, minced – 1 tsp.
- Green chilies, thinly chopped – 1 tsp.
- Cilantro leaves, coarsely chopped – 1½ tbsps.
- Curry leaves, chopped – 8 leaves.
- Cumin seeds – ½ tsp.
- Black pepper – ¼ tsp crushed.
- Grated coconut – 2 tbsps.
- Clarified butter – 4 tbsps.
- Salt - ¾ tsp.

Directions:
Put the oats into a grinder and make a fine flour. Mix the oat flour with semolina and rice flour. Add fresh curd to the mixed flour with a little water. Stir well to make a smooth batter without any lumps. Now, add the chopped onions, coriander leaves, ginger, green chilies, curry leaves, cumin seeds, crushed black pepper, grated coconut, salt and combine well. Keep the batter aside to set for 10 minutes. Check whether the consistency of the batter is smooth and flowing to make the dosa. If not, keep adding water.

Now on a cast iron pan spread some clarified butter and bring to medium-low heat. When the pan becomes hot, stir and pour a ladle full of batter at the center of the pan and slowly spread outward in a circular motion. Drizzle some clarified butter on the edges of the dosa and spread on the top. When the base becomes golden and crisp, flip the dosa using a spatula and cook the other side until the based become crisp. Fold the dosa on the pan and serve hot. You can also use a non-stick dosa pan to make the dosa. If using a non-stick dosa pan, do not spread clarified butter/oil on the pan.

Potato Paratha

Cooking Time: 30 minutes | Serves: 9| Per Serving: Calories 213, Carbs 28g, Fat 9g, Protein 5g

Ingredients for paratha dough:
- Wheat flour – 2 cups
- Clarified butter – 1 tbs
- Salt - ½ tsp.
- Water - ½ cup plus for kneading
-

Ingredients for the potato fill:
- Potatoes - 4 medium size.
- Onions – 2 large size. Thinly chopped.
- Green – 2. Thinly chopped
- Red chili powder – ½ tsp.
- Dry mango powder – 1 tsp.
- Cilantro leaves, coarsely chopped - 2 tbsps.
- Salt – 1 tsp.

Directions:
Rinse all vegetables before using them. Cut the potatoes into halves and boil in a pressure cooker with water 1 inch above the potato level for three whistles under medium-high heat. After the third whistle, turn off the stove and allow the cooker to settle down the pressure naturally. Then, drain the water, peel the potatoes, and mash them. Add the onions, green chilies, chili powder, coriander leaves, dry mango powder, and salt to the mashed potatoes and keep it aside.

Combine the wheat flour with salt in a bowl and make a dent in the center of the flour. Pour clarified butter and some water into it and mix to make a soft dough. The dough should not get sticky and keep kneading for 8 to 10 minutes and leave it aside for 20 minutes. Make 9 or 10 small balls out of the dough. Spread some flour on the working table and place the round ball on the working table and spread with your fingers initially and roll it to a round paratha using a rolling pin. Scoop the potato filling at the center of the paratha and spread it 1 inch away from the edge. Make another paratha and place it on top of it. Crimp the edges with fingers. Sprinkle some flour on the paratha and roll it using the roller pin, making a round paratha.

Heat the cast iron pan on medium-low temperature and cook the paratha on it. When the base has cooked partially, flip the paratha using a spatula. Spread clarified butter on it and flip again and cook until the brown spot appears. Similarly, spread some clarified butter on the other side and continue cooking until both sides are cooked well and a brown spot appears. Serve the hot parathas with mango pickle or with dhal. Press the paratha and its edges with a spatula to get it cooked well. Serve hot.

Cottage Cheese Paratha

Cooking Time: 30 minutes | Serves: 9 | Per Serving: Calories 236, Carbs 20g, Fat 15g, Protein 6g

Ingredients for the paratha:

- Whole wheat flour - 2½ cups.
- Clarified butter - 1 tsp.
- Salt - ½ tsp.
- Water - ½ cup.

Ingredients for the paneer stuffing:
- Cottage cheese – 7 oz. Grated.
- Green chilies - 2. Finely chopped.
- Mango powder - ½ tsp dry.
- Garam masala powder - ½ tsp.
- Red chili powder - ½ tsp.
- Salt - ½ tsp.

Directions:
Mix salt with wheat flour in a bowl and add clarified butter to it. Combine it adding water to make a smooth dough. Knead it for some time and keep it aside for 20 minutes covered. Now, put the grated cottage cheese in a separate container and add chili powder, garam masala, dry mango powder, chopped green chilies, salt, and mix well.

Make 18 small balls from the dough and start spreading 2 balls at a time. On your working table, spread some flour and roll the balls to make round paratha. Place the cottage cheese mix at the center of the paratha and spread 1 inch away from the edges. Make another paratha using the second ball and place it on top of the cottage cheese mixture and crimp to seal the edges with fingers. Now sprinkle some flour over it and roll it out to make a round paratha.

Place a cast-iron pan on the stove and bring to medium-high heat. When the pan is hot enough, place the cottage cheese paratha on it. Flip the side when it is cooked partially at the base and spread some clarified butter on it. Flip again and cook until brown spots appear. Cook the other side also by applying clarified butter until brown spots appear. Press the paratha and its edges with a spatula to cook it evenly. Keep spreading clarified butter when required as you cook it. Once the cooking is over, serve hot.

No Yeast Appam

Cooking Time: 30 minutes | Serves: 4| Per Serving: Calories 389, Carbs 59g, Fat 16.9g, Protein 10g

Ingredients:
- Regular rice - 1 cup.
- Husked black gram - 3 tbsps.
- Fenugreek seeds - ¼ tsp.
- Cooked rice - 1¼ cups.
- Coconut milk - 1 cup.
- Coconut water - ¼ cup.
- Salt - 1½ tsps.
- Baking soda - ⅛ tsp.
- Coconut oil – 2 tbsps.

Directions:
Rinse regular rice, husked black gram, and fenugreek seeds until the water turns clear and soak it for 6 hours. After soaking, drain the water and put the soaked rice, cooked rice, black gram, fenugreek seeds, coconut water, coconut milk into a wet grinder and make a smooth batter. Transfer the batter into a large bowl. Combine salt andsugar into the batter and leave it aside to ferment overnight or for at least 12 hours. The batter will begin to rise after fermentation.

The consistency of the batter will be thinner than the dosa batter. You can manage the consistency of the batter by adding water or coconut water. Now add the baking soda to the batter and stir well. Leave it aside for 20 minutes until bubbles start to rise.

Place a shallow, deep-pan (appam pan) on the stove and bring to medium-low heat. When the pan heats up sufficiently, pour a ladle full of batter evenly to the center of the pan. Reduce the heat to low. Then hold the pan with the handles and swirl it so that it spreads out evenly onto the pot in a thin layer. After swirling, you can increase the heat and let it cook well. Sprinkle some coconut oil and cover the pan with a lid until it cooks well and the base turns golden brown. Take off the top and using a spatula lift the appam, beginning from the edges to the middle. Serve the appam hot with coconut chutney, stew, gravy, or korma.

Pongal Breakfast

Cooking Time: 20 minutes | Serves: 3| Per Serving: Calories 292, Carbs 40g, Fat 11g, Protein 8g

Ingredients:
- Rice - ½ cup.
- Split green gram - ¼ cup.
- Cumin seeds - ½ tsp.
- Hing - ⅛ tsp.
- Ginger, minced - 1 tsp.
- Water - 3½ cups, divided.
- Salt - ½ tsp.

For tempering:
- Cumin seeds – 1 tsp.
- Black pepper - 1 tsp crushed.
- Curry leaves - 12.
- Cashew nuts – 12.
- Clarified butter - 3 tbsps.

Directions:
Sort and fry the split green gram in the pan at medium-low heat until it releases the aroma. Put in a bowl, and to this, add the rice. Rinse them thoroughly until the water becomes clear and drain. Put it in a pressure cooker and add the cumin seeds, hing, chopped ginger, salt, with 3¼ cups of water. Let it pressure cook for 7 whistles. Increasing whistle time will reduce consistency. So, it is better always to cook for shorter whistle time. After the whistle, allow it to de-pressure the cooker naturally. Open the cooker and check the consistency. If the consistency looks like pulao, you can add about 1 cup of water and mix well. Heat for some more time and make sure that the

rice and green gram cooked well. You can also mash the rice and green gram slightly. Once the cooking is over, pour ¼ cup of hot water, mix well, and leave it aside.

Now let us make the tempering. Pour clarified butter in another pan and bring to medium-low heat. Add the cumin seeds to the clarified butter and let them sizzle. Then add the cashew nuts, black pepper, curry leaves and sauté until the cashew nuts become a golden color. Add this to the Pongal mixture and combine well. Close the pressure cooker and leave it for about 5 minutes, so that it can absorb the tempting aroma. Serve it hot with sambar or coconut chutney.

Poori Bhaji

Cooking Time: 25 minutes | Serves: 5| Per Serving: Calories 263, Carbs 33g, Fat 11.7g, Protein 7g

Ingredients:

- Potatoes – 4 medium size.
- Mustard seeds - 1 tsp.
- Onions – 2 medium size, finely chopped
- Green chili – 2, chopped.
- Cumin seeds - 1 tsp.
- Black gram - 1 tsp.
- Ginger, minced - 1 tsp.
- Curry leaves - 6.
- Turmeric powder - ¼ tsp.
- Hing - ⅛ tsp.
- Coriander leaves - 2 tbsps coarsely chopped. Divided.
- Water - ¾ cup.
- Peanut oil – 3 tbsps.
- Salt – 1 tsp

Directions:
Rinse the potatoes and boil them. After boiling, peel the skin and chop them. Pour oil in a pan and bring to medium-low heat. When the oil becomes hot, add mustard seeds and let them splutter. Then, put the cumin seeds in to sizzle. After that, add the black gram sauté until it becomes golden brown. Add the finely chopped onions to it and sauté until it turns soft. At this point, add ginger, curry leaves, green chilies, and stir fry for 2 minutes until the flavor emanates. Now add turmeric powder, hing, salt and sauté them on a medium-low heat. To this, add the chopped potatoes along with 1 tablespoon of coriander leaves and stir gently. Add ¾ cup of water, stir gently, and cook for about 6 minutes on a low heat until the liquid is absorbed. Garnish it with 1 tablespoon of coriander leaves and serve it hot with Pooris.

Fenugreek Leaves Paratha

Cooking Time: 30 minutes | Serves: 9 | Per Serving: Calories 184, Carbs 21g, Fat 9g, Protein 4g

Ingredients:
- Whole wheat flour - 2 cups.
- Fenugreek leaves - 1 cup.
- Green chilies - 2 thinly chopped.

- Garlic, minced - 1½ tsps.
- Oil - 2 tbsps.
- Water - ½ cup.
- Salt – 1 tsp.
- Clarified butter – 4 tbsps.

Directions:
Rinse, pat dry and coarsely chop the fenugreek leaves and keep them aside. For making the dough, mix wheat flour and salt in a large bowl. Then add the chopped fenugreek leaves, chopped chilies, minced garlic, oil to the wheat flour and mix well. Pour water gradually and knead to make a smooth dough. The dough should not be sticky.

Make 9 balls out of the dough and keep it ready for making the paratha. Sprinkle some flour on the working table and also spread some flour over it. Using a rolling pin, roll the dough balls into parathas. Heat a pan on a medium temperature and place the fenugreek paratha in it for frying. Flip the paratha when one side ¼ cooked. Spread some clarified butter on the paratha and flip again. Cook until brown spots appear on the paratha. When one side is cooked well, spread oil on the paratha and cook until brown spots appear. With the spatula, press the edges so that it can get cooked well evenly. Serve the fenugreek paratha with butter, curd, yogurt or mango pickle.

Spinach Paratha

Cooking Time: 30 minutes | Serves: 9 | Per Serving: Calories 197, Carbs 20g, Fat 12g, Protein 4g

Ingredients:
- Whole wheat flour - 2 cups.
- Spinach Leaves – 1 cup.
- Green chilies – 2 thinly chopped.
- Carom seeds - ¼ tsp.
- Hing - ⅛ tsp.
- Oil – 2 tbsps.
- Clarified butter – 6 tbsps.
- Salt – 1 tsp
- Water - ¾ cup

Directions:
Rinse, then boil the spinach, and after boiling drain it and make a smooth puree in a blender. In a large bowl, mix wheat flour, salt, green chilies, hing, and carom seeds. Add spinach puree into it and pour two tablespoons of oil. Pour ¾ cup of water gradually and mix the flour to make a smooth dough.

Make 9 balls from it and roll to make a small circle using a rolling pin. Spread some clarified butter on the rolled dough. Fold it from both sides and apply some clarified butter on it. Again, fold the sides to make a square shape. Now roll it to make a medium-size round paratha.

Place the paratha on a hot pan at a medium-low temperature. Once the base has cooked a little, flip it and spread some clarified butter. When the other side is also half cooked, flip again and spread clarified butter. For even cooking, press the edges and top of the paratha with a spatula. Flip it 2 or 3 times until golden spots appear on both sides. Serve it hot with pickle, korma or yogurt

Rice Batter Dosa

Cooking Time: 30 minutes | Serves: 18 | Per Serving: Calories 82, Carbs 8g, Fat 4.8g, Protein 1g

Ingredients:
- Parboiled rice - ½ cup.
- Regular rice - ½ cup.
- Fenugreek seeds - ⅛ tsp.
- Split black gram - ¼ cup
- Water - 2¼ cups divided into 1½ cups for soaking Water-¾ cup for grinding
- Salt - ½ tsp.
- Oil to spread on the pan – 6 tbsps.

Directions:

Preparing the dosa batter:
Put parboiled rice, regular rice, split gram and fenugreek seeds in a bowl and rinse 2 or 3 times. Soak the mix for 6 hours. Drain the ingredients and put it in a wet grinder and add ¾ cup of water. Blitz the ingredients to make a smooth batter. You may grind the ingredients in one batch or two batches depending on the grinder's capacity. Transfer the whole dough into a large bowl. Add salt and mix thoroughly. Cover the pot and keep it fermenting for about 10 hours. Fermentation will smoothen the batter and also double the volume of the batter.

Dosa making:
Before making the dosa, stir the batter. Place a flat cast iron pan on the stove and bring to a medium-low heat. Spread ¼ tsp. of oil on the pan. You can also use a clean kitchen towel to spread the oil, which can reduce oil consumption. If you are using a non-stick pan, no need to spread the oil, and if you spread the oil, the batter will start rolling. So do not spread oil on a non-stick pan.

Spoon a full ladle of batter on the pan and pour at the center. Slowly spread it round, starting from the center to outwards. Adjust the flame according to the thickness and size of the pan. Sprinkle ½ tsp. of oil at the dosa's edge when the center top is cooked well and spread it on the dosa with the spoon. Cook until the base gets cooked well and becomes a golden color. Using a spatula, remove the dosa by folding as per your style or serve as it is. Continue making repeating the same process.

Masala Dosa

Cooking Time: 30 minutes | Serves: 20 | Per Serving: Calories 337, Carbs 47g, Fat 14.2g, Protein 16g

Ingredients:

For the batter:
- Parboiled rice - 1½ cups.
- Split black gram - 1 cup

- Chickpea – 1 tbsp.
- Fenugreek seeds - ½ tsp.
- Water for grinding – 1½ cups
- Salt - ½ tsp.

For making the potato filler:
- Potatoes – 4 medium size
- Oil – 2 tsps.
- Split chickpeas – 1 tbsp.
- Onions, thinly sliced – 2 medium size
- Ginger, minced – 1 tsp.
- Curry leaves – 1 twig
- Green chilies, chopped – 2
- Turmeric powder - ¼ tsp.
- Hing - ⅛ tsp.
- Water - ½ cup
- Cilantro leaves, coarsely chopped – 3 tbsps.
- Salt - ¾ tsp.

Directions:
Making the batter:
Rinse and soak the rice, split black gram, chickpeas, and fenugreek in one bowl for 5 hours. Rinse the soaked the chickpeas separately for making potato filling for 5 hours.

Drain the rice, lentils, fenugreek, put it in a wet grinder with 1½ cups of water, and make a smooth batter. Transfer it to a large bowl, add salt and mix well. Cover the pot and keep aside for fermenting 8 or 10 hours. Ideally, it would be better to keep it fermenting overnight.

Making the potato masala:
Rinse the potatoes in running water and cut into halves. Pressure cook the potatoes in 2 cups of water for 5 whistles. Let the pressure settle down naturally. Open the cooker and drain the potatoes and allow it to cool down. After cooling, peel the skin, chop the potatoes and keep it aside.

Drain the chickpeas and keep aside. In a saucepan, pour oil and bring to medium-low heat. Wait until the oil becomes hot, and after that, put mustard seeds to splutter and then add the soaked chickpeas. Stir fry until the chickpeas become golden. At this point, add curry leaves, sliced onions, minced ginger, chopped chilies, and sauté until the onions become translucent. Add hing, turmeric powder, and sauté for a minute. Pour water and continue cooking for about 3 minutes until the gravy becomes thick. Now add the boiled potatoes, add some salt, and combine to mix. Continue cooking in low heat until the mix becomes thick. Turn off the stove and spread chopped cilantro leaves. Keep it aside.

Making the masala dosa:
Stir the batter before making the dosa. Place the cast iron pan on the stove and bring to a medium-low heat. Smear some oil on the surface and spoon one ladle full of batter to the pan's center. Spread it from the center to outward in a circular motion slowly to make the dosa. Drizzle some oil at the edges and center and spread with a spoon. When the base becomes golden, remove it using a spatula and spread potato masala on the center, Fold the dosa serve hot.

You can also make dosa on a non-stick pan. Do not spread oil on the non-stick pan to make the dosa. Spreading oil will spoil the dosa as the batter starts to roll up.

Finger Millet Dosa

Cooking Time: 25 minutes | Serves: 3| Per Serving: Calories 318, Carbs 42g, Fat 13.8g, Protein 8g

Ingredients:
- Millet Flour - 1 cup
- Gram flour - ¼ cup
- Ginger, minced - ½ tsp.
- Onions, thinly sliced - ½ cup
- Green chili, chopped -1
- Cilantro leaves, coarsely chopped – 3 tbsps.
- Hing - ⅛ tsp.
- Curry leaves, chopped – 1 twig
- Cumin seeds - ½ tsp.
- Freshly grated coconut - 3 tbsps.
- Buttermilk - ½ cups
- Clarified butter – 2 tbsps.
- Water - 1½ cups
- Salt - ½ tsp.

Directions:
In a bowl, mix gram flour with chopped onions, ginger, green chilies curry leaves, and coriander leaves. Add cumin seeds, grated coconut, hing, and salt to the bowl and mix well. Add buttermilk and combine it very well to make a dosa batter. Cover it for about 20 minutes and let it set.

Smear some clarified butter on the flat pan and bring to a medium-low heat. Stir the batter and spoon a ladle full of batter and pour in the center of the pan. Spread it slowly from the center to outward in a circular motion with the spoon. When the base becomes crisp, smear some clarified butter on the dosa and spread with a spoon. Sprinkle some clarified butter on the edges of the dosa. Using a spatula, flip the dosa and cook both sides crisp. Follow the same cooking process. Serve finger millet dosa with coconut chutney.

Set Dosa

Cooking Time: 30 minutes | Serves: 4 | Per Serving: Calories 313, Carbs 42g, Fat 12.9g, Protein 7g

Ingredients:
- Parboiled rice - 2 cups.
- Split black gram – 2 tbsps.
- Water to grind - 1½ cups.
- Salt - ¾ tsp.
- Baking soda - ¼ tsp.
- Clarified butter – 4 tbsps.

Directions:
Rinse rice, split black gram, and soak in a large bowl for 8-10 hours. Drain the water and put it in a wet grinder with water. Grind it to make a soft batter. Transfer it into a large bowl, cover and keep aside for 10 hours for fermenting. After 10 hours, before making the dosa add baking soda and salt and mix well. Allow it rest for another 10 minutes. If the batter is too thick, add some more water and mix well.

Place a cast-iron pan on the stove and bring to medium-low heat. Smear some clarified butter. Stir the batter. Spoon a ladle full of batter and pour at the center of the pan. Spread it with the spoon towards the outside from the center in a circular motion. The dosa should be a bit thicker than the regular masala dosa. To make it crisper, add some clarified butter from the edges and spread it on the dosa. When it becomes golden brown from the bottom, flip it with the spatula. When both sides become crisp, remove it to a plate. Continue the cooking process for the remaining batter and enjoy it with chutney.

Mysore Masala Dosa

Cooking Time: 50 minutes | Serves: 10 | Per Serving: Calories 329, Carbs 59g, Fat 10.5g, Protein 8g

Ingredients:

For dosa batter:
- Regular rice – 2 cups
- Split black gram - ½ cup
- Fenugreek seeds - ¼ tsp.
- Salt - ¾ tsp.
- Water for grinding - ¾ cup

For making dosa:
- Clarified butter – 4 tbsps.

For potato filling:
- Potato, boiled - 3 medium size.
- Onions, chopped - ¾ cups.
- Ginger, minced – 1 inch.
- Garlic, minced – 1 tbsp.
- Curry leaves – 1 twig.
- Green chili, thinly chopped – 1.
- Mustard seeds - ½ tsp.
- Turmeric powder - ½ tsp.
- Chili powder - ¼ tsp.
- Hing - ⅛ tsp.
- Lemon juice – 1 tsp.
- Water - ½ cup
- Oil -1 tsp.
- Cilantro leaves, coarsely chopped – 2 tbsps.

- Salt - ¾ tsp.

To make red chutney:
- Split chickpeas, roasted – 2 tbsps.
- Garlic – 5 pods.
- Dry chili – 5.
- Tamarind, de-seeded – 1 tsp.
- Onion, chopped - ¼ cup.
- Salt - ¼ tsp.
- Water, to grind – 4 tbsps.

Directions:
Sort split black gram and rinse along with rice and fenugreek until the water turns clear. Soak the rice, fenugreek, and split black gram for 5 hours. After it has soaked well, drain and put in a wet grinder with water to make a smooth batter. Transfer it into a large bowl and mix in salt. Keep it aside for about 10 hours for fermentation.

For making the potato filling, boil the potatoes in a pressure cooker for 5 whistles. Allow it to settle the pressure. Peel the potato skin, crumble, and keep aside. In a deep pan, pour oil and bring to a medium-low heat. When the oil becomes hot, add mustard seed until it splutters. Add curry leaves until they sizzle and put in the chopped onion. Stir fry the onion until it becomes soft. Now add garlic paste, minced ginger, green chili, turmeric powder, salt, red chili powder, and sauté for about 3 minutes. If the mix becomes too tight/dry, add some water. Add the crumbled potato and cook for about 2 minutes. Maintain the consistency of the liquid as you want. Sprinkle lemon juice and add chopped cilantro leaves and mix well. Keep it aside.

For making the red chutney, put all the ingredients in a wet chutney grinder and blitz to make a smooth paste. Maintain the liquid consistency as per your preference. Keep it aside.

Now let us make the Mysore masala dosa. In a thick frying pan, spread some clarified butter and bring to a medium-low heat. Stir the dosa batter, spoon one full ladle of batter, and pour it in the pan's center. Spread it slowly from the center towards outside in a circular motion. Smear some clarified butter on the edge and spread on the dosa. When the base becomes golden, flip it using a spatula. When it is cooked well, flip back and place a scoop of potato masala on the center and fold the dosa. Continue the same process for the remaining batter. Serve it with red chutney.

You can use a non-stick frying pan also to make the dosa. If you are using a non-stick pan, do not use oil or clarified butter to make the dosa during the initial stage, except for roasting.

Wheat Dosa

Cooking Time: 20 minutes | Serves: 6 | Per Serving: Calories 154, Carbs 26g, Fat 4.8g, Protein 4g

Ingredients:
- Wheat – 1 cup.
- Rice flour - ½ cup.
- Water - 2½ cups.
- Curry leaves, chopped – 1 tsp.

- Shallots, sliced – 5.
- Ginger, minced - ½ tsp.
- Hing - ⅛ tsp.
- Cumin - ½ tsp.
- Lime juice – 1 tsp.
- Salt - ¾ tsp.
- Clarified butter – 2 tbsps.

Directions:
Mix wheat and rice flour in a large bowl, adding salt. Add sliced shallots, and all other ingredients and mix to make a dosa batter without any lumps. Try using a wired whisk to make the batter, so that it can be free of any lumps. Allow the dough to rest for 30 minutes.

Place a cast-iron pan on the stove and bring it to a medium heat. When the pan is hot, smear some clarified butter and spread evenly on the pan using a small clean kitchen towel. Keep a cotton towel exclusively for spreading oil/butter. Stir the batter before you begin to make the dosa. Spoon a ladle full of batter in the center of the pan and spread it slowly towards the outside in a circular motion. When the top portion of the dosa is cooked well, smear some clarified butter on top and spread on the dosa with a spoon. Flip the side and cook until it becomes crisp. Remove it with a spatula and serve.

It's possible to also make wheat dosas by using a non-stick pan. When using the non-stick pan, do not spread oil/clarified butter. You can spread the butter on top to make it crisp while flipping.

Cheese Dosa

Cooking Time: 20 minutes | Serves: 6 | Per Serving: Calories 150, Carbs 15g, Fat 7.9g, Protein 5g

Ingredients:
- Parboiled rice - 1½ cups.
- Split black gram – 1 cup
- Onion, thinly sliced – 1 large
- Tomato, thinly chopped – 1 large
- Ground pepper - ½ tsp.
- Cheese, grated - ½ cup
- Basil leaves, coarsely chopped – 3 tbsps.
- Dried oregano – 2 tsps.
- Clarified butter – 4 tbsps.

Directions:
Rinse split black gram and rice until the water turns clear and soak it for 10 hours. When the ingredients have been soaked well, drain and put into a wet grinder and make smooth dosa batter. Transfer it into a large bowl, cover and keep aside for 10 hours or overnight for fermenting. When you are ready to make the dosa, stir it 2 or 3 times.

Heat a cast-iron pan on a medium-low temperature, spread some clarified butter on it and spread it using a cooking brush or a clean kitchen towel. Spoon a full ladle of batter and pour it at the center of the pan and spread outward in a circular motion. Sprinkle chopped onion on top, followed by chopped tomatoes, chopped basil, and dried oregano. Scatter grated cheese on top while you continue cooking. Spread clarified butter at the edge of the dosa. Continue cooking in low heat until the base becomes golden, and the dosa gets cooked well. Using a spatula, fold the dosa overlapping one portion over the other. Serve with chutney.

Butter Roast Dosa

Cooking Time: 20 minutes | Serves: 4 | Per Serving: Calories 384, Carbs 62g, Fat 12.2g, Protein 6g

Ingredients:
- Parboiled rice -1½ cups.
- Split black gram - ½ cup.
- Split chickpeas – 1 tbsp.
- Fenugreek seeds - ½ tsp.
- Salt - ½ tsp.
- Water for grinding rice – 1¼ cups.
- Clarified butter – 4 tbsps.

Directions:
Sort, rinse split black gram and chickpeas, and keep aside. Similarly, rinse rice until the water turns clear and put all the pulses along with fenugreek in a large bowl and soak for 5 hours. Drain the ingredients and place them in a wet grinder. Make a smooth batter by adding 1¼ cups of water. Check the consistency of the batter and, if required, add more water. Transfer it in a large bowl. Cover the pot and let it ferment for 10 hours. Before making the ghee roast, add salt and stir the batter.

Heat a cast-iron pan at a medium-low temperature and sprinkle some clarified butter. Spread the clarified butter on the pan using a cooking brush or a cotton kitchen towel. Spoon a full ladle of batter and pour at the center of the pan. Spread it outward slowly in a circular motion to make a full round shape. When the dosa is cooked well, on the top, sprinkle a little clarified butter at the edge and spread it all over. Cook until the base becomes golden and using a spatula flip the dosa. Let the dosa crisp thoroughly before serving. Serve hot with chutney.

Yogurt Dosa

Cooking Time: 30 minutes | Serves: 4 | Per Serving: Calories 195, Carbs 17g, Fat 12.7g, Protein 4g

Ingredients:
- Parboiled rice – 1 cup.
- Split black gram – 2 tbsps.
- Yogurt - ½ cup.
- Water - 1½ cups.
- Sugar - ½ tsp.
- Salt - ¾ tsp.
- Clarified butter – 4 tbsps.

Directions:

Rinse rice and split black gram, and soak for 10 hours or overnight. Drain the ingredients, put it in the wet grinder, with yogurt and water, and make a smooth batter. Transfer it into a large bowl. Add sugar and salt. Cover the pot and let it ferment for 10 hours.

Place a cast-iron pan on the stove and bring to a medium-low heat. Stir the batter before making the dosa. Smear some clarified butter on the pan and spread it with a cooking brush or cotton towel. Pour a full ladle of batter at the center of the pan and spread it outward in a circular motion. Cover the pan with a lid. When the top has cooked well, spread some oil at the dosa's edge and spread over with a spoon. Continue cooking until the base turns golden. Repeat the process for the remaining batter. Serve with chutney.

Idli-South Indian Style

Cooking Time: 25 minutes | Serves: 30 (idlis) | Per Serving: Calories 65, Carbs 12g, Fat 1.3g, Protein 2g

Ingredients:
- Parboiled rice - 2 cups.
- Split black gram - ½ cup.
- Water for grinding split black gram - ½ cup.
- Water for grinding rice - 1 cup.
- Salt - 1 tsp.
- Oil for applying on idli molds – 2 tbsps.
- Water for steaming idli - 2½ cups.

Directions:
Rinse the rice and split black gram separately. Soak them in separate bowls for 10 hours or overnight. First, drain the black gram, make a batter in a wet grinding jar adding ½ cup of water, and transfer it to a large bowl. Then, drain the rice and make a smooth batter in a wet grinder by adding 1 cup of water and transfer to the same bowl of black gram batter. Combine both batters by adding salt and keep aside for fermenting about 10 hours or overnight. Fermenting will let the idli smooth and double the dough.

Put the idli steamer or pressure cooker on the stove and bring the heat to a medium-high. Bring the water into a rolling boil. Now grease your idli molds with oil. Pour some batter into it. Now steam the idli mold putting in an idli steamer or pressure cooker. If you are using a pressure cooker, keep open the pressure vent. Steam it for 12 - 15 mins. Serve hot with sambar and coconut chutney.

Instant Semolina Idli

Cooking Time: 12 minutes | Serves: 7 (idlis) | Per Serving: Calories 189, Carbs 20g, Fat 10g, Protein 5g

Ingredients:
- Semolina – 1 cup.
- Yogurt - ½ cup.
- Baking soda - ⅛ tsp.
- Water - ½ cup.
- Cashew nuts – 12.
- Green chili – 1.

- Ginger, minced – 1 tbsp.
- Clarified butter, for roasting semolina – 4 tbsps. Divided.
- Salt - ½ tsp.

Tempering ingredients:
- Oil – 2 tsps.
- Mustard-1 tsp.
- Split chickpeas – 1 tsp.
- Curry leaves – 1 twig
- Hing - ⅛ tsp.

Directions:
In a thick pan, pour 3 tablespoons of clarified butter and bring to a medium-low heat. When the butter becomes hot, add semolina and stir fry until it begins to change the color to gold. Transfer the roasted semolina on a flat plate and allow it to cool down. After that put it in a wet grinder

In the same pan add 1 tbsp. of clarified butter and roast the cashew nuts to a golden brown. Transfer them to the roasted semolina bowl. Add 1 more teaspoon of oil, put mustard to splutter, and then add split chickpeas, hing and curry leaves. When the chickpeas become a golden color, transfer all the mix into the semolina bowl. Now add the yogurt, green chilies, minced ginger, and salt. Pour water and make a smooth thick batter. Add water as required to maintain the batter consistency instead of pouring in the entire water. Transfer it to a large bowl, cover and keep aside for about 30 minutes.

Make ready the idli cooker or pressure cooker by steaming water to a rolling boil. Spread some oil in the idli molds and pour the batter into the molds. If you are using a pressure cooker, keep the vent open. Allow the cooker to steam for 12 minutes. Remove it from the molds and serve with chutney.

Chapter 2 Snacks

Vegetable Pancake

Cooking Time: 8 minutes |Serves: 15 |Per Serving: Calories 24, Carbs 4g, Fat 1g, Protein 1g

Ingredients:
- Oat flour - ½ cup.
- Brown rice flour – 2 tbsps.
- Zucchini, thinly chopped - ¼ cup.
- Carrots, shredded - ¼ cup.
- Onions – thinly chopped - ¼ cup.
- Cilantro, coarsely chopped – 2 tbsps.
- Garlic, minced – 2 cloves.
- Ginger, grated - ½ tsp.
- Water - ½ cup
- Baking soda - ¼ tsp.
- Baking powder - ¼ tsp.
- Lemon juice, fresh - 2½ tsps.
- Salt - ½ tsp.
- Vegetable oil – 2 tbsps. for cooking.

Directions:
In a large bowl, combine oat and rice flour. Add all other ingredients as per the given order and mix well to make a smooth batter. Check the salt, lemon level, and, if required, add as per your taste.

Place a large pancake pan on the stove at medium-low heat and spread some oil. Then, pour a ladle full of batter in the pancake slot. Make sure the batter does not overflow. You can pour 2 or 3 pancakes at a time to cook, depending on the type of pan. Continue cooking until the base of the pancake becomes golden brown and crisp. Spread some vegetable oil on the top and flip the pancake to cook the other side too until it becomes golden brown. After cooking, let it cool and serve with your favorite sauce.

Crispy Vegetable Pakoras

Cooking Time: 15 minutes |Serves: 4 |Per Serving: Calories 160, Carbs 16g, Fat 18g, Protein 2g

Ingredients:
- Okra – 4.
- Green beans – 12.
- Red bell pepper – ½.
- Yellow lentil powder - ⅓ cup
- Corn starch – 2 tbsps.
- Rice flour – 2 tbsps.

- Ground coriander – 2 tsps.
- Mango powder – ¼ tsp.
- Red chili powder – ¼ tsp.
- Baking soda – ⅛ tsp.
- Salt – ½ tsp.
- Oil – 6 tbsps. For frying.

Directions:
Rinse all the vegetables before using them. Cut the okra vertically and slice into 4 pieces. Chop the greens beans into halves and again cut vertically. Then, julienne the bell pepper into 4 parts. In a large bowl, mix all the dry ingredients and baking soda. Put all these mixtures into a dry grinder and blitz. Sprinkle this dry mixture over the vegetables by adding a little water so that it can coat the vegetables.

Pour oil in a pan and bring to a medium-high heat. When the oil becomes hot, put in the coated vegetables, one after the other. Fry the pakoras by frequently flipping until they turn golden-brown. Transfer the cooked pakoras onto a tissue paper laced plate to absorb the excess oil. Serve it hot with desired condiments.

Spinach Pakora

Cooking Time: 10 minutes |Serves: 4 |Per Serving: Calories 301, Carbs 18g, Fat 23.5g, Protein 6g

Ingredients:
- Spinach, coarsely chopped – 2 cups.
- Chickpea flour – 1 cup.
- Corn starch – 2 tbsps.
- Chili flakes – 2 tsps.
- Coriander, crushed – 2 tsps.
- Mango powder – ½ tsp.
- Cumin seeds – ½ tsp.
- Salt – ½ tsp.
- Hing - ⅛ tsp.
- Oil – 1 tsp.
- Oil – 6tbsps for frying.

Directions:
Rinse the spinach, dry, and coarsely chop. Then, combine all the ingredients with spinach in a large bowl. Add water to the bowl and make a sticky dough. Spread some oil on a plate and keep it ready. Pour 6 tablespoons of oil in a pan and bring the heat to medium-high. Slightly oil your palm and take 2 tablespoons of dough. Roll it to make patties and place them on the oiled plate. Repeat the same process to make the remaining patties. Put the patties in the hot oiled pan without overlapping. Fry the pakoras by flipping and turning until both sides have become golden brown. It is better to fry the pakoras in batches by repeating the same process.

Spicy Corn Salad

Cooking Time: 10 minutes |Serves: 4 |Per Serving: Calories 152, Carbs 17g, Fat 8.7g, Protein 5g

Ingredients:
- Corn kernels – 2 cups.
- Oil – 1 tsp.
- Salt – ½ tsp.
- Cumin seeds – ½ tsp, roasted.
- Cilantro leaves, coarsely chopped – 2 tbsps.
- Green chili – 1 tbsp, thinly chopped.
- Red bell pepper – 2 tbsps., thinly chopped.
- Lemon juice – 1 tsp.
- Cream cheese – ¼ cup.

For garnishing:
- Feta cheese – ¼ cup.

Directions:
In a flat and heavy frying pan, sparingly spread some oil and bring to a medium-high heat. Add some corn kernels and stir fry continuously for about 5 minutes. When the frying is in progress, some of the kernels pop, some may change their color to brown or golden. Now turn off the heat and add the rest of the ingredients, except feta cheese and combine well. Scatter, shredded feta cheese on the corn kernels, and serve hot.

Vegetable Samosa

Cooking Time: 15 minutes |Serves: 4 |Per Serving: Calories 166, Carbs 28g, Fat 5g, Protein 3g

Ingredients:

For the filling:
- Potatoes – 4 large size, boiled and peeled.
- Coriander powder – 4 tbsps.
- Cumin powder – 1 tbsp.
- Lemon juice - 1½ tbsps.
- Garam masala powder – 1 tbsp.
- Red chili powder – 1 tbsp.
- Salt – 1½ tsps.

For the dough:
- All-purpose flour – 2 cups.
- Carrom seeds – 1 tbsp.
- Salt – 1 tsp.
- Vegetable oil – 5 tbsps.

Directions:
In a pressure cooker, boil potatoes by adding 4 cups of water for 3 whistles. After boiling, allow to settle down the pressure naturally. Open the pressure cooker, drain the water and remove the potatoes into a bowl to cool down. After cooling, peel the potatoes and mash them using a potato masher or spoon. To it, add all the ingredients given in the filling section. Keep it aside.

Now let us make the dough. Put the all-purpose flour, carrom seeds, salt in a large bowl, and combine it well. Now add water gradually and make the dough. Keep the dough aside for about 15 minutes. Make 16 balls out of the dough and roll in your palm. Spread some flour on the working table and spread it flat round shape using a rolling pin. Do a moon cut through the center. Make a triangle out of the moon cut and crimp and seal the edges with wet fingers. Hold the triangle in the palm and make it like a cone shape. Seal also inside of the cone by wetting your fingers. Fill the cone with the potato filler and seal the cone by crimping the edges firmly. Make all the samosas and prepare for frying.

In a frying pan, pour oil and bring to medium-low heat. When the oil is hot enough, place the samosas one by one. You can fry 3 or 4 samosas at a time. Fry until both sides become golden brown by flipping. Serve hot with ketchup.

Roasted Caramelized Fox Nuts

Cooking Time: 15 minutes | Serves: 4 | Per Serving: Calories 298, Carbs 40g, Fat 13.3g, Protein 6g

Ingredients:
- Fox nuts – 4 cups.
- Oil – 3 tbsps. Divided.
- Salt – 1 tsp.
- Sugar – 6 tbsps.
- Almonds – 2 tbsps.

Directions:
Use a large and heavy pan for this recipe to avoid fox nuts popping out of the pan. Add the fox nuts in the pan and pour 1 tablespoon of oil and salt over it. Combine it well. Turn on the heat to medium-high and keep stir-frying for about 8 minutes, until the fox nuts turn a little golden in color. Remove the nuts from the pan and transfer them into another bowl. Wipe the pan clean from the remainder of the salt.

In the same pan, pour 2 tablespoons of oil and set the heat to medium-low. Put all the sugar in it and keep stirring until the sugar melts to form a caramelized syrup. Once done, switch off the flame. Add the almonds and fox nuts in the syrup and keep stirring for even coating. Use a spatula and let the syrup coat every nut in the bowl, and it is ready to serve.

Cauliflower Fritters

Cooking Time: 20 minutes | Serves: 4 | Per Serving: Calories 112, Carbs 23g, Fat 0.9g, Protein 4g

Ingredients:
- Cauliflower florets – 3 cups.

- Gram flour - ⅓ cup.
- Corn starch – 3 tbsps.
- Ground coriander – 1 tsp.
- Cumin seeds - ½ tsp.
- Red chili powder - ¼ tsp.
- Baking soda - ⅛ tsp.
- Salt - ½ tsp.
- Ginger paste – 1 tsp.
- Green chili - 1 thinly chopped.
- Cilantro leaves – 2 tbsps. coarsely chopped.
- Oil – 10 tbsps.

Directions:
Rinse all the vegetables before using them. Cut the cauliflower florets into 1-inch pieces. Boil cauliflower about 5 minutes on medium heat until it becomes tender. Stop boiling, drain the water, and transfer it a large bowl to cool down. Mix the corn starch, gram flour, red chili powder, baking soda, green chili, minced ginger, cilantro leaves, and salt in a large bowl. Scatter the dry mixture over the cauliflower and mix it gently to coat. Sprinkle ¼ cup of water while mixing the dry ingredients for better coating.

Pour oil into the frying pan and bring to medium-low heat. Put the coated cauliflower in the pan and sauté for about 8 minutes by flipping it occasionally until it becomes golden brown. Remove it with a slotted spoon and place on a tissue paper layered plate to absorb the oil.

Coconut Fudge

Cooking Time: 20 minutes | Serves: 6 | Per Serving: Calories 211, Carbs 22g, Fat 13g, Protein 3g

Ingredients:
- Milk – 1¾ cups.
- Coconut powder – ¾ cup.
- Sugar – ½ cup.
- Cardamom powder – ⅛ tsp.
- Clarified butter – 4 tbsps.
- Pistachios – 1 tbsp, sliced.

Directions:
Put the coconut powder in the boiling milk and let it soak for about 30 minutes. Melt 1 teaspoon of clarified butter and sugar in a thick flat-bottom pan under a medium-high heat by sautéing continuously. Continue stirring the mix on medium-high heat for about 4 minutes until the sugar changes to a light brown color. As soon as the syrup turns brown, switch off the heat and slowly add milk to it while you continue stirring to avoid any lumps.

If the sugar-milk mixture becomes lumpy, then set the heat to medium-low and continue stirring until the sugar dissolves completely and the liquid will change the color to light brown. By adding the remaining butter gradually, keep stirring and scraping the edges for about 15 minutes. By now, the mixture will turn to look like a soft dough. Transfer it into a butter spread flat plate and flatten it with a butter coated backside of a spoon. Scatter pistachios on top and allow it to sit for about 4 hours. Cut into square pieces and serve.

Indian Savory Crackers

Cooking Time: 20 minutes |Serves: 6 |Per Serving: Calories 252, Carbs 20g, Fat 18.3g, Protein 3g

Ingredients:
- All-purpose flour – 1 cup
- Semolina flour – 2 tbsps.
- Salt – ½ tsp.
- Black pepper - ¼ tsp. Crushed.
- Cumin seed – ¼ tsp.
- Oil – 8 tbsps. Divided.
- Chilled water - ½ cup
- Lemon juice – ¼ tsp.

Directions:
Combine flour, salt, semolina flour, cumin seeds, black pepper, lemon drops, and 2 tablespoons of oil in a large bowl. Add chilled water and continue mixing it to make a smooth dough. The dough should be soft; hence, no need to knead it further. Let it season for 15 minutes. Make 20 small balls out of the dough and pierce through it using a fork to prevent puffing. Pour 6 tablespoons of oil in a frying pan at low-medium temperature and place the roll in the pan. Fry the rolls until they become golden-brown and place them in a paper towel to absorb the oil.

Corn Fritters

Cooking Time: 15 minutes |Serves: 4 |Per Serving: Calories 433, Carbs 70g, Fat 14.5g, Protein 9g

Ingredients:
- Yellow corn – 2 cups.
- Fennel seeds – 1 tsp.
- Salt – ½ tsp.
- Ginger, minced – 1 tsp.
- Green chili – 1 tbsp. Finely chopped.
- Cilantro – 1 tbsp. Thinly chopped.
- Mango powder – 1 tsp.
- Rice flour – ¼ cup.
- Oil – 3 tbsps. For frying.
- Water - ¼ cup.

Directions:
Grind the corn to make a coarse paste by adding water. Put the fennel seed, ginger, green chili, cilantro, mango powder, and salt to a mixing bowl, and transfer the corn paste into it. Combine the mix thoroughly. Add the rice flour and combine it to make a smooth dough. If the consistency of the dough is too thin, add a little more rice flour and make it tight. Make 12 equal parts of the dough like a bullet shape. On a medium-low heat, pour oil in a frying pan. Put the cutlets into the

frying pan and fry them flipping sides until they become golden brown for about 7 minutes. Using a slotted spoon, transfer them onto a parchment laced plate. Serve hot.

Spicy Snack

Cooking Time: 20 minutes |Serves: 6 |Per Serving: Calories 101, Carbs 16g, Fat 2g, Protein 5g

Ingredients:
- Black chickpeas – 1 cup.
- Vegetable oil – 2 tbsps.
- Ginger, minced – 1 tbsp.
- Green chili, thinly chopped – 1 tbsp.
- Ground coriander – 1 tbsp.
- Tamarind pulp - ¼ cup.
- Red chili powder – 1 tsp.
- Salt – 1 tsp.
- Sugar – 1 tbsp.
- Ground cumin seed – 2 tsps., roasted.
- Potato – 2 medium sized.
- Cucumber, chopped into small pieces - ½ cup
- Tomatoes, chopped - ½ cup.

For garnishing:
- Ginger, minced – 1 tbsp.
- Green chilies, thinly chopped – 1 tbsp.
- Lemon – 6 wedges.

Directions:
Rinse all vegetables and black chickpeas before using them. Soak the black chickpeas for a minimum of 4 hours or overnight. Peel the potatoes, cut into cubes, and pressure cook for 3 whistles. After the 3rd whistle, do a quick release and remove the cooked potatoes into a bowl. Pressure cook black chickpeas in 3 cups of water for 5 whistles. After the 5th whistle, turn off the stove and let the pressure subsidize naturally. Open the cooker and check the tenderness of the black chickpeas. If they are not tender enough, cook for 1 more whistle. Drain and keep aside.

Pour oil in a saucepan and bring to medium-high heat. Transfer the cooked black chickpeas into the hot pan. Add coriander powder, green chili, ginger, and sauté for about 2 minutes. Then add salt, red chili powder, tamarind pulp, sugar, and continue cooking for about 4 minutes by stirring at a low heat occasionally. Check the moistness and, if required, add some water. It should not be too dry or watery. Switch off the stove and transfer the cooked black chickpeas into a bowl and add the cooked potatoes. Add the chopped tomatoes and cut cucumber. Sprinkle roasted cumin powder and mix all the ingredients gently. Before serving, garnish with thinly sliced chilies and minced ginger. Finally, on top decorate with lemon wedges.

Potato Patty

Cooking Time: 1 minute |Serves: 4 |Per Serving: Calories 429, Carbs 59g, Fat 17.3g, Protein 12g

Ingredients:

For Patty:
- Potatoes – 4 cups, boiled, peeled and crumbled.
- Corn starch – 2 tbsps.
- Salt – 1 tsp.
- Cilantro – 2 tbsps. Coarsely chopped.
- Oil – 8 tbsps.

For topping sauce:
- Chickpea canned – 15 oz.
- Oil – 2 tbsps.
- Chickpea flour – 2 tbsps.
- Green chili – 2 tbsps. Finely chopped.
- Ginger – 2 tbsps. Minced.
- Salt – 1 tsp.
- Ground cumin seed – 1 tsp, roasted.
- Garam masala – 1 tsp.
- Mango powder – ½ tsp.

Directions:
Boil the potatoes, without overcooking. After cooling, peel off the skin and crumble the potatoes. The potato should not be mushy, and it should be firm and cooked well. Add salt, cilantro, and corn starch to the crumbled potato and mix them lightly with hands. Do not knead it. Then, make 8 equal parts out of it and roll them into patties. Place the patties in a container, cover, and refrigerate for about 5 hours. This process will let you have crispy patties.

Chickpea topping:
Rinse and mash the chickpeas in a blender with 1 cup of water. It should not be pasty. Pour oil in a pan and bring to medium-low heat. Then, add chickpea flour into the pan and stir fry continuously until it becomes golden color. Add green chili, ginger, and stir for about 1 minute. Then, add ground cumin seeds, chickpeas, mango powder, garam masala, and salt. Stir fry it on low heat for 10 minutes. The consistency of the chickpea should be like a dosa batter. Add water if required to maintain the consistency. After cooking, remove it from the stove.

Crispy potato patties:
In a shallow frying pan, pour oil enough to fry the patties and bring to a medium-low heat. Fry the patties when the oil becomes hot and flip sides after every 2 minutes for even cooking. Continue frying until both sides become golden brown. Serve it with the chickpea topping.

Masala Vada

Cooking Time: 20 minutes |Serves: 16 |Per Serving: Calories 76, Carbs 11g, Fat 2.5g, Protein 3g

Ingredients:
- Split chickpeas – 1 cup.
- Rice flour – 1 tbsp.
- Potatoes – 1 cup. Boiled, peeled, and mashed.

- Salt – 1 tsp.
- Fennel seeds – 1 tsp.
- Mango powder – 1 tsp.
- Black pepper – ½ tsp, crushed.
- Hing – ¼ tsp.
- Ginger paste – 1 tbsp.
- Green chilies, chopped – 2 tbsps.
- Cilantro, coarsely chopped – ¼ cup.
- Oil – 8 tbsps, for frying.

Directions:

Wash and soak the split chickpeas overnight or for a minimum of 4 hours. After soaking, drain the chickpeas and keep aside 2 tablespoons of chickpeas. Grind the remaining chickpeas coarsely without water and transfer into a large bowl. Boil, peel the potatoes and mash it, using a potato masher and transfer into the bowl.

Put all other ingredients in the bowl, including the soaked chickpeas, and combine them with the coarsely ground chickpea and mashed potato. Make 16 balls out of the mix. Slightly wet your palms and flatten the balls into a round shape in your palm. Create a small dent in the center. Pour oil in a frying pan and bring it to medium-low heat and place the vadas in the hot oil. Fry both the sides for about 7 minutes until it turns golden-brown and using a slotted spoon remove it to a tissue laced plate to absorb the excess oil.

Gram Flour Dhokla

Cooking Time: 1 minute |Serves: 6 |Per Serving: Calories 202, Carbs 31g, Fat 6.9g, Protein 5g

Ingredients:

For batter:
- Gram flour – 1½ cups.
- Semolina – 1 tbsp.
- Ginger paste – 1 tsp.
- Green chili paste – 2 tsps.
- Turmeric powder - ¼ tsp.
- Hing - ⅛ tsp.
- Baking soda - ¾ tsp.
- Salt – 1 tsp.
- Lime juice – 1 tsp.
- Water – 1 cup

For tempering:
- Oil – 2 tbsps.
- Water - ⅓ cup
- Mustard seeds – 1 tsp.
- Cumin seeds – 1 tsp.
- White sesame seeds – 2 tsps.

- Curry leaves – 1 twig
- Green chili, chopped – 1.
- Lime juice – 1 tsp.
- Sugar – 2 tsps.

For garnishing:
- Coriander leaves – 2 tbsps. Coarsely chopped.
- Coconut – 2 tbsps. Grated.

Directions:

In a steamer pan, spread about ½ teaspoon of oil. In a bowl, add gram flour, other ingredients of the batter except for semolina and add water to make a thick batter. Add semolina in this mix and continue stirring without any lumps in the batter. The mixture should be thick yet flowing.

Boil 3 cups of water in the steamer. While the water is boiling, stir in baking soda to the batter and stir quickly. Pour the batter on the greased pan and place the pan in the steamer pan. You can also use a pressure cooker to steam the dhokla. While using a pressure cooker, keep open the pressure vent. Steam the steamer cooker for about 20 minutes under a medium-high heat. In the pressure cooker, it will be ready within 17 minutes. Insert a toothpick on the dhokla to check if it's done. If it comes out clean, it is ready to serve, otherwise, steam it for some more time. After the cooking is over, invert the pan onto the plate. It will come off quickly since it has been greased well.

Now let us do the tempering. For that, in a small pan pour 2 tablespoons of oil and bring to a medium-low heat. When the oil becomes hot, add the mustard seed to splutter. After crackling the mustard seeds, add cumin seeds to sizzle, followed by curry leaves, sliced green chilies, and stir well. Now add sesame seeds and sauté until it changes its color. Pour ⅓ cup of water into the pan and add 2 teaspoons of sugar. Stir well until it boils and pour it over the dhokla. Garnish with grated coconut and coriander leaves. Cut the dhokla into pieces and serve.

Vegetable Cutlet

Cooking Time: 20 minutes |Serves: 12 |Per Serving: Calories 93, Carbs 10g, Fat 4g, Protein 2g

Ingredients:

For cutlet:
- Potatoes, cut into cubes – 2 cups.
- Green peas – ½ cup.
- Carrot, cut into cubes – 1 cup.
- Beans, chopped – 3 cups.
- Cilantro leaves, coarsely chopped – 3 tbsps.

For crumb coating:
- Breadcrumbs – ½ cup.
- Chickpea flour – 2 tbsps.

Other ingredients:
- Salt – ½ tsp.

- Ginger, grated – ¾ tsp.
- Green chilies – 2, finely chopped.
- Garam masala – ¾ tsp.
- Breadcrumbs – 6 tbsps.
- Oil – 4 tbsps.

Directions:
Rinse and boil the vegetables until they become fork tender. Add them to a mixing bowl and mash until they become a smooth mix. Add grated ginger, breadcrumbs, chilies, garam masala, salt, and mix the mashed vegetables. Keep the mix aside.

Divide the dough into 12 equal parts and roll them as balls and flatten them to make thick patties. Keep it on a greased plate. On another plate, take some breadcrumbs. In a bowl, add the chickpea flour with some water and make a thin batter. Dip the cutlet in the chickpea batter and then dredge in the breadcrumbs.

In a shallow frying pan, pour 1 teaspoon of oil and bring to a medium-low heat. Then, place the cutlets in the pan when the oil becomes hot. Before placing the cutlet on the pan, shake it to remove excess breadcrumbs. Flip frequently and fry until each side becomes golden brown. Serve warm with desired sauce.

Mushroom Cutlet

Cooking Time: 20 minutes |Serves: 12 |Per Serving: Calories 40, Carbs 8g, Fat 1.3g, Protein 1g

Ingredients:
- Mushrooms – 1 cup, sliced.
- Onion – 1 large, thinly sliced.
- Potato – 1, large, boiled, and crumbled.
- Chickpeas flour – 6 tbsps.
- Mint leaves, chopped – 2 tsps.
- Green chilies – 4, chopped.
- Garam masala - ½ tsp.
- Salt - ½ tsp.
- Ginger garlic paste – 1 tsp.
- Breadcrumbs - 1¼ cups.
- Oil – 8 tbsps. For frying.

Directions:
Mix all the ingredients such as chopped mushrooms, chilies, potatoes, onions, mint, ginger garlic paste, garam masala, and salt in a large bowl and keep it aside 5 minutes to season the flavor. Add chickpea flour to the mixture and combine well. Then, heat oil in a deep-frying pan at a medium-low temperature. Grease your palms and make small thin mushroom patties and dredge in the breadcrumbs to coat thoroughly. Fry the patties until they become golden brown from all sides. After frying, remove them to a tissue laced plate to absorb excess oil.

Cottage Cheese Cutlet

Cooking Time: 25 minutes |Serves: 4 |Per Serving: Calories 231, Carbs 15g, Fat 14g, Protein 10g

Ingredients:
- Cottage cheese – 1 cup
- Potato – ¾ cup, boiled & mashed.
- Green chilies – 3, finely chopped.
- Breadcrumbs – ¼ cup
- Ginger paste – 1 tsp.
- Cumin seed – ¼ tsp.
- Onion – 1 medium size, thinly chopped.
- Turmeric powder – ⅛ tsp.
- Garam masala – ¾ tsp.
- Coriander leaves – 2 tbsps., coarsely chopped.
- Salt – ¾ tsp.
- Oil – 2 tbsps., for frying.

Directions:

Peel potato and boil it until it becomes soft. After boiling, transfer it a bowl to cool down and mash it thoroughly using a potato masher. Add cottage cheese, cumin, turmeric, ginger paste, coriander leaves, garam masala, chilies, breadcrumbs, salt, and combine to make a dough. If the mixture becomes too fluid, add a little more breadcrumb to make it tight.

Now make patties in moderate thickness using the dough. Heat a pan under a medium-low temperature and pour in some oil. When the pan becomes hot, place the patties and fry them flipping sides occasionally until both sides become crispy and golden brown. Transfer them to a tissue paper laced plate to absorb the excess oil. Serve with ketchup or chutney.

Vegetable Kabab

Cooking Time: 15 minutes |Serves: 10 |Per Serving: Calories 101, Carbs 16g, Fat 2g, Protein 5g

Ingredients:
- Potatoes – ¾ lb.
- Coriander leaves, chopped – ½ cup.
- Green peas – 1 cup.
- Chilies – 3, thinly chopped.
- Spinach - ½ cup
- Chickpea flour – 3 tbsps.
- Breadcrumbs - ¼ cup
- Ginger garlic paste - 1½ tsps.
- Salt – 1 tsp.
- Garam masala - ½ tsp.
- Lemon juice – 1tbsp.
- Oil – 3 tbsps.

Directions:
Rinse and pat dry all the vegetables well before using them. Boil potatoes and peas together to make them tender. The potatoes should not be mushy. Roast the chickpea flour dry until it starts to release the aroma and keep aside. Heat 1 teaspoon of oil in a pan and sauté ginger garlic paste until it gets rid of the raw aroma. Add chilies and peas to the pan and mix them well until the peas become tender. Add spinach in the same pan and continue to sauté until it wilts. Now, add salt and garam masala. Stir fry for a moment until the aroma starts to release and switch off the stove. Leave it aside and let it cool.

Combine this in a blender to make a smooth paste by adding cilantro leaves and peas. Mash the potatoes and add to the spinach paste. Add the roasted chickpea flour and combine to create a neat dough. The dough should not be sticky. If it is sticky, add breadcrumbs.

Divide the dough into 10 equal parts and make patties by flattening each portion. In a pan pour 1 teaspoon of oil and place in the patties, when the pan becomes hot. Fry them until both sides become crisp and golden brown. Do not overlap the patties while frying. You can fry all the remaining patties in the same process. Serve with chutney or ketchup.

Crispy Cauliflower Manchurian

Cooking Time: 25 minutes | Serves: 3 | Per Serving: Calories 460, Carbs 32g, Fat 36g, Protein 5g

Ingredients:

For the Manchurian gravy:
- Oil – 1½ tbsps.
- Garlic – 1 tbsp. Minced.
- Ginger - ½ tbsp. Finely grated.
- Green chili – 1, thinly chopped.
- Onion – 1 medium size, thinly sliced.
- Bell pepper - ¼ cup, thinly chopped.
- Soy sauce – 1 tbsp.
- Red chili sauce – 3 tbsps.
- Tomato ketchup – 2 tbsps.
- Red chili powder - ½ tsp.
- Vinegar - ½ tbsp.
- Sugar – 1 tsp.
- Salt - 1½ tsp, divided.
- Water – 4 tbsps.
- Ground black pepper - ¾ tsp.
- Spring onion – 2 tbsps., for garnishing.

For cauliflower Manchurian:
- Cauliflower florets – ½ lbs.
- All-purpose flour – 6 tbsps.
- Corn flour – 3 tbsps.

- Red chili powder – 1 tsp.
- Ground black pepper - ¼ tsp.
- Oil – 6 tbsps., for frying.

Directions:
Rinse and dry all the vegetables before using them. Cut and boil the cauliflower florets for 5 minutes until it becomes tender; drain and keep it aside with no moisture. In a large bowl, mix all-purpose flour, corn flour, red chili powder, ground black pepper, ½ teaspoon salt, and mix thoroughly to make a smooth batter by adding water gradually. The batter should have a medium consistency. It should not be runny or too tight. Then, add the boiled cauliflower florets into the batter and mix well.

In a deep-frying pan, pour oil and bring to medium-low heat. When the oil becomes hot, put in the batter coated florets batch by batch. Fry the florets until they become crispy and golden. After frying, remove them using a slotted spoon and place on a tissue laced plate to drain the excess oil.

Now make the cauliflower Manchurian by mixing red chili powder with 3-4 tablespoons of water. In a pan heat oil at medium-low temperature. Add garlic, green chilies, ginger, when the oil becomes hot and sauté for 2 minutes. Then, add soy sauce, tomato ketchup, red chili paste, vinegar, sugar, and continue sautéing for another 2 minutes. Add ground pepper, water, 1 teaspoon salt, and sauté until the sauce becomes thick. The texture of the sauce should be a mix of hot, sweet, and a bit sour. Let the sauce cool for about 2 minutes and add the fried cauliflower and gently mix to coat the sauce. Garnish with chopped spring onion. Serve hot.

Black Gram Fritters

Cooking Time: 40 minutes |Serves: 8 |Per Serving: Calories 291, Carbs 34g, Fat 13g, Protein 11g

Ingredients:
- Split black gram – 2 cups.
- Cumin seeds – 1 tsp.
- Black pepper – 1 tsp, crushed.
- Onion – 1 large. Cut into thin slices.
- Green chilies – 2, chopped.
- Oil – 6 tbsps.
- Cilantro leaves, coarsely chopped – 1 tsp.
- Coconut – ½ cup, chopped.
- Ginger, minced – 1 tbsp.
- Curry leaves – 2 twigs.
- Peppercorns – 1 tsp.
- Water, for grinding - ¼ cup.
- Salt – ½ tsp.

Directions:
Soak the gram overnight. Drain the gram and put it in a grinder to make a smooth batter. Add the required amount of water while grinding. Add all the spices, vegetables, and salt in the batter and mix it well. Make round shaped fritters by creating a hole in the middle like a donut. While making the fritters, moisten your hand so that batter won't stick with your hand. Heat some oil at a

medium-high temperature in a deep non-stick frying pan for deep-frying the fritters. Once the oil becomes very hot, start placing these fritters in the pan, one by one. Fry all the fritters in the same way and keep them on a paper towel to absorb the oil. Serve the fritters with warm sambar or chutney.

Dry Chili Paneer

Cooking Time: 10 minutes |Serves: 3 |Per Serving: Calories 325, Carbs 28g, Fat 18.7g, Protein 13g

Ingredients:

For batter:
- Corn starch – 2 tbsps.
- All-purpose flour – 3 tbsps.
- Ginger paste – ½ tsp.
- Garlic paste – ½ tsp.
- Ground black pepper – ¼ tsp.
- Red chili powder – ¼ tsp.
- Salt – ¼ tsp.
- Water – ¼ cup.

For fry paneer:
- Oil – 3 tbsps.
- Cottage cheese, cubed – ½ lbs.

For gravy:
- Spring onion – 3, chopped.
- Green chilies – 3, julienned.
- Ginger, minced – 2 tsps.
- Garlic, minced – 2 tsps.
- Bell pepper, sliced - ½ cup.
- Soy sauce – 2 tsps.
- Chili sauce – 1 tsp.
- Ground black pepper - ¼ tsp.
- Red chili powder - ½ tsp.
- Sugar – 1 tsp.
- Salt - ½ tsp.
- Water - ⅔ cup
- Cornstarch – 1 tbsp.
- Water – 3 tbsps. for mixing cornstarch.
- Vinegar – ½ tsp.
- Spring onion, finely chopped – 3 tbsps.

Directions:

For making the batter:

In a bowl, add 2 tablespoons of corn starch and 3 tablespoons of all-purpose flour and mix them well. Put all other batter ingredients in the bowl and whisk until every spice has mixed thoroughly in the flour. Pour water as needed in this mix and create a smooth batter without any lumps. To this batter, add the cottage cheese cubes by running a spoon until every piece gets an even batter coating.

Pour oil in a frying pan, bring to a medium-low heat and fry the marinated cottage cubes until they turn golden in color, flipping frequently. Transfer them onto a tissue paper laced plate to absorb the excess oil.

In the same pan, add ginger, garlic, chilies, and sauté them for a minute. Add the spring onions and cook at medium-high heat for about 4 minutes. Reduce the heat, add sliced bell pepper and sauté for 2 minutes. Add red chili powder, soy sauce, chili sauce, salt, and stir to mix with the ingredients. Now add water, give a gentle stir and simmer on a medium-high heat for 3-4 minutes. Add sugar and check the salt level. If required, add some more salt, as per your taste. Simmer the gravy until it becomes slightly thick and the corn starch is cooked well. Check the gravy and make sure there is no raw taste of the corn starch.

Add the fried cottage cheese cubes into the gravy. Turn off the stove and pour vinegar and stir gently. Garnish with chopped spring onions, mix well and serve hot.

Easy Cottage Cheese Tikka in a Pan

Cooking Time: 15 minutes |Serves: 3 |Per Serving: Calories 316, Carbs 11g, Fat 22g, Protein 17g

Ingredients:

Main ingredient:
- Paneer – ¾ lbs.
- Onion – 1 medium, diced.
- Bell pepper – 1, diced.

For marination:
- Yogurt – 1 cup
- Ginger, minced – 1 tbsp.
- Red chili powder – 2 tsps.
- Turmeric powder - ½ tsp.
- Ground cumin – 1 tsp.
- Ground coriander – 1 tsp.
- Garam masala powder - ½ tsp.
- Carom seeds – 1 tsp.
- Dry mango powder – 1 tsp.
- Chaat masala – 1 tsp.
- Ground black pepper - ½ tsp.
- Lemon juice - 1½ tsp.
- Mustard oil – 1 tbsp.
- Salt – ½ tsp.
- Mustard oil for brushing.

Directions:
Cut the paneer cheese and other vegetables in cubes and keep them aside. Whisk the yogurt in a bowl until it turns smooth and adds all the spices, ginger-garlic paste, salt, carom seeds, mustard oil, and lemon juice. Combine it thoroughly and add more salt if required. Add the vegetables and paneer cheese into the marinade and gently combine to get them coated. Close the bowl and refrigerate it to marinate for 2 hours.

After 2 hours, thread the veggies and cottage cheese alternatively on soaked bamboo skewers. Before start baking, preheat the oven to 230°C for 20 minutes. Then, line a baking tray with a parchment paper or aluminum foil. Place the threaded cottage cheese skewers on the tray without overlapping. Brush some mustard oil on the veggies and cottage cheese. Place the baking tray on the top rack of the oven and bake for about 10 minutes at 230°C. Turn the skewers after 10 minutes and continue baking for another 5 minutes, until the edges of the paneer cheese become golden. Do not bake for an extended period, as it may harden the paneer cheese. In between, check the baking level of the paneer cheese; if required, you can increase or decrease the heat. After baking, transfer the paneer cheese tikka to a serving plate. Dust the chaat masala on it and drizzle lemon juice before serving.

Instant Semolina Dhokla

Cooking Time: 20 minutes |Serves: 4 |Per Serving: Calories 337, Carbs 62g, Fat 4g, Protein 10g

Ingredients:

Main ingredient:
- Semolina – 2 cups.
- Ginger, paste – ½ tsp.
- Green chili, paste - ½ tsp.
- Water – 1 cup.
- Oil – 1 tsp.
- Sugar – ½ tsp.
- Turmeric powder – ¼ tsp.
- Lemon juice – 1¼ tbsp.
- Baking soda – 1 tsp.
- Salt – ¾ tsp.
- Water – 4 cups for boiling

For tempering:
- Mustard seeds – ½ tsp.
- Cumin seeds – ½ tsp.
- Sesame seeds – 1 tsp.
- Curry leaves – 10.
- Hing - ¼ tsp.
- Water – 3 tbsps.
- Oil – ½ tbsp.

For garnishing:

- Coconut, grated – 2 tbsps.
- Coriander leaves, coarsely chopped – 2 tbsps.

Directions:
Keep aside the baking soda and in a large bowl, combine all the ingredients listed in the main ingredient section by adding 1 cup of water and whisk them well to make a smooth batter. Keep it aside for 20 minutes to settle in. In a steamer, add about 4 cups of water and heat to boiling.

In the meantime, spread oil in a pan and keep it ready. Sprinkle baking soda in the batter and stir the batter briskly so that it will not bubble. Transfer the batter on to the greased pan and spread evenly. Place the pan in the steamer to steam it for about 20 minutes. Do a toothpick test to check the doneness of the dhokla. If not cooked well, steam for some more time. Invert the dhokla pan onto a plate and allow it cool a little.

Meanwhile, let us prepare for the tempering. Pour oil in a pan and bring to a medium-low heat. When the oil becomes hot, add mustard and let it crackle. Then, add cumin seeds to pop and crackle. Add the other ingredients in the pan now and let it stay for a couple of seconds. Switch off the stove and add 3 tablespoons of water in it. Pour this mixture over the semolina dhokla and add the garnish before serving.

Cauliflower Manchurian Dry

Cooking Time: 20 minutes | Serves: 4 | Per Serving: Calories 332, Carbs 38g, Fat 18g, Protein 5g

Ingredients:

For cauliflower florets:
- Cauliflower – 1 medium size.
- All-purpose flour – 1 cup
- Corn starch – 4 tbsps.
- Black pepper powder – ¼ tsp.
- Red chili powder – ½ tsp.
- Soy sauce – 1 tsp.
- Water – 1 cup plus 1 tbsp.
- Oil – 6 tbsps.
- Water – as needed

Other ingredients:
- Spring onion, chopped – ¾ cup.
- Bell pepper, thinly chopped - ½ cup.
- Ginger, minced – 3 tsps.
- Garlic, minced – 3 tsps.
- Green chili – 2, chopped.
- Celery - ½ tbsp, finely chopped.
- Soy sauce - 1½ tbsps.
- Tomato ketchup – 1 tbsp.
- Rice vinegar – 1 tsp.

- Ground black pepper – ½ tsp.
- Salt – ¾ tsp.
- Oil – 6 tbsps. For frying.

Directions:
Cut the cauliflower florets into a medium size. Rinse, boil it in saltwater, and blanch for about 20 minutes. After that, drain and keep it in a large bowl for cooling.

In a large bowl, mix all-purpose flour, black pepper, corn starch, red chili powder, soy sauce, and salt. Add ¾ cup of water and make a smooth batter with no lumps. Now in a frying pan pour oil and bring to a medium-high heat. Dip the florets in the batter and fry in the oil pan. Flip the florets frequently for even cooking until they become golden brown. Using a slotted spoon, remove the fried florets into a tissue paper laced plate to absorb the excess oil.

In the same saucepan, under a medium-low heat, put the chopped green chilies, minced ginger, and sauté for 2 minutes until the raw smell of the ginger and garlic disappear. Then, add chopped bell pepper, chopped celery, and spring onions. Change the heat to a medium-high and sauté until the bell pepper becomes tender. At this point, add tomato ketchup, salt, soy sauce, black pepper, and stir well. Now add the fried cauliflower. Stir fry to combine and having a luxurious spice sauce coating on the fried florets. Finally, drizzle with vinegar and turn off the stove. Garnish with spring onion greens and serve hot.

Spinach Kabab
Cooking Time: 20 minutes |Serves: 8 |Per Serving: Calories 96, Carbs 11g, Fat 4g, Protein 3g

Ingredients:

For blanching spinach:
- Spinach leaves – 2 cups.
- Water – 2 cups, for blanching.
- Coldwater - 1½ cups.

For cooking green peas and potatoes:
- Potatoes – 2 large size.
- Green peas - ½ cup.
- Water – 2 cups, for pressure cooking.

Other ingredients:
- Chickpea flour – 4 tbsps.
- Green chili – 1
- Ginger, minced – 1 tsp.
- Chaat masala powder – 1 tsp.
- Dry mango powder – 1 tsp.
- Garam masala powder - ¼ tsp.
- Salt - ½ tsp.
- Cashew nuts – 8, halved.
- Oil – 3 tbsps.

Directions:
Rinse the spinach and put it in boiled water for 2 minutes. After that, put it in the cold water for 1 minute and take it out, and coarsely chop and keep it aside.

In a small frying pan, roast the chickpea flour until it releases the aroma and begins to change the color. Do not let it brown. Boil peas and potatoes in a pressure cooker with 2 cups of water for three whistles. Allow the pressure to settle down naturally and drain the water. Transfer the peas into a bowl and allow it to cool down. Before using the potatoes, peel them and crumble. Make a paste of green chili and ginger.

In a bowl, put the crumbled potatoes, cooked peas, chopped spinach, chili-ginger paste and combine well using a kabab mixture. To this mixture, add the roasted chickpea flour, all dry spices, and salt. Gently mix the ingredients. Make round patties.

In a pan pour cooking oil and bring to medium-low heat and fry the round patties until they become a crisp and golden color. Serve hot with ketchup or coriander chutney.

Chapter 3 Salads

Vegetable Salad

Cooking Time: 3 minutes |Serves: 3 |Per Serving: Calories 221, Carbs 15g, Fat 16.1g, Protein 7g

Ingredients:
- Carrots – 2 medium size.
- Cucumber – 2 medium size.
- White Indian radish – 1 small, tender.
- Tomato – 1 large.
- Spring onions – 3.
- Pumpkin seeds – 3 tbsps.
- Sunflower seeds, roasted – 1 tbsp.
- Sesame seeds - ½ tbsp.
- Cashew nuts, chopped – 1 tbsp.
- Almonds, chopped – 1 tbsp.
- Walnuts – 1 tbsp.
- Pistachios – 1 tbsp.

For the vegetable dressing:
- Olive oil, extra virgin – 1 tbsp.
- Lemon juice, fresh – 1 tsp.
- Basil, chopped – 4 leaves.
- Celery, coarsely chopped 1 tsp.
- Salt - ½ tsp.
- Pepper - ½ tsp.

Directions:
Rinse and dry all the vegetables before using them. Scrub radish, carrots and peel the cucumber. Then, cut the vegetables into small bite-size and put in a bowl. Chop spring onion, tomato, and put in the vegetable bowl. In a pan, roast all the nuts and seeds until they become crisp. Keep them aside. In a small bowl, toss all the ingredients for the dressing. Transfer the dressing ingredients into the vegetable bowl. Toss the vegetables to mix with the dressing. Scatter roasted seeds and nuts on it. Serve fresh.

Tropical Fruit Salad

Cooking Time: 10 minutes |Serves: 2 |Per Serving: Calories 438, Carbs 31g, Fat 32g, Protein 14g

Ingredients:
- Mangoes – 2 large.
- Bananas – 2 medium sized.
- Sapota – 3 medium sized.
- Papaya – 1 small.

- Cashew nuts – 2 tbsps.
- Mint leaves – 1 tbsp.

Directions:
Peel and chop the fruits into bite sizes. Put all the cut fruits into a medium bowl and toss to mix. Then, in a pan, dry roast the nuts until they become crisp. Scatter the dry fruits on top of the fruits. Garnish with mint leaves and serve fresh.

Sprout Salad

Cooking Time: 15 minutes |Serves: 2 |Per Serving: Calories 136, Carbs 29g, Fat 0g, Protein 7g

Ingredients:
- Sprouted green gram – 2 cups.
- Onion – 1 small, thinly sliced.
- Tomato – 1 medium size, chopped.
- Green chili – 1, chopped.
- Chili powder - ¼ tsp.
- Lemon juice – 1 tsp.
- Cilantro leaves, coarsely chopped – 1 tbsp.
- Lemon – 1 sliced into wedges
- Salt - ½ tsp.

Directions:
Soak the green gram and wrap in a cotton cloth for one day to sprout. Rinse the sprouts in water and boil to cook. Strain the sprouted green gram in a large bowl. Put chopped onion and tomato into it. Then add chopped green chili, red chili powder, and toss well to mix. Add salt and sprinkle lemon juice on top of it. Garnish with cilantro leaves and decorate with a lemon wedge while serving.

Corn Salad

Cooking Time: 15 minutes |Serves: 3 |Per Serving: Calories 142, Carbs 30g, Fat 2g, Protein 5g

Ingredients:
- Corn cobs – 2 cups.
- Onion – 1, finely chopped.
- Cucumber – 1 medium, chopped.
- Red chili powder - ¼ tsp.
- Cumin powder, roasted - ¼ tsp.
- Cilantro leaves, coarsely chopped – 1 tbsp.
- Lemon juice – 1 tsp.
- Salt - ½ tsp.

Directions:

Pressure cook the corn cobs for 5 whistles in 1½ cups of water. After cooking, allow the pressure to settle down naturally. Transfer them to a bowl and allow them to cool. Then scrap the corn kernels using a knife.

Put the corn kernels in a mixing bowl. Add chopped onion, chopped cucumber, chopped parsley, and chopped cilantro. Then, put roasted cumin powder and also chili powder into the jar. Add salt and sprinkle lemon juice into the bowl. Toss the ingredients to mix well. Serve fresh.

Potato Salad

Cooking Time: 20 minutes |Serves: 3 |Per Serving: Calories 305, Carbs 27g, Fat 19g, Protein 5g

Ingredients:
- Water – 4 cups.
- Salt – 1 tsp.
- Sugar – 1 tsp.
- Apple cider vinegar – 1 tsp.
- Potatoes - 1¼ lbs. Peeled and cubed.

For the dressing:
- Vegan mayonnaise – 6 tbsps.
- Dijon mustard – 1 tsp.
- Sugar - ½ tsp.
- Lemon juice – 1 tsp.
- Onions, chopped – 2 tbsps.
- Parsley, thinly chopped – 1 tbsp.
- Green olives – 6, pitted, and sliced.
- Red chili powder - ¼ tsp.
- Ground black pepper - ¼ tsp.
- Salt – 1 tsp.

For garnishing:
- Parsley, thinly chopped – 1 tsp.
- Red chili powder - ¼ tsp.

Directions:
In a bowl, mix vinegar, salt, sugar, and keep it ready. Then, rinse, peel, and cube the potatoes. After cubing, put in the vinegar-sugar-salt mixed water and boil for about 15 minutes until they are fork-tender. Drain the water and keep the potatoes ready to use. Wash all the remaining vegetables before cutting into the required size. In a bowl mix Dijon mustard with vegan mayonnaise. Add the chopped vegetables, salt, and gently mix. Season with ¼ teaspoon sugar, ¼ teaspoon red chili powder, and combine very well. Check the taste and, if required, add lemon juice, or Dijon mustard or chili powder or salt as needed.

Now add the boiled potatoes into the mayonnaise mixture and combine gently. After that, sprinkle ground black pepper and mix gently. Garnish with red chili powder and chopped parsley. Serve fresh.

Avocado Salad

Cooking Time: 15 minutes |Serves: 3 |Per Serving: Calories 267, Carbs 14g, Fat 24g, Protein 3g

Ingredients:
- Extra virgin olive oil – 1 tbsp.
- Lemon – 1, small. Wedged.
- Lemon juice – 2 tsps.
- Black pepper, crushed - ¼ tsp.
- Garlic, minced – 1 tsp.

Other ingredients:
- Onion, chopped – 1 small, finely chopped.
- Tomatoes – 1 medium, finely chopped.
- Cilantro, coarsely chopped – 1 tbsp.
- Avocados – 2 medium size, chopped
- Salt - ½ tsp.

Directions:
Rinse all the vegetables before using them. Put the lemon wedges, olive oil, and lemon juice in a medium bowl. Add crushed black pepper, red chili powder, minced garlic, and mix well. Keep the dressing mix aside.

In another bowl, put the chopped onion, parsley, avocado, tomatoes, and mix gently. Sprinkle salt and toss well. Stir the already prepared dressing and pour over the vegetable mix and toss gently. Serve fresh.

Yellow Lentil & Split Chickpeas Salad

Cooking Time: 15 minutes |Serves: 4 |Per Serving: Calories 113, Carbs 11g, Fat 6.3g, Protein 4g

Ingredients:
- Yellow lentils - ¼ cup.
- Cucumber, skinned and chopped - 1½ cups.
- Coconut, grated – 3 tbsps.
- Green chili – 1, chopped.
- Cilantro leaves, finely chopped – 2 tbsps.
- Lemon juice - ½ tsp.
- Salt - ¼ tsp.

For tempering:
- Oil – 2 tsps.
- Mustard seeds - ½ tsp.
- Hing - ⅛ tsp.
- Curry leaves – 1 twig.

Directions:
Rinse and dry all the vegetables before using them. Wash the yellow lentils 2 or 3 times and soak them for about 2 hours. After soaking, drain the lentils and keep them ready to use. To the bowl, add grated coconut, sliced cucumber, chopped green chili, chopped cilantro leaves, salt, and toss well. Sprinkle lemon juice over it and toss again.

For tempering the salad, pour mustard oil in a small pan and select the stove heat to medium-low. When the oil becomes hot, put the mustard seeds in to splutter. Then, add hing and curry leaves. Turn off the stove and transfer the mix to the mix vegetable bowl. Toss well and serve fresh.

Onion, Tomato & Cucumber Salad

Cooking Time: 15 minutes |Serves: 1 |Per Serving: Calories 178, Carbs 36g, Fat 1g, Protein 7g

Ingredients:
- Onion – 1 medium size, finely chopped.
- Tomatoes – 2 medium sized, finely chopped
- Cucumber – 2 small sized, peeled and chopped.
- Mint leaves – 5, chopped.
- Cilantro leaves, chopped - ¼ cup
- Lemon juice – 1 tsp.
- Lemon – 1, cut into wedges.
- Cumin powder - ½ tsp, roasted.
- Green chili – 1, chopped.
- Salt – 1 tsp.

Directions:
Wash all the vegetables before using them. Add all the chopped vegetables in a large bowl. Add, chopped cilantro leaves, chopped mint leaves, chopped green chili and toss to mix. Then, scatter roasted cumin powder, and sprinkle lemon juice. Sprinkle salt and toss well. Decorate with lemon wedges and serve fresh.

Chery Tomato Salad

Cooking Time: 10 minutes |Serves: 3 |Per Serving: Calories 56, Carbs 3g, Fat 4g, Protein 2g

Ingredients:

For dressing:
- Extra virgin olive oil – 1 tbsp.
- Apple cider vinegar – 2 tsps.
- Basil, fresh, chopped - ½ tbsp.
- Parsley, fresh, chopped - ½ tbsp.
- Sugar - ¼ tsp.
- Black pepper, crushed - ¼ tsp.
- Salt - ¼ tsp.

Main ingredients:
- Cherry tomatoes - ½ lbs.

Directions:
Rinse, dry, and chop the tomatoes into quarters. Keep them ready to use.

In a medium bowl, mix apple cider vinegar and olive oil. Add salt, sugar, chopped basil, chopped parsley, crushed black pepper in a medium bowl. Transfer the chopped tomatoes into the bowl and toss well to mix. Serve fresh.

Carrot Salad

Cooking Time: 5 minutes |Serves: 3 |Per Serving: Calories 89, Carbs 10g, Fat 5.5g, Protein 1g

Ingredients:
- Carrots – 4 medium sized, scrubbed and grated.
- Mustard seeds – 1 tsp.
- Sesame seeds – 1 tsp.
- Oil – 3 tsps.
- Green chili – 1, chopped.
- Turmeric powder - ¼ tsp.
- Hing - ⅛ tsp.
- Lemon juice – 1 tsp.
- Salt - ¾ tsp.

Directions:
Heat oil in a pan at a medium-low temperature. When the oil becomes hot, add mustard to splutter. Then add sesame seeds to sizzle for few moments. After that, add chopped green chili and sauté for a half minute. Now, sprinkle hing and turmeric powder and sauté for 1 minute. Finally, add grated carrots and sauté for about 4 minutes on a medium-low heat. Turn off the stove. Drizzle lemon juice, sprinkle salt, and toss to mix well. Do not cook the carrot too much. It should taste crispy. Serve fresh.

Bean Sprout & Bell Pepper Salad

Cooking Time: 1 minute |Serves: 4 |Per Serving: Calories 22, Carbs 2g, Fat 1.3g, Protein 1g

Ingredients:
- Beans sprouts - 1½ cups.
- Bell pepper, finely sliced - ¼ cup.
- Salt - ½ tsp.

For making the spice dressing:
- Oil - 1½ tsps.
- Garlic, minced - 1 tsp.
- Vinegar - 2 tsps.
- Sugar - ½ tsp.

- Soy sauce - 1 tsp.
- Chili powder - ½ tsp.
- Roasted peanut, coarsely crushed - 1½ tbsps.
- Salt - ½ tsp.

To Garnish:
- Spring onion greens, sliced - 1 tbsp.
- Cilantro leaves, shredded - 1 tbsp.

Directions:

For the dressing:
In a thick non-stick cooking pan, heat some oil and put in garlic. Sauté it for 15 seconds on medium heat. Transfer it from the cooking pot to a bowl and let it cool. In a medium bowl, mix peanuts, vinegar, soy sauce, chili powder, and sugar. Keep it ready for use.

Making the salad:
In a bowl, mix bean sprouts, spicy dressing, capsicum, and salt. Mix them well by tossing. Serve the dish soon or refrigerate it at least for half an hour to serve chilled.

Beetroot and Carrot Salad

Cooking Time: 5 minutes |Serves: 2 |Per Serving: Calories 86, Carbs 9g, Fat 5g, Protein 3g

Ingredients:
- Beetroot cubes - ½ cup.
- Red bell pepper cubes - ½ cup.
- Carrot, cut into diagonal pieces - ½ cup.
- Red pumpkin - ½ cup.
- Sea salt - ½ tsp.
- Zucchini, cut into cubes - ½ cup.
- Paneer cheese cubes - ¼ cup.
- Mushroom, cube cuts - ½ cup.
- Arugula leaves – 1 cup.
- Alfalfa sprouts -2 tbsps.

Dressing ingredients:
- Olive oil - 1 tbsp.
- Lemon juice – 1 tsp.
- Honey - ½ tsp.
- Balsamic vinegar - 1 tsp.
- Ground black pepper - ½ tsp.
- Salt - ½ tsp.

Directions:
Sauté carrot, beetroot, and red pumpkin by adding salt in a thick non-stick pan on medium heat. Transfer it into a bowl and keep aside. Now add Zucchini with salt in the same pan and sauté on

medium heat. Add paneer cubes and toss the pan on a medium-high heat for 1 min. Switch off the stove and add all the other items and gently mix. Finally, add the dressing and toss well before serving.

Chickpea Salad

Cooking Time: 20 minutes |Serves: 2 |Per Serving: Calories 214, Carbs 36g, Fat 3.3g, Protein 12g

Ingredients:
- White chickpeas - 1 cup.
- Tomato cubes - ¾ cup.
- Cucumber cubes - 1 cup.
- Spring onion, white and green parts - ¾ cup.
- Salt - ¼ tsp.

For the mint dressing:
- Fresh mint leaves, chopped - ½ cup.
- Coriander, coarsely chopped - ½ cup.
- Low-fat yogurt - 2 tbsps.
- Sugar - ½ tsp.
- Salt- ¼ tsp.
- Crushed black pepper - ½ tsp.

Directions:

For mint dressing
Mix all the items one by one into a big bowl. Transfer it into a blender and make a fine paste adding some water. Keep it aside.

For salad making:
Soak the chickpeas overnight. Pressure cook them for 2 whistles and allow it to settle the pressure naturally. After opening the lid, drain the chickpeas and combine all items in a big bow. Now transfer the mint dressing over it and toss well. Serve fresh or chilled.

Fruit & Vegetable Salad

Cooking Time: 10 minutes |Serves: 2 |Per Serving: Calories 99, Carbs 21g, Fat 1.1g, Protein 3g

Ingredients:
- Iceberg lettuce, shredded to pieces - 1 cup.
- Bell pepper, cut into cubes - ¼ cup.
- Apple, cut into cubes - 2 cups.
- Shredded carrot - ½ cup.
- Celery, cut into thin pieces - 2 tbsps.
- Orange carpels, cut into halves - ½ cup.
- Raisins, chopped - 2 tbsps.

For the dressing:
- Low- fat yogurt - ½ cup.
- Chili sauce - 1 tsp.
- Tomato ketchup - 1½ tbsps.
- Ground mustard - ¼ tsp.
- Bell pepper, chopped - 2 tsps.
- Green chilies, finely chopped -1 tsp.
- Onions, finely sliced - 1 tsp.
- Sugar - 1 tsp.
- Salt - ½ tsp.
- Low- fat milk - 2 tbsps.

Directions:
Mix all the fruit and vegetable items in a large kitchen bowl and also mix the dressing ingredients. Toss to combine well and serve immediately.

Potato Herb Salad

Cooking Time: 20 minutes |Serves: 3 |Per Serving: Calories 96, Carbs 18g, Fat 2.4g, Protein 2g

Ingredients:
- Potatoes, medium sizes, boiled - 3.
- Olive oil, extra virgin - 1 tbsp.
- Coarsely chopped fresh mix herbs of celery, basil, and parsley - ¼ cup.
- Salt - ½ tsp.
- Crushed black pepper – ½ tsp.
- Shredded fresh lettuce, for garnishing – 1 tsp.

Directions:
Boil the potatoes and peel the skin. Cut the potatoes into pieces and put them in a large bowl. Add the fresh mixed herbs into the bowl along with pepper and salt. Drizzle them with virgin olive oil. Gently mix the potatoes with the added spices until they get an even coating. Serve fresh by garnishing with shredded lettuce.

Cucumber Salad

Cooking Time: 3 minutes |Serves: 3 |Per Serving: Calories 103, Carbs 5g, Fat 8.5g, Protein 3g

Ingredients:
- Cucumbers, thin sliced - 2 cups.
- Grated coconut, fresh - ¼ cup.
- Roasted peanuts - ¼ cup.
- Green chili, chopped -1.
- Cilantro leaves, coarsely chopped - 1 tbsp.
- Lemon juice - 1 tsp.
- Salt - ½ tsp.
- Sugar - ¾ tbsp.

Ingredients for tempering:
- Sunflower oil - 1 tbsp.
- Mustard seed - ½ tbsp.
- Curry leaves - 2 twigs.

Directions:
In a shallow pan, roast the peanuts on a medium-low heat. Stop cooking and transfer them to a bowl when the black spot appears on the peanuts and allow them to cool. Rinse cucumber under running water and slice it. Keep them aside in a container for 15-20 minutes.

Hand rub the cooled peanuts to remove the skin and place them in a dry grinder for making a coarse powder. Now squeeze water from the cucumber, put in the coarse peanut powder, chop the chili, grated coconut, and lemon juice in a bowl. Add the shredded cilantro leaves and toss well.

For tempering, pour 1 tablespoon of oil into a deep skillet and bring to medium-low heat. Put mustard seeds in until they splutter and add curry leaves. Turn off the stove and transfer the tempering mix into the cucumber mix and gently mix. Sprinkle with salt, sugar, and serve.

Mango Salad

Cooking Time: 15 minutes |Serves: 5 |Per Serving: Calories 15, Carbs 4g, Fat 0.1g, Protein 0g

Ingredients:
- Raw mangoes, finely cubed - 1 cup.
- Onions, thinly cubed - ¼ cup.
- Ground red chili - ½ tsp.
- Roasted ground cumin seeds - ½ tsp.
- Sugar - 2 tsps.
- Salt - ½ tsp.
- Cilantro leaves, fresh, coarsely chopped - 1 tbsp.

Directions:
Rinse and peel the skin of the mangoes. Chop the mangoes into small cubes. Put the chopped mangoes and cubed onion into a big bowl. Now put ground cumin, red chili powder, salt, and sugar into the bowl and combine it. Allow it to season for 15 minutes. By this time, the mango salad will become soft to consume. Garnish with cilantro leaves and serve.

Watermelon and Mint Salad

Cooking Time: 15 minutes |Serves: 3 |Per Serving: Calories 45, Carbs 9g, Fat 1.2g, Protein 1g

Ingredients:
- Watermelon cubes - 3 cups.
- Black olives - 2 tbsps.
- Mint leaves - ¼ cup

Lemony-honey dressing:

- Lemon juice - 2 tsps.
- Olive oil - 1 tsp.
- Honey - 1 tbsp.
- Salt - ½ tbsp.

Directions:
First of all, mix all the ingredients except for the lemony-honey dressing in a large bowl and toss well. After that, transfer lemony-honey dressing in the mix and combine it well. Serve fresh or serve refrigerated.

Onion Ring Salad

Cooking Time: 10 minutes | Serves: 3 | Per Serving: Calories 11, Carbs 2g, Fat 0.1g, Protein 0g

Ingredients:
- Onion, finely sliced - 1 large.
- Ground red chili - ¼ tsp.
- Lemon juice - 1 tsp.
- Cilantro leaves, coarsely chopped - 1 tbsp.
- Salt - ½ tsp.

Directions:
Slice the onion into rings. Put it into a medium bowl and add chili powder, and cilantro leaves. Sprinkle lemon juice and add salt. Combine the ingredients gently and serve fresh.

Potato and Pomegranate Salad

Cooking Time: 30 minutes | Serves: 4 | Per Serving: Calories 87, Carbs 12g, Fat 4g, Protein 2g

Ingredients:
- Fresh Potatoes, medium-sized, diced and boiled – 2.
- Pomegranate arils - ½ cup.
- Onion small, thinly sliced - 1.
- Tomato, medium sized, thinly chopped – 1.
- Mint leaves, coarsely chopped - 1½ tbsps., divided.

For dressing:
- Ground red chili - ¼ tsp.
- Mix (chaat) masala powder - 1 tsp.
- Ground roasted cumin - 1 tsp.
- Lemon juice - 2 tbsps.
- Sunflower oil - 2 tbsps.
- Salt - ½ tsp.

Directions:
In a medium bowl, combine onion, diced potatoes, tomatoes, chopped mint leaves, and pomegranate arils gently. Put all dressing ingredients in a medium bowl and mix slowly. If needed,

add more spices. Now transfer the dressing mixture into the large salad bowl and toss well. Garnish with mint leaves and serve fresh.

Roasted Mushroom and Bell Pepper Salad

Cooking Time: 15 minutes |Serves: 3 |Per Serving: Calories 16, Carbs 3g, Fat 0.2g, Protein 1g

Ingredients:
- Mushrooms - 2 cups.
- Bell pepper, green – 1.
- Bell pepper, red - 1.
- Bell pepper, yellow – 1.
- Rosemary, dried - 1 tsp.
- Thyme, dried - ½ tsp.
- Lemon juice - 1½ tsp.
- Salt - ½ tsp.

Directions:
Rinse and dry the mushroom. Preheat the oven at 200°c for 5 minutes and bake the mushroom for 10 minutes or until they become light brown. Flip them while baking every 5 minutes to have them evenly baked. Remove and allow them to cool. After cooling, cut, and remove the stem. Chop the mushrooms into cubes and keep aside. Roast the bell peppers until their skin becomes black. Allow them to cool and remove the burnt skin, stem, and seeds. Cut them into cubes and keep aside. Now mix the cubes of mushrooms and cubes of bell peppers. Add lemon juice, thyme, rosemary, salt, and toss the mixture. Serve fresh.

Spinach and Paneer Cheese Salad

Cooking Time: 15 minutes |Serves: 4 |Per Serving: Calories 31, Carbs 3g, Fat 1.6g, Protein 2g

Ingredients:
- Spinach, blanched, shredded - 1½ cups.
- Paneer cheese cubes - ½ cup.
- Green chilies, chopped - 1 tbsp.
- Tomatoes, thinly chopped - 1 cup.
- Powdered sugar - 1 tsp.
- Lemon juice - 1 tbsp.
- Tomato ketchup - 2 tbsps.
- Soy sauce - 1 tsp.
- Chili sauce - 1 tsp.

Directions:
In a large bowl, mix all the ingredients and toss gently. Serve fresh.

Tomato and Lettuce Salad

Cooking Time: 20 minutes |Serves: 6 |Per Serving: Calories 11, Carbs 1g, Fat 0.8g, Protein 0g

Ingredients:
- Fresh lettuce, chopped - 2 cups.
- Quartered tomatoes – 2.
- Green peas, boiled - 1 cup.
- Celery, coarsely chopped - 2 tbsps.
- Bell pepper, sliced - ¼ cup.
- Paneer cheese cubes - ½ cup.

For the dressing:
- Garlic, finely sliced - 2 tsps.
- Fresh basil leaves, finely chopped - 2 tsps.
- Lemon juice - 3 tbsps.
- Paprika flakes - ½ tsp.
- Olive oil - 2 tsps.
- Ground black pepper – 1 tsp.
- Salt - ¾ tsp.

Directions:
In a large salad bowl, combine all the ingredients and refrigerate. In another bowl, mix all the dressing ingredients and transfer onto the refrigerated items and toss well before serving. Serve immediately after dressing.

Tomato Basil and Feta Cheese Salad

Cooking Time: 15 minutes |Serves: 2 |Per Serving: Calories 118, Carbs 4g, Fat 10g, Protein 4g

Ingredients:
- Tomato deseeded cubes - 1 cup.
- Fresh basil, cut into pieces - ¼ cup.
- Feta cheese, crumbled - 5 tbsps.
- Green cucumber cubes - ¾ cup.
- Olive oil - 2 tsps.
- Ground black pepper - ½ tsp.
- Salt – ½ tsp.

Directions:
Mix up all the ingredients in a large bowl. Toss well and serve it instantly.

Cabbage Salad

Cooking Time: 5 minutes |Serves: 2 |Per Serving: Calories 27, Carbs 4g, Fat 1.4g, Protein 1g

Ingredients:

For salad
- Cabbage, shredded - 2 cups.

- Green chilies, thinly chopped -1 tsp.
- Cilantro leaves, coarsely chopped - 2 tbsps.

For dressing:
- Lemon Juice - 1 tsp.
- Coriander powder - 1 tsp.
- Olive oil - 1 tsp.
- Chili powder - ¼ tsp.
- Black salt - ¼ tsp.
- Asafetida - ¼ tsp.
- Salt - ¼ tsp.

Directions:
Mix all the ingredients in a large salad bowl along with the dressing ingredients. Serve fresh.

Chapter 4 Stew/Soups

White Pumpkin Stew

Cooking Time: 15 minutes |Serves: 2 |Per Serving: Calories 207, Carbs 24g, Fat 11.1g, Protein 7g

Ingredients:
- Deseeded, white pumpkin tender – 2 cups.
- Onion, finely sliced – ¼ cup.
- Green chilies, julienned – 4.
- Curry leaves – 1 twig.
- Ginger, minced - ½ tbsp.
- Coconut oil – 1 tbsp.
- Coconut milk, whole fat – 1 cup.
- Water – ½ cup.
- Salt - 1 tsp.

Procedure:
Rinse pumpkin in running water and cut into small cubes. Put in a cooking bowl along with sliced onion, chilies, curry leaves, and minced ginger. Add water and salt. Cover it with the lid and cook at medium-low heat. Once the vegetables become soft, add coconut milk. Simmer it and warm for 5 minutes. Add coconut oil and curry leaves. Close it till use.

Sambar

Cooking Time: 40 minutes |Serve: 4 |Per Serving: Calories 307, Carbs 48g, Fat 12.1g, Protein 8g

Ingredients:

Vegetables:
- Potato – 1 large, peeled and cubed.
- Tomato – 4 large, quartered.
- Carrot – 1, scrubbed and cubed.
- Drumstick – 1, cut into 1-inch length.
- Eggplant – 1, cubed.
- Onion, sliced - 1 large.
- Green chilies, julienned – 2.
- Split pigeon peas - ½ cup.

Spices ingredients:
- Turmeric powder – ½ tsp.
- Tamarind pulp – 2 tbsps.
- Cilantro leaves, chopped – 2 tbsps.
- Red chili powder – 1 tsp.
- Coriander powder – 1 tbsp.

- Sambar Powder – 3 tsps.
- Mustard Seeds – ½ tsp.
- Fenugreek - ½ tsp.
- Red chilies – 3, cut into halves.
- Curry leaves – 1 twig.
- Hing – ½ tsp.
- Coconut oil – 3 tbsps.
- Water – 3 cups.
- Salt – 2 tsps.

Directions:
Rinse all vegetables before using them. Heat 1 teaspoon of coconut oil in the pressure cooker. When the oil becomes hot, add sliced onions, green chilies, and garlic for about 2 minutes. Add the pigeon peas, turmeric powder, salt, all the cut vegetables into the pressure cooker. Pour water above the vegetable level and cook for 2 whistles.

Soak the tamarind pulp in ½ cup of water. After the 2nd whistle, release the pressure manually. Open the cooker and add tamarind juice. Stir gently and simmer for about 5 minutes. Check the salt level and, if required, add more. Then, add the chopped cilantro leaves, hing, and simmer at a low heat for 2 minutes. Now, you can remove it from the stove and keep aside.

Now let us do the tempering. In a frying pan, pour the remaining oil and bring to medium-low heat. When the oil becomes hot, put the mustard seeds in to splutter. Then add fenugreek, dry chilies, split shallots, curry leaves, and fry for about 1 minute. Mix coriander powder, sambar powder, chili powder, and sauté for about 2 minutes under a medium-low heat. Transfer the entire mix to the sambar in the pressure cooker. Stir gently and cook under medium-low heat for 2 minutes. Stop cooking and serve with rice.

Red Lentils and Clarified Butter Soup

Cooking Time: 15 minutes |Serve: 4 |Per Serving: Calories 136, Carbs 16g, Fat 5.6g, Protein 7g

Ingredients:
- Split red lentils (masoor dal), rinsed & drained – ¼ cup.
- Low fat paneer cut into cubes – ¼ cup.
- Oil – 1 tbsp.
- Sliced onions – ½ cup
- Minced garlic – ½ cup
- Ground chili – ¼ tsp.
- Chopped tomatoes – ¾ cup.
- Lemon juice – 2 tsps.
- Salt - ½ tsp.

Directions:
Heat oil in a pressure cooker. When the oil becomes hot, sauté onions for 1 to 2 minutes on a low-medium heat. Add chili powder, garlic, and sauté until it starts to emanate the flavor. Put red lentils and tomatoes along with 2 ½ cups of water in the cooker. Give a gentle mix and pressure cook for

3 whistles. Switch off the cooker and allow it to settle the pressure. When the ingredients become heat-free, puree it in a mixer grinder. Transfer the puree into a nonstick pan and stir in salt. Bring to boil the puree and simmer it for 2 minutes. Finally, add low fat paneer cheese cubes, lemon juice, and give a gentle stir. Serve immediately.

Green Gram Soup

Cooking Time: 20 minutes |Serve: 4 |Per Serving: Calories 130, Carbs 8g, Fat 10.9g, Protein 2g

Ingredients:
- Green gram (moong) - ½ cup.
- Water – 3¼ cups divided.
- Oil – 1 tbsp.
- Cumin – ½ tsp.
- Hing – ¼ tsp.
- Green chilies, finely chopped – ½ tsp.
- Curry leaves – 4 or 5 leaves.
- Lemon juice – 2 tsps.
- Salt - ½ tsp.
- Coriander leaves, coarsely chopped – 1 tbsp.

Directions:
Soak the green gram for 8 hours and drain before using. In a pressure cooker, pour 3 cups of water and green gram. Pressure cook it for 3 whistles. Let the pressure settle naturally. Open the cooker and blend the green gram using a hand blender. In a pan pour oil and bring to low-medium heat and put cumin seeds in to splutter. Add hing, chiles, curry leaves, and sauté for some time on a low-medium heat. Now transfer the blended mixture to the pan. Add ¼ cup water, salt and cook for 4 or 5 minutes. Stir well by adding lemon juice. Serve hot by garnishing it with coriander leaves.

Carrot Soup

Cooking Time: 13 minutes |Serves: 4 |Per Serving: Calories 51, Carbs 9g, Fat 1.1g, Protein 2g

Ingredients:
- Carrots, finely grated – 2 cups.
- Onions, sliced – ½ cup.
- Water - ¾ cup divided.
- Yellow split gram – 1 tbsp.
- Low-fat milk – ¾ cup
- Salt - ½ tsp.

Directions
Rinse and drain yellow split gram, and keep ready to use. Put carrots, onions, ¼ cup of water, and yellow split gram in a pressure cooker. Stir it gently and pressure cook for 3 whistles. Stoop the cooker and allow the pressure to settle down naturally before you open the lid. Transfer the mixture to a blending bowl and make a smooth puree. In a deep nonstick pan, add milk, salt,

pepper, ½ cup of water, and cook it on a medium-low heat for 2-3 minutes by stirring occasionally. Serve it immediately and hot.

Tomato Soup

Cooking Time: 20 minutes |Serves: 2 |Per Serving: Calories 180, Carbs 29g, Fat 6.2g, Protein 5g

Ingredients
- Medium to large tomatoes – 4.
- Garlic, finely chopped – ½ tsp.
- Onion, finely sliced – ¼ cup.
- Bay leaf – 1.
- Corn flour – 1 tsp.
- Water - 2 tbsps.
- Butter – 1 tbsp.
- Water – 1 cup
- Fat cream – 1 tbsp.
- Sugar – ½ tbsp.
- Brown or white bread – 2 slices.
- Ground black pepper - ½ tsp.
- Salt - ½ tsp.
- Coriander leaves, coarsely chopped for garnishing – 1 tbsp.

Directions:

Preparing the tomato puree:
Rinse the tomatoes and keep them aside. Pour 5 or 6 cups of water in a saucepan, put in some salt and bring it to boil. Add the tomatoes to the boiled water and turn off the stove. Let the tomatoes stay in the boiled water for 20-30 minutes. Drain the water after cooling. Peel the tomatoes and remove the eye portion, once they have cooked well. Chop the tomatoes and put them inside the jar along with chopped garlic and sliced onions. Blend it into a smooth puree.

Bread toasting:
Place the bread on a hot frying pan and roast until it becomes golden brown from both sides. Slice it into cubes and keep aside.

Making the tomato soup:
Make a smooth paste of corn flour by mixing 1 tsp. flour with 2 tablespoons of water. Melt butter in a saucepan and sauté bay leaf for 2 seconds. Add garlic on a medium-low heat and sauté until it becomes slightly brown. Put sliced onions in and sauté until they become translucent. Stir in the tomato puree and add water, pepper, and salt. When the soup starts to boil, add the corn flour mixture. Simmer it for 4 minutes until the soup becomes thick. Add sugar, cream, and simmer for a minute. Add the bread croutons, garnish with coriander, and serve hot.

Vegetable Soup

Cooking Time: 20 minutes |Serves: 3 |Per Serving: Calories 116, Carbs 15g, Fat 5.2g, Protein 4g

Ingredients

- Garlic, finely chopped - ½ tsp.
- Minced ginger – ¾ tsp.
- Onions, finely sliced – ¼ cup.
- Cabbage, finely chopped – ½ cup.
- Carrots, finely grated – ⅓ cup.
- Bell pepper, finely chopped – ⅓ cup.
- French beans, finely chopped – ¼ cup.
- Oil – 1 tbsp.
- Water- 3 cups.
- Ground black pepper – ¼ tsp.
- Nutmeg powder – 1 tsp.
- Salt - ½ tsp.
- Spring green onions for garnishing – 1 tbsp.

Directions:
Pour 1 tbsp. of oil into a saucepan and bring to medium-low heat. When the pot becomes hot, add ½ teaspoon of finely chopped ginger and garlic. Sauté them until they become golden brown. Then stir in cabbage, carrots, bell pepper, and French beans. Add 3 cups of water, ground black pepper, and season it with salt. Cover the pan and simmer on medium heat. Add some veggies for the crunch. Garnish with spring onions and serve hot.

Corn Soup

Cooking Time: 20 minutes |Serves: 2 |Per Serving: Calories 166, Carbs 22g, Fat 8.1g, Protein 3g

Ingredients:
- Olive oil – 1 tbsp.
- Spring onions, chopped – 1 tbsp.
- Corn starch – ½ tbsp.
- Water - 1½ cups.
- Celery, finely chopped – 1 tsp.
- Corn cob – 1 large size.
- Ground black pepper – ½ tsp.
- Salt - ½ tbsp.

Directions:

Making the corn paste:
Boil the corn in a medium bowl and scrape the corn kernels. Keeping 2 tablespoons of corn kernels aside, blend the corn kernels in some water and make a smooth paste.

Making the corn soup:
Heat oil in a pan and sauté the spring onions until they are transparent. Add the chopped celery and sauté for few minutes. Transfer the corn paste into the pan and stir. Pour water and bring it to boil. Put ground black pepper, remaining 2 tablespoons of kernels, salt, and simmer for 2 or 3 minutes. Add the corn flour paste until the soup becomes thick. Garnish it with celery and serve hot.

Spinach Soup

Cooking Time: 20 minutes | Serves: 2 | Per Serving: Calories 192, Carbs 8g, Fat 17.6g, Protein 2g

Ingredients:
- Chopped spinach – 2 cups.
- Chopped onions - ¼ cup.
- Garlic pod, minced – 3.
- Gram flour – 1 tbsp.
- Ground cumin - ¼ tsp.
- Bay leaf – 1 small size.
- Water – 2 cups.
- Butter – 1½ tbsps.
- Ground black pepper - ½ tsp.
- Salt - ½ tsp.
- Clarified butter for garnishing – 2 tbsps.

Directions:

Cooking the spinach mixture:
In a saucepan, heat oil and sauté bay leaf for 2 or 3 seconds. Add garlic and sauté until it becomes golden brown. Put chopped onions and stir until it becomes brown. Add the spinach, season with ground black pepper. Put gram flour along with 2 cups of water and stir to mix. Bring it to boil for 3 or 4 minutes. Add the cumin powder and stir well. Let the mixture cool.

Making the soup:
Discard the bay leaves and combine the mixture using a hand blender. Add more salt if needed. If the soup is thick, add about ¼ cup of water and let it simmer for 2 or 3 minutes. Garnish with fresh spring onions, clarified butter, and serve hot.

Mushroom Soup

Cooking Time: 20 minutes | Serves: 3 | Per Serving: Calories 174, Carbs 9g, Fat 13.7g, Protein 4g

Ingredients:
- Clarified butter – 2 tbsps.
- Bay leaves – 1 leaf.
- Onions, finely sliced – ⅓ cup.
- Minced garlic – ½ tsp.
- Button mushrooms – ½ pound,
- Whole wheat flour – 1 tbsp.
- Ground black pepper – ½ tsp.
- Water- 1 cup.
- Whole milk kept at room temperature - 1 cup.
- Salt - ½ tsp.
- Low fat cream- 6 tbsps.

- Cilantro, coarsely chopped – 2 tbsps.

Directions:

Stir-frying garlic and onions:
Melt clarified butter in a heavy saucepan. When the butter becomes hot, put in the bay leaf and stir fry for about 3 minutes until the fragrance starts to release. Add finely sliced onions, garlic, and sauté until the onions turn soft and translucent.

Cooking the mushrooms:
Remove the lower portion of the mushroom stems and quarter them. Put the chopped mushrooms into the saucepan and sauté at medium-low heat until they release water. Continue cooking until they become dry and golden brown. Add flour and sauté on a medium heat for 3 or 4 minutes. Add ground black pepper and mix well.

Making the soup:
Pour water and then milk into the saucepan. Add salt and stir. Simmer it on a medium heat for about 4 or 5 minutes. As the soup thickens, keep stirring occasionally. When the soup becomes thick, add cream and parsley. Sprinkle ground nutmeg and stir. Stop cooking and serve hot.

Broccoli Soup

Cooking Time: 25 minutes |Serves: 2 |Per Serving: Calories 372, Carbs 44g, Fat 17.1g, Protein 14g

Ingredients
- Broccoli – ½ pound.
- Clarified butter – 2 tbsps.
- Sliced onions – ¼ cup.
- Garlic, minced – 3 cloves.
- Whole wheat flour – 1½ tbsp.
- Vegetable stock – 1½ cups.
- Full fat milk – 1½ cups.
- Dry oregano – ¼ tsp.
- Ground nutmeg – ⅛ tsp.
- Salt - ½ tsp.
- Ground black pepper – ½ tsp.

Directions:

Blanching the broccoli:
Cut the broccoli florets into bite-sized pieces. Boil in a bowl adding ¼ teaspoon of salt and switch off the cooking. Put the chopped florets in the boiled water for about 20 minutes until it becomes soft to the fork. Drain the water and keep aside a few florets for later use. Doing the blanching is an excellent method to neutralize the insects and pesticide residues.

Making the broccoli soup:
Heat butter in a thick saucepan and sauté onions until they turn golden brown. Add flour and stir well for 2 minutes. Put the drained broccoli along with the vegetable stock. Mix it and cover the

lid. Slightly warm the milk on the stove and using an immersion blender puree the soup in the saucepan. Add hot milk to the puree. Simmer on a low heat for about 6 minutes. Sprinkle in dry oregano and season with ground nutmeg and black pepper. Serve hot.

Hot and Sour Soup

Cooking Time: 30 minutes | Serves: 3 | Per Serving: Calories 150, Carbs 20g, Fat 6.2g, Protein 5g

Ingredients:
- Oil – 1 tbsp.
- Onions, finely sliced – ¼ cup.
- Garlic, minced – 1 tsp.
- Ginger, finely grated – 1 tsp.
- French beans, finely chopped – ¼ cup.
- Sliced mushrooms – ¾ cup.
- Grated carrots – ¼ cup.
- Shredded cabbage – ¼ cup.
- Celery, chopped - ¼ cup.
- Corn starch flour – 2 tbsps.
- Water – 3 tbsps.
- Ground black pepper – ¾ tsp.
- Soy sauce – 3 tsps.
- Salt - ½ tsp.
- Rice vinegar – 2 tsps.
- Coriander leaves, coarsely chopped – 3 tsps.

Directions:

Frying veggies:
Heat oil in a thick saucepan and add onion, garlic, and ginger. Sauté them on high heat for 2 or 3 minutes until the onion becomes translucent. Add chopped French beans and mushrooms. Let the mushrooms fry until golden brown. Add cabbage, celery, and carrots after the mushrooms are golden brown. Stir fry on a high heat for 2 or 3 minutes. Make the corn starch paste by mixing corn starch flour with water, and keep it aside.

Making the soup:
Add water and soy sauce into the fried vegetable pan and stir well. Stir in salt and bring the soup to simmer. Add corn starch paste and mix well. Allow the soup to thicken on a medium flame. Add black pepper and vinegar once soup becomes thick. Switch off the stove and garnish with coriander leaves. Serve hot.

Pumpkin Soup

Cooking Time: 25 minutes | Serves: 2 | Per Serving: Calories 375, Carbs 24g, Fat 30.6g, Protein 6g

Ingredients:
- Pumpkin – ½ pound.
- Onions, chopped – ⅓ cup.

- Garlic cloves, minced – 3.
- Water – ¾ to 1 cup.
- Olive oil - 2 tbsps.
- Dry oregano – ¼ tsp.
- Ground black pepper - ¼ tsp.
- Salt - ¼ tsp.
- Grated cheese – 1 tbsp, for garnishing.

Directions:

Pumpkin cooking:
Wash, peel, and chop pumpkin and put it into a pressure cooking along with garlic and onions. Pour water and cook on medium heat for 2 whistles. Open the lid once the pressure settles. Blend the whole mixture with a hand blender to become a smooth puree.

Making the soup:
Put the pressure cooker on a medium heat and pour oil. When the oil becomes hot, put the thyme, oregano, and black pepper in. Transfer the puree into the cooker and add salt to taste. Bring the soup to simmer and turn off the stove when the soup becomes hot. Garnish with grated cheese and serve hot.

Lemon Coriander Soup

Cooking Time: 20 minutes |Serves: 3 |Per Serving: Calories 194, Carbs 27g, Fat 7.6g, Protein 8g

Ingredients:
- Sesame oil – 1 tbsp.
- Ginger, finely chopped – 1 tsp.
- Garlic, minced – 1 tsp.
- Onions, sliced – ¼ cup.
- Carrots, finely chopped – ¼ cup.
- Mushrooms, cut into pieces – 1¼ cups.
- Green chili, chopped – 1 .
- Lemongrass stalk, chopped – 1.
- Ground black pepper powder - ½ tsp.
- Vegetable stock – 4 cups.
- Lemon Juice – 2 tbsps.
- Coriander leaves, coarsely chopped – ¼ cup.
- Shredded spring onions for garnishing - ¼ cup.

Directions:

Cooking vegetables:
In a thick saucepan, heat oil on a medium heat and sauté garlic, chili, and ginger. Stir fry until they are golden brown. Add onions and sauté until they becomes translucent and add the other vegetables. Stir fry until they become brown. Pour 4 cups of vegetable stock, chopped lemongrass, and add black pepper and salt.

Making the soup:
Cover the saucepan and cook the vegetables on a medium-low heat. Add lemon juice and coriander leaves when the vegetables are cooked. If you want to reduce the sourness of the soup, use only 1 tablespoon of lemon juice. Stir and then switch off the stove. Discard lemongrass and garnish with spring onions and serve hot.

Creamy Corn Veg Soup

Cooking Time: 15 minutes |Serves: 4 |Per Serving: Calories 163, Carbs 26g, Fat 5.1g, Protein 7g

Ingredients:
- Corn kernels – 2 cups.
- Milk, kept at room temperature – 1½ cups. Divided.
- Sugar- ½ tsp.
- Butter – 1 tbsp.
- Onions, finely sliced – 2 tbsps.
- Carrots, finely grated – 4 tbsps.
- French beans, chopped – 2 tbsps.
- Celery, finely shredded – 1 tsp.
- Water – 1½ cups.
- Ground black pepper – ½ tsp.
- Salt - ½ tsp.

Directions:
Steam the corn cobs in a pressure cooker and scrape off the corn kernels. Put them in a blender. Blend it to make a smoothie by adding sugar and 1 cup of milk. Melt butter in a thick saucepan and add all chopped veggies. Sauté them on a medium heat. Add celery and transfer corn puree. Stir and sauté for a minute. Add water, the remaining ½ cup of milk, and continue stirring. Simmer on low heat. Stir in salt and black pepper. Serve hot.

Vegetable Stew

Cooking Time: 30 minutes |Serves: 4 |Per Serving: Calories 328, Carbs 28g, Fat 24g, Protein 6g

Ingredients:
- Carrots, peeled and chopped – 2 medium size.
- Potato, peeled and chopped - 1 large.
- Peas – 1 cup.
- Beans – 3 ounces.
- Onion, finely sliced -1 large.
- Ginger garlic paste – 1 tsp.
- Green chilies – 3.
- Cloves – 3.
- Cinnamon – 1½ inch.
- Pepper, crushed - 1 tsp.
- Thin coconut milk – 2½ cups.

- Thick coconut milk – 1 cup.
- Curry leaves – 1 twig.
- Coconut oil – 2 tbsps.
- Salt – ¾ tsp.

Directions:
Pour coconut oil in a pan and bring to medium-low heat. When the oil becomes hot, add the spices and sauté until the fragrance emanates. Add ginger-garlic paste, green chilies, onions, curry leaves, and sauté until the onions get a golden color. Put the chopped veggies in and sauté. Now pour thin coconut milk and salt to cook the vegetables until they become tender. Finally, add thick coconut milk and simmer for a few minutes and turn off the stove. Serve hot.

Vegetable Stew South Indian Style

Cooking Time: 40 minutes |Serves: 5 |Per Serving: Calories 346, Carbs 40g, Fat 19.4g, Protein 7g

Ingredients:
- Potatoes, peeled and cubed – 2 large.
- Carrot, scrubbed and diced – 1.
- French beans – 15.
- Green peppers – 2.
- Coconut milk – 2 cups.
- Ground pepper – 1 tsp.
- Sugar - 1 tsp.
- Curry leaves – 1 sprig.
- Coconut oil – 2 tsps.
- Salt - ½ tsp.

Directions:
Rinse, and cut the vegetables, and steam them in a large bowl. Keep aside for later use. In a saucepan add coconut milk, curry leaves, green chilies, and cooked vegetables. Stir well and bring it to boil. Add salt for taste. If the gravy is thick, add a little water. Finally, add coconut oil and cook on a medium-low heat for a few minutes. Turn off the stove and allow the stew to stand for about 10 to 15 minutes. Serve hot with your favorite dish.

Malabar Vegetable Stew

Cooking Time: 35 minutes |Serves: 4 |Per Serving: Calories 295, Carbs 19g, Fat 25.1g, Protein 5g

Ingredients:
- Vegetable oil – 3 tbsps.
- Cloves – 3.
- Cinnamon stick – 1 inch.
- Onion, thinly sliced – 1 large.
- Tomato, finely chopped – 1 medium size.
- Green chili, julienned – 1.
- Ginger, minced – 1 tbsp.

- Turmeric powder – ⅛ tsp.
- Carrot, scrubbed and cubed – 1 cup.
- Cauliflower, cut into small florets – 2 cups.
- Green beans, long cut – 5½ ounces.
- Curry leaves – 1 twig.
- Water – ¾ cup.
- Salt - ¾ tsp.
- Coconut milk – 1 cup.
- Ground black pepper – ½ tsp.
- Cilantro leaves, finely chopped - 2 tbsps.

Directions:
In a saucepan, pour oil and bring to a medium-low heat. Add spices and fry for few seconds until the fragrance emanates. Put in chopped onions and sauté until transparent and, at this point, add minced ginger, chopped tomatoes until the tomatoes become soft and juicy. Then add all the veggies and stir for 5 minutes. Add water, salt and simmer for 10 minutes until the vegetables are cooked well. Pour coconut milk in and continue cooking for 2 minutes on a low heat. Finally, add pepper powder and curry leaves. Before serving, garnish with chopped coriander leaves.

Mughal Vegetable Stew

Cooking Time: 15 minutes |Serves: 4 |Per Serving: Calories 86, Carbs 6g, Fat 6.9g, Protein 1g

Ingredients:
- Potato – 1 medium size.
- Cauliflower florets – 1 cup.
- French beans, long cuts – 1 cup.
- Bell pepper – 1.
- Yogurt, beaten – ½ cup.
- Cashew nuts, broken up – ½ cup.

Spices and tempering
- Coriander powder – 1 tsp.
- Turmeric powder - ½ tsp.
- Red chili powder - ½ tsp.
- Rosewater – 1 tsp.
- Salt – 1 tsp.
- Cumin seed – ½ tsp.
- Cinnamon stick – 1 inch.
- Green cardamom – 2.
- Cloves – 4.
- Peppercorns – 5.
- Bay leaves – 1.
- Green chilies, julienned – 3.
- Grated ginger – ½ tsp.
- Clarified butter – 2 tbsps.

Directions:
Rinse all vegetables, before chopping them into bite sized pieces. Heat oil at a medium-low temperature in a saucepan and deep fry all the veggies till they become soft. Soak cashew nuts for about 20 minutes and make a smooth paste in a grinder.

In another pan add 2 tablespoons of clarified butter and bring to a medium-low heat and add cumin seed. When it sizzles, add all other spices and sauté until they start to produce the aroma. Now add the green chilies and minced ginger. Stir fry until the raw aroma of the ginger disappears. Add coriander powder and turmeric and stir fry for a minute. Turn off the stove and add yogurt and mix well. Add cashew nut paste, water, turn on the stove and bring to the boil. Now, add all the vegetables and salt. Stir gently and set the heat to a medium-low and cook until oil precipitates on the side and top. Drizzle with rose water and serve hot.

Panjabi Kadhi

Cooking Time: 20 minutes |Serves: 4 |Per Serving: Calories 109, Carbs 8g, Fat 6.9g, Protein 4g

Ingredients:
- Chickpea flour – 2 tbsps.
- Fresh yogurt – 1½ cups.
- Garlic, minced - 1 tsp.
- Onion, finely sliced – ¼ cup.
- Turmeric powder – ¼ tsp.
- Cloves – 2.
- Cumin seeds – 1 tsp.
- Hing – ⅛ tsp.
- Curry leaves – 1 twig.
- Oil – 1 tbsp.
- Green chilies, coarsely chopped – ½ tsp.
- Salt – ¾ tsp.
- Cilantro leaves, chopped – 2 tbsps.

Directions:
Whisk yogurt and chickpea flour in a medium bowl without any lumps and keep aside. In a pan pour oil and bring to a medium-low heat. Put in cumin seeds; when they sizzle, stir in cloves. After that, add hing, curry leaves and garlic and continue sautéing until they start to produce the aroma. Now, add onions and sauté until they are transparent. Reduce the heat to the minimum and add the yogurt mixture, water, turmeric powder, and cook for about 3 minutes. Now add salt, chilies and simmer for 10 minutes to thicken the gravy. Garnish with chopped cilantro leaves while serving.

Dal Makhani

Cooking Time: 1 hour |Serves: 4 |Per Serving: Calories 386, Carbs 39g, Fat 10.2g, Protein 13g

Ingredients:

- Whole black gram – ¾ cup.
- Kidney beans – ¼ cup.
- Water – 3 cups.
- Onion, thinly chopped – ½ cup.
- Green chilies, chopped – 2.
- Ginger-garlic paste – 2 tsps.
- Tomatoes, pureed – 2.
- Cumin seeds – ½ tsp.
- Cloves – 3.
- Cardamom – 3.
- Cinnamon – 1 inch
- Bay leaf – 1
- Red chili powder – ½ tsp.
- Low fat cream – ½ tsp.
- Fenugreek leaves – ¼ tsp.
- Clarified butter – 3 tbsps.
- Salt - ¾ tsp.

Directions:
Soak black gram and kidney beans overnight or for 8 hours. Pressure cook them in 3 cups of water for 20 whistles. In a mixer jar, add tomatoes and make a smooth puree. Heat up a pan add clarified butter. When the butter becomes hot, add all the spices and sauté well until they start to release the aroma. Add chopped onions and sauté until they becomes golden brown. Now add ginger-garlic paste and stir fry until the raw smell goes. Add green chilies and stir. After that, add tomato puree, red chili powder, and sauté at a medium-low heat until it starts to release oil on the gravy surface. Now, put black gram and kidney beans in, and continue cooking. If the gravy is thick, add the required amount of water to maintain the consistency. Stir well and simmer for about 25 minutes. After that, add the low-fat cream, stir well, and turn off the stove. Finally, garnish with chopped fenugreek leaves and mix well. The dish is ready to serve with any of your favorite bread.

Split Chickpeas Stew

Cooking Time: 40 minutes |Serves: 5 |Per Serving: Calories 338, Carbs 72g, Fat 2g, Protein 12g

Ingredients:
- Split chickpeas – ½ cup.
- Shallots, peeled and halved– 10.
- Potatoes, peeled and quartered – 8 medium sized.
- Elbow macaroni - ¼ cup.
- Green chilies – 4.
- Ginger, minced – 1 tbsp.
- Cumin seeds, roasted – 1 tsp.
- Tomatoes, chopped – 2 medium size.
- Garam masala powder – ½ tsp.
- Lemon, cut into small wedges – 1.
- Salt - ¾ tsp.
- Chili powder – ½ tsp.

- Ground coriander – 1 tsp.
- Ground cumin - ½ tsp.
- Ground pepper - ½ tsp.
- Onion, thinly sliced – 1 small.

Directions:
In a large bowl, rinse split chickpeas and cook with 6 cups of water for about 20 minutes. Add shallots, potatoes, tomatoes, macaroni, salt, coriander, chili powder, minced ginger, and cumin powder. Mix well and cook until the split chickpeas and veggies are cooked well. Sprinkle with pepper, roasted cumin seeds and garnish with coriander leaves, sliced onions, and lemon wedges.

Spiced Red Lentil Stew

Cooking Time: 45 minutes |Serves: 5 |Per Serving: Calories 219, Carbs 31g, Fat 6.8g, Protein 11g

Ingredients:
- Red lentils – 1 cup,
- Onion, sliced – 1 large,
- Sweet potatoes, diced – 2½ cups,
- Oil – 2 tbsps.
- Ginger, minced – 1 tbsp.
- Garlic cloves, crushed – 2.
- Ground coriander – 1 tbsp.
- Ground cumin – 1 tsp.
- Turmeric powder – ½ tsp.
- Ginger paste – 1 tsp.
- Tomato, coarsely chopped – 1 cup.
- Cilantro leaves, coarsely chopped – 2 tbsps.
- Salt - ½ tsp.
- Water – 4 cups.

Directions:
In a saucepan pour oil and bring to a medium-low heat. When the oil becomes hot, add onions and sauté until it becomes golden brown. Add sweet potato, minced ginger, crushed garlic, and stir well. After that, add chili, lentils, ground coriander, ground cumin, and turmeric powder. Stir well continuously until the flavor emanates. Now add tomatoes and 4 cups of water. Cook for 30 minutes until lentils and potatoes are soft. Add salt and simmer it to thicken for 10 minutes. Garnish with cilantro and serve hot.

Spring Onion Soup

Cooking Time: 15 minutes |Serves: 4|Per Serving: Calories 261, Carbs 32g, Fat 14g, Protein 5g

Ingredients:
- Spring onions, chopped – 4½ cups, divided.
- Potatoes, peeled and cut into bite-sized pieces – 2 medium size.
- Garlic, chopped – 4.

- Soy sauce – 2 tsps.
- Dry oregano – ½ tsp.
- Water – 6 cups.
- Olive oil – 3 tbsps.
- Ground pepper – 1 tbsp.
- Salt - ¾ tsp.
- Bread, cut into cubes - ½ cup.
- Clarified butter – 1 tbsp.

Directions:
Rinse all the vegetables before chopping. Now, on a low heat, warm the olive oil in a saucepan and fry garlic for 2 minutes. Add spring onions and sauté for 5 minutes at a medium-low heat. Now add, chopped potatoes, salt, ground pepper, and sauté well. Pour 4 cups of water in and stir to mix well. Cover the pan and simmer until the potatoes are soft. Switch off the stove and allow the mixture to cool down. With a hand blender, blend to make a smooth soup. Add soy sauce, dried oregano, and simmer for 5 minutes. Check the soup's consistency and, if required, add more water and cook until it boils. In a frying pan, pour some clarified butter, bring to medium-low heat and fry the bread cubes. Garnish the onion soup with chopped spring onions and fried bread. Serve hot.

Chapter 5 Main Meals

Vegan Cheesy Flatbread

Cooking Time: 16 minutes |Serves: 4 |Per Serving: Calories 369, Carbs 34g, Fat 22.3g, Protein 10g

Ingredients
- Wheat pastry flour- 1 cup plus 1 tsp.
- Oat flour - ⅓ cup.
- Baking powder - 1½ tsps.
- Garlic powder - ½ tsp.
- Ground coriander - ½ tsp.
- Kosher salt - ½ tsp.
- Cashew yogurt - ½ cup.
- Olive oil, extra virgin - ¼ cup.
- Vegan mozzarella cheese, shredded - ½ cup.
- Butter flavored coconut oil - ¼ cup.

Directions
Make dough by mixing, wheat pastry flour, baking powder, oat flour, garlic powder, ground coriander, kosher salt, cashew yogurt, and olive oil. Keep it covered for 30 minutes. Make 4 balls out of the dough and flatten them. Place cheese at the center of the flattened ball and fold it. Flatten the dough again. Heat a thick pan with coconut oil on a medium-low heat and gently place the flatbread onto it. Flip each side gently after 3 or 4 minutes, until it cooked well. Repeat with other portions.

Carrot Chickpea Curry

Cooking Time: 55 minutes |Serves: 2 |Per Serving: Calories 293, Carbs 36g, Fat 14.2g, Protein 10g

Ingredients:
- Carrots - 10½ ounces.
- Cooked chickpeas - 8¾ ounces.
- Tinned tomatoes – 7 ounces.
- Onion – 1 large.
- Cloves garlic, minced – 4.
- Ginger, minced – 2 tbsps.
- Coconut milk – 6 ounces
- Cooking oil - 1 tbsp.
- Ground chili - 1 tsp.
- Ground coriander- 1 tbsp.
- Ground turmeric - ½ tsp.
- Ground cumin - ½ tsp.
- Ground black pepper - ¼ tsp.
- Ground cinnamon - ⅛ tsp.
- Dried fenugreek leaves - 1 tbsp.

- Salt - ¾ tsp.

Directions:

Rinse, peel and cut the carrots into lengthwise 3cms and split cut into 4 pieces. Dice the onion. Pour oil in a saucepan and bring to medium-low heat. When the oil becomes hot, put the chopped carrots and sauté for 10 minutes and keep aside. Now, fry onions for 5 minutes in a medium-low heat. Put garlic and ginger into it and stir fry for a minute. Sprinkle all the spices into the pan except fenugreek and keep stirring. Add the tomatoes, coconut milk, chickpeas, and gently stir for a minute. Now, stir in the fried carrot. Finally, sprinkle the fenugreek, salt, and cover with the lid. Let it simmer for 40 minutes on a low heat.

Rice and Butter Cauliflower

Cooking Time: 20 minutes |Serves: 4 |Per Serving: Calories 454, Carbs 72g, Fat 13.6g, Protein 12g

Ingredients
- Basmati rice - 1 cup.
- Water – 2 cups.
- Butter, unsalted - 3 tbsps.
- Cloves garlic, minced – 3.
- Onion, diced – 1 small size.
- Ginger, minced - 1 tsp.
- Garam masala powder - 2 tsps.
- Ground chili - 1 tsp.
- Ground cumin - 1 tsp.
- Tomato paste - ¼ cup.
- Tomato sauce – 8 ounces.
- Vegetable stock - 2 cups.
- Kosher salt – 1 tsp.
- Ground black pepper – 1 tsp.
- Cauliflower, cut into florets – 1.
- Heavy cream - ½ cup.
- Fresh cilantro leaves, coarsely chopped - ¼ cup.

Directions

Rinse rice 2 or 3 times until the water becomes clear, drain and keep aside. In a deep cooking bowl, pour 2 cups of water and cook the rice until the water evaporates entirely in a medium-low heat. Make sure not to burn the rice.

Heat butter in a large saucepan. Put garlic and onion into the pan when the butter becomes hot and sauté for 3 minutes. Add ginger, garam masala, ground chili, cumin, tomato paste, and cook for one minute under a medium-low heat. Stir in tomato sauce and vegetable stock with them. Add salt, pepper and continue sautéing for about 7 minutes in a low heat. Add the chopped cauliflower and cook for about 10 minutes until it becomes tender. Stir in heavy cream for 1 minute, scatter chopped cilantro leaves. Finally, add salt and pepper, and gently mix. Serve with rice.

Rice and Cauliflower Lentil Curry

Cooking Time: 30 minutes |Serves: 4 |Per Serving: Calories 462, Carbs 73g, Fat 15.3g, Protein 14g

Ingredients
- Brown rice – 1 cup.
- Petite yellow lentils - ½ cup.
- Coconut oil - 1 tbsps.
- Shallots, sliced thinly - 2 medium.
- Grated ginger - 2 tbsps.
- Cloves Garlic, minced – 2.
- Green curry paste - 5 tbsps.
- Cauliflower, chopped - 2 cups.
- Coconut milk – 5 ounces.
- Water - ¼ cup
- Coconut aminos - 2 tbsps.
- Maple syrup- 1 tbsp.
- Kale, chopped - 4 cups.
- Lime juice, fresh - 2 tbsps.

Directions

Rinse rice until the water becomes clean and drain. In a rice cooking bowl, pour in 4 cups of water and bring to the boil. Put in the rice and cook well until the rice becomes soft. Switch off the stove and drain the rice and keep aside.

Soak petite yellow lentils overnight or for 1 hour. Put oil, shallots, ginger, and garlic into a hot skillet and fry for about 3 minutes. Add curry paste into it and cook for another 2 minutes stirring occasionally. Now, put in the chopped cauliflower and fry for a few minutes. Stir in coconut milk. Add soaked petite yellow lentils, coconut aminos, maple syrup, and stir well and cook for about 20 minutes. Finally, add kale 5 minutes before you turn off the stove. Drizzle with lime juice and gently stir. Serve with brown rice.

Vegetable Biriyani with Baked Tofu

Cooking Time: 1 hour 10 minutes |Serves: 8 |Per Serving: Calories 323, Carbs 37g, Fat 16.4g, Protein 11g

Ingredients:

For rice:
- Vegan butter - 2 tbsps.
- Onions, thinly sliced - 2 medium.
- Basmati rice - 2 cups.
- Raisins - ½ cup.
- Garlic cloves, minced – 2.
- Ginger, grated - 2 tsps.
- Black peppercorns – 10.
- Green cardamom pods – 5.
- Cloves – 5.

- Cinnamon sticks – 2.
- Star anise – 2.
- Bay leaves – 2.
- Ground coriander - 1 tsp.
- Ground cumin - 1 tsp.
- Ground turmeric - ½ tsp.
- Cumin seeds - ½ tsp.
- Cayenne pepper - ¼ tsp.
- Water - 3¾ cups.
- Salt - 1½ tsps.

For spicy baked tofu:
- Soy sauce - 3 tbsps.
- Lemon juice - 1 tbsp.
- Maple syrup - 1½ tbsps.
- Garam masala - 1 tsp.
- Garlic clove, minced - 1
- Canola oil - 1 tsp.
- Tofu, cut into ½ inch cubes – 1 packet (7 ounces)

For roasted vegetables:
- Russet potato - 1 medium size.
- Cauliflower florets - 2 cups.
- Green beans- 1 cup.
- Canola oil - 1 tbsp.
- Cashews - 1 cup.
- Fresh cilantro, chopped - ½ cup.
- Coconut, shredded - ¼ cup.

Directions
Rinse the rice, then soak it for 20 minutes. Fry the onions for 4-5 minutes in a saucepan with melted butter, until they become golden brown. Remove the onions onto a plate and put peppercorns, cayenne pepper, cumin seeds, ground cumin, star anise, cinnamon sticks, raisins, ginger, garlic, cloves, cardamom, bay leaves, coriander, and turmeric into the pan and sauté on a low heat. Stop sautéing when the flavors start to release and transfer the spices into a plate.

Drain the rice and put it in a rice cooking bowl with 3¾ cups of water and cook on a low heat. Put the roasted spices, fried onions and salt into the pan and give it a gentle stir. Increase the heat and bring to boil the liquid. After boiling, reduce the heat, close the lid and let it simmer for 20 minutes or until the water evaporates completely. Once the water evaporates completely, turn off the stove and let it sit for 5 minutes.

When cooking is in progress, start working on tofu. Pour maple syrup, soy sauce, lemon juice, oil, garam masala, and garlic into a shallow dish, and stir to mix them. Put the chopped tofu into the mix and toss well to coat. Let it marinate for 20 minutes. Roast the tofu by flipping sides for about 40 minutes on a medium-low heat until the sides become brown.

For making the roasted vegetables, pour oil in a large skillet, put the chopped potatoes, green beans, cauliflower, and toss well to coat. Place the coated vegetables in the oven and bake for 20 minutes until it becomes fork-tender.

Open the rice cooker lid, fluff the rice and put baked tofu, roasted vegetables, coconut, cashews, and chopped cilantro leaves. Stir gently and remove the spices like; bay leaves, star anise, and cinnamon sticks before serving.

Garlic Naan

Cooking Time: 45 minutes |Serves: 12 |Per Serving: Calories 136, Carbs 17g, Fat 5.8g, Protein 3g

Ingredients:
- All-purpose flour - 4 cups.
- Sugar - 1 tbsp.
- Active dry yeast - 2¼ tsps.
- Warm water - ¼ cup.
- Warm milk - ¾ cup.
- Plain yogurt - ¾ cup.
- Kosher salt - 1 tsp.
- Butter, melted – 4 ounces.
- Cloves Garlic, minced – 4.
- Cilantro, coarsely chopped – 2 tbsps.

Directions:
Mix yeast, sugar, and water in a bowl and keep it aside to become foamy. Add milk, yogurt into it and combine it well. Mix salt and flour and make a well in the center. Pour the yeast mixture into the well. Knead well to make it a smooth dough. Keep the dough aside for 1 hour after transferring it into a lightly oiled bowl and cover it with a dampened cloth.
Roll the dough into 12 medium-sized balls and place them on a floured workstation. Flatten them there and transfer them onto a medium-high heat thick skillet. Smear butter over the bread and cook for around 2 minutes and flip sides when it begins to form bubbles. Continue cooking the other side also for about 2 minutes until it becomes golden in color. Transfer the remaining butter into a microwave-safe bowl add minced garlic. Microwave it for about 15 seconds and brush the garlic butter over the naan and sprinkle with cilantro. Serve hot.

Palak Paneer

Cooking Time: 30 minutes |Serves: 4 |Per Serving: Calories 260, Carbs 17g, Fat 17.7g, Protein 14g

Ingredients
- Olive oil - 6 tbsps. Divided.
- Cloves garlic, minced – 2.
- Ginger root, grated - 1 tbsp. Divided.
- Red chili peppers, dried – 2.
- Onion, sliced - ½ cup.
- Ground cumin - 2 tsps.
- Ground coriander - 1 tsp.

- Ground turmeric - 1 tsp.
- Sour cream - ¾ cup.
- Spinach, coarsely chopped - 3 lbs.
- Quartered tomato - 1 large.
- Cilantro leaves, coarsely chopped – 4 sprigs.
- Ricotta cheese - 4 ounces.
- Salt - ½ tsp.

Directions:
Pour 3 tablespoons of olive oil into a thick saucepan and bring to medium-low heat. Sauté ½ tablespoon of grated ginger, garlic, onion, and dry red chilies until the onion becomes brown. You can mix the cumin, coriander, turmeric, and sour cream in a medium bowl after that. Add spinach into it and cook it for 15 minutes. Let it cool.

Combine tomato, balanced ginger, and cilantro with the spinach mixture in a blender for about 30 seconds. Transfer it to the saucepan and simmer it on low heat. Pour 3 tablespoons of olive oil into a frying pan and bring to a medium heat. Sauté cheese until it becomes brown. Drain and add to the spinach mixture and cook on a low heat for about 10 minutes. Add salt to taste and serve.

Potato and Cauliflower Spice Mix

Cooking Time: 15 minutes | Serves: 4 | Per Serving: Calories 273, Carbs 54g, Fat 4.1g, Protein 7.5g

Ingredients:
- Cauliflower - 1 head.
- Potatoes – 3.
- Olive oil - 1 tbsp.
- Cumin seeds - 1 tsp.
- Tomatoes, diced – 2.
- Onion, sliced – 1.
- Salt - 1 tsp.
- Curry powder - 1 tsp.

Directions:
Rinse, peel, and cut the potato into 1-inch cubes. Similarly, cut cauliflower into 1-inch florets. Microwave on high cauliflower and potatoes separately for 3 minutes and 4 minutes, respectively. In a large skillet heat olive oil. Add cumin seeds and sauté until they become golden brown. Add the sliced onions and stir for about 3 minutes on a medium-high heat until the onion becomes translucent. Put in tomato and stir fry for about 5 minutes. Add cauliflower and potato and gently fold the mixture. Season with salt, curry powder and continue cooking for about 4 minutes. Serve warm.

Black Chickpeas with Potato

Cooking Time: 1 hour 20 minutes | Serves: 6 | Per Serving: Calories 285, Carbs 43g, Fat 9.2g, Protein 9g

Ingredients:
- Black chickpeas - 1 cup.

- Salt - 1½ tsps.
- Baking soda - ½ tsp.
- Water – 6 cups + 3 tbsps. Divided.
- Onion, large, sliced – 1.
- Clove garlic, minced - 1 tbsp.
- Ginger, grated - 1 tbsp.
- Vegetable oil - 3 tbsps.
- Cumin seeds - ¼ tsp.
- Asafetida powder - ½ tsp.
- Potatoes, cubed – 4.
- Ground coriander - 1 tsp.
- Garam masala - 1 tsp.
- Ground turmeric - ¼ tsp.
- Cayenne pepper - ¼ tsp.
- Tamarind paste - 3 tbsps.

Directions

Sort, rinse chickpeas, and drain. In a large bowl, put drained chickpeas, baking soda, ½ tsp. salt, and soak it in 4 cups of water overnight or 24 hours. In a blender, combine onion, garlic, and ginger by adding 3 tablespoons of water to make a paste. Pour vegetable oil in a large skillet and bring it to medium-low heat. When the oil becomes hot, add cumin seeds and asafetida to the skillet and sauté for 1 minute. Continue the stir-frying by adding onion paste and cook for 5 minutes on medium-low heat. Drain the chickpeas and transfer them into the onion-cumin mixture. Stir in potatoes, coriander, turmeric, garam masala, cayenne pepper, and 1 teaspoon of salt. Pour 2 cups of water and cook it on low heat for 1 hour with the lid. Once the chickpeas become tender, add tamarind paste into the mixture, stir gently, and cook for about 10 to 12 minutes.

Ghee Rice

Cooking Time: 15 minutes | Serves: 2 | Per Serving: Calories 593, Carbs 108g, Fat 13.9g, Protein 12g

Ingredients
- Basmati rice - 1 cup.
- Clarified butter - 2 tbsps.
- Onion, sliced – 1 medium.
- Water - 1¾ cups.
- Green chilies, julienned – 1.
- Salt - ½ tsp.
- Cashew nuts – 14.
- Raisins- 14.
- Cinnamon- 2 inch.
- Cloves – 4.
- Green cardamoms – 4.
- Mace - 1 strand.
- Star anise – 1.
- Bay leaf – 1.

Directions
Rinse rice 3 times until the water becomes clear, drain and keep aside. In a thick saucepan, add 2 tablespoons of clarified butter and bring to medium-low heat. Put cashews and raisins into the pan and sauté. Once done, remove them onto a plate. In the same pan, fry onions until they turns brown and keep them aside for garnishing.

In a pressure cooker, pour the left-over butter and sauté all the remaining spices on a medium-low heat until the aroma begins to release. Add drained rice, julienned chilies and fry on a medium-low heat for about 4 minutes. Now, pour 1¾ cups of water and add salt. Stir gently and close the pressure cooker with the pressure vent on and cook on low heat for 1 whistle. Switch off the stove and allow the pressure to release naturally. Open the lid and fluff the rice using a fork. Serve ghee rice onto the plates by garnishing with fried onions, cashews, and raisins.

Mint Rice

Cooking Time: 20 minutes |Serves: 3 |Per Serving: Calories 329, Carbs 53g, Fat 12.5g, Protein 7g

Ingredients:
- Rice - 1½ cups.
- Mint, finely chopped - 1 cup.
- Coriander leaves, coarsely chopped – 2 tbsps.
- Green chilies – 2.
- Ginger, minced - 1 tbsp.
- Garlic - 3 small pods.
- Coconut, shredded - ¼ cup.
- Salt- ¾ tsp.
- Oil – 2 tbsps.
- Water - 2½ cups.
- Lemon juice - 2 tbsps.
- Carrots, peas, potatoes, beans - 1½ cups.

Mint rice spices:
- Bay leaf – 1
- Star anise – 1
- Mace – 1 strand
- Cumin - ½ tsp.
- Cloves – 6.
- Cinnamon - 2 inch.
- Green cardamoms – 4.

Directions:
Rinse rice 3 times until the water becomes clear and soak it for 15 minutes. Wash green chilies, coriander, and mint leaves. Blend them in a mixer grinder along with ginger, garlic, coconut without adding water.

Heat a saucepan with 2 tablespoons of oil. Add bay leaf, star anise, mace, cumin, cloves, cinnamon, and green cardamoms to the pan and sauté until they begin to sizzle. Transfer the mint-coriander paste into the pan and fry for about 3 minutes on a medium-low heat. Add the mixed vegetables and stir-fry for another 2 minutes. Pour water and add salt. Add the rice and cook at a low temperature.

Rice Flour Bread

Cooking Time: 15 minutes | Serves: 4 | Per Serving: Calories 183, Carbs 37g, Fat 2.4g, Protein 3g

Ingredients:
- Rice flour- 1 cup.
- Water – 1 cup.
- Shallots, coarsely chopped – 1.
- Coconut grated - 3 tbsps.
- Carrot, grated – 3 tbsps.
- Green chili, thinly chopped – 2.
- Coriander leaves, coarsely chopped - 2 tbsps.
- Cumin - ½ tsp.
- Salt - ⅓ tsp.
- Ginger, minced - ½ tsp.
- Oil - 1 tbsp.

Directions:
Make a soft dough using flour, salt, cumin, chopped shallots, chilies, coriander leaves, coconut, and carrots using a mixing bowl by adding water part by part. Make 4 equal balls out of the dough and keep it covered by a damp cloth to prevent drying. On a foil place the dough ball and spread it with fingers to make a round bread. Spread some oil on a thick frying pan and bring it on medium-high heat. Place the bread gently on it and cook until it becomes firm. Flip sides and apply some oil and cook well until the brown spots appear. Repeat the same process for making the remaining bread.

Tomato Broth

Cooking Time: 20 minutes | Serves: 4 | Per Serving: Calories 479, Carbs 89g, Fat 10.2g, Protein 9g

Ingredients
- Potatoes, peeled and cubed – 2.
- Beans, chopped – 8.
- Beetroot, scrubbed and cubed - ¼ cup.
- Large onion, sliced – 1.
- Tomatoes, deseeded and chopped - 2 large.
- Green chilies, julienned – 1.
- Coriander leaves, chopped - 3 tbsps.
- Garlic paste - 1 tbsp.
- Red chili powder - ¼ tsp.

- Peppercorn - ½ tsp.
- Turmeric powder - ¼ tsp.
- Oil - 3 tbsps.
- Salt- ½ tsp.
- Basmati rice - 1½ cups.
- Water – 2¾ cups.

For the spices:
- Bay leaf – 1.
- Star anise – 1.
- Green cardamoms – 4.
- Cloves – 6.
- Cinnamon stick 1 inch – 2.
- Peppercorns – 6.
- Cumin - ½ tsp.

Directions
Rinse and dry all vegetables before cutting/slicing. Soak the rice for 30 minutes after rinsing until the water becomes clear. Pour oil into a pressure cooker and bring to a medium-low heat. Put all the spices in and sauté for 2 minutes until the flavor starts to release. Stir in the onions until they become translucent. Now, add garlic paste, tomatoes, salt, turmeric, pepper powder, and red chili powder and stir fry for 2 minutes. Add other vegetables and stir fry for about 4 minutes. Now, start cooking the rice by pouring water into the cooker and bringing it to the boil. Put in the soaked rice, give a gentle stir, and close the lid. Stop cooking after 1 whistle and let the pressure settle naturally. After the pressure has released fully, open the cover and fluff the rice gently.

Bell Pepper Rice
Cooking Time: 25 minutes |Serves: 4 |Per Serving: Calories 411, Carbs 84g, Fat 4.2g, Protein 8g

Ingredients
- Rice – 2 cups.
- Water - 3¼ cups + 2 tbsps.
- Oil - 2 tbsps.
- Onion, sliced - 1 medium.
- Green chili, julienned – 1.
- Garlic paste - 1 tbsp.
- Green peas - ½ cup
- Bell pepper, chopped - 2 cups.
- Coriander leaves, coarsely chopped - 2 tbsps.
- Mint leaves - ¼ cups.
- Salt - 1¼ tsps.
- Lemon juice - 2 tbsps.

Spices for bell pepper rice:
- Curry leaves - 1 sprig.

- Cumin - ½ tsp.
- Garam masala - 1½ tsps.
- Red chili powder- ½ tsp.
- Turmeric, powder - ¼ tsp.

Directions
Rinse the rice until the water becomes clear and cook in a pressure cooker for 1 whistle on a medium-high heat. After cooking, let it release the pressure naturally. Open the lid and fluff the rice. Keep it aside. In a thick saucepan, pour oil and bring to a medium-low heat. Sauté cumin and curry leaves. Stir in onions, chili, garlic paste, until the onion becomes tender. Add capsicum and green peas along with 2 tablespoons of water and stir fry for 3 minutes. Put mint, coriander, chili powder, garam masala, salt, and sauté on a medium-low heat until the aroma emanates. Transfer the cooked grainy rice into the capsicum mixture and stir well.

Spicy Veg Pulao

Cooking Time: 20 minutes | Serves: 3 | Per Serving: Calories 455, Carbs 92g, Fat 6.2g, Protein 10g

Ingredients
- Basmati rice - 1 cup.
- Oil - 1 tbsp.
- Onion – 1, medium, sliced.
- Potatoes, peel and cubed – 1 small
- Tomato, chopped – 1.
- Cauliflower, floret cuts - ½ cup.
- Beans, chopped – 6.
- Carrot, scrubbed and cubed – 1.
- Green peas - ¼ cup.
- Salt - 1 tsp.
- Garlic paste - 1 tsp.
- Green chili, thinly sliced – 1.
- Coriander leaves, coarsely chopped - 2 tbsps.
- Water – 1¾ cups.

Dry spices for pulao:
- Bay leaf - 1
- Cumin - ½ tsp.
- Cloves – 4.
- Cinnamon stick - 2 inch.
- Black cardamom - 1
- Green cardamoms – 4.

Spice powder for pulao:
- Turmeric powder - ¼ tsp.
- Red chili powder - ¼ tsp.
- Ground coriander - 1 tsp.
- Ground cumin - ½ tsp.

- Garam masala - ½ tsp.

Directions

Rinse rice until the water becomes clear and soak it for 30 minutes. Rinse all vegetables before you process for cooking. In a pressure cooker, pour oil and bring to medium-low heat. Put in cumin, bay leaf, cardamoms, cloves, cinnamon, onions, chili, garlic paste and sauté well for about 3 minutes. After that, stir in coriander powder, garam masala, cumin, turmeric, cumin powder, and salt. Add all vegetables and stir fry for about 3 minutes. Now drain the rice and put it into the cooker. Pour water and gently mix once. Close the lid and cook for 1 whistle on a medium-high heat. Let the pressure release naturally. After that, open the lid and fluff the rice by sprinkling cilantro leaves. Cover the cooker for 5 minutes and serve.

Vegetable Pulao

Cooking Time: 20 minutes |Serves: 3 |Per Serving: Calories 486, Carbs 98g, Fat 6.6g, Protein 10g

Ingredients:
- Basmati rice - 1½ cups.
- Clarified butter - 2 tbsps.
- Onion, sliced - 1 medium.
- Green chilies, thinly chopped – 2.
- Carrots, beans, peas, potatoes - 1½ cups.
- Salt - ¾ tsp.
- Water - 2¾ cups.
- Mint, chopped - 3 tbsps.
- Garlic paste - 1½ tsps.

Spices for veg pulao:
- Bay leaf – 1.
- Star anise – 1.
- Mace - 1 strand.
- Cumin - ½ tsp.
- Green cardamoms - 4
- Cloves – 6.
- Cinnamon stick - 2 inch.
- Nutmeg – 1 small piece.
- fennel seeds - ¼ tsp.
- Stone flower - 2 pinches

Directions

Rinse the rice until the water turns clear and soak for 15 minutes. After 15 minutes, drain it and keep aside. Rinse and dry all vegetables before chopping/shredding. Meantime, in a pressure cooker, pour in clarified butter and bring to a medium-low heat. Put all the spices in and sauté until they start to release the aroma. Add onions, chilies, garlic paste, and continue sautéing until the onion becomes tender. Stir in mint and vegetables for about 3 minutes. Pour water into the pressure cooker and add salt. Put in the drained rice, close the lid, lock the vent and pressure cook for 1 whistle under a medium-high heat. After the whistle, stop cooking and wait to release the pressure naturally. Open the lid and fluff the rice with a fork. Serve hot.

Indian Vegetable Roll

Cooking Time: 15 minutes |Serves: 5 |Per Serving: Calories 100, Carbs 18g, Fat 2.1g, Protein 3g

Ingredients:
- Wheat flour – 1¼ cups.
- Salt - ½ tsp.
- Water - ⅓ cup.
- Oil - 1 tsp.

For the filling:
- Potato, peeled and cubed - 1 medium.
- Capsicum, peas, cauliflower, carrot, etc. - 1 cup.
- Oil - 1 tbsp.
- Cumin - ½ tsp.
- Mustard - ½ tsp.
- Asafetida - ¼ tsp.
- Onion, sliced – 1.
- Garlic paste - ¾ tsp.
- Ground coriander - ¾ tsp.
- Red chili powder - ½ tsp.
- Garam masala - ½ tsp.
- Turmeric - ⅛ tsp.
- Salt - ½ tsp.
- Cilantro leaves, chopped – 2 tbsps.
- Sauce - 3 tsps.

Directions:
Boil the potato and keep aside. Put the wheat flour, salt, oil, and required amount of water in a mixing bowl and make the dough. Knead well to let the dough become soft. Cover the dough with a damp cloth for 20 minutes so that it can retain the moisture. Now make 5 equal balls from the dough and spread some wheat flour on the rolling table and flatten the ball on it. Place a thick pan on the stove and bring to medium-high heat. Keep the flattened bread over it and cook until the bread develops bubbles. When it starts to develop bubbles, flip sides and press with a spatula. When both sides cook well with golden brown spots, spread some clarified butter over it. Place a parchment paper or kitchen cloth on a plate and keep the baked bread over it. Continue cooking the remaining bread.

For making the filling, sauté mustard and cumin in an oiled saucepan until it splutters. Stir in hing, onions, and salt until the onion becomes translucent. Add garlic paste and continue sautéing until the raw smell disappears. Now put all the vegetables, excluding the steamed potato. Finally, stir in turmeric, chili powder, coriander powder, garam masala and stir fry for 2 minutes. Cover the pan and cook on a medium-low heat. When the vegetables are cooked, add in the boiled potatoes and stir to mix gently.

Spread sauce on the bread. Place the cooked veggies on one side of the bread and roll it tightly. Prick it with a toothpick to hold the roll firmly. Serve warm.

Biriyani Rice

Cooking Time: 30 minutes |Serves: 4 |Per Serving: Calories 265, Carbs 50g, Fat 5g, Protein 6g

Ingredients:
- Basmati rice – 2 cups.
- Water - 3¾ cups.
- Clarified butter - 2½ tbsps.
- Onion, thinly sliced - ½ cup.
- Garlic paste - 1 tbsp.
- Tomato, deseeded and chopped - ½ cup.
- Salt- 1 tsp.
- Mint leaves, chopped – 2 tbsps.
- Curd - ¼ cup.

Spices for biriyani rice:
- Bay leaf – 1.
- Cloves – 6.
- Green cardamoms – 6.
- Star anise – 1.
- Cumin - ½ tsp.
- Mace - 1 strand.
- Cinnamon – 1.
- Turmeric powder - ¼ tsp.
- Red chili powder - ½ tsp.
- Biriyani masala powder - 1½ tsps.

Directions

Rinse the rice until the water turns clear and soak it for 20 minutes. After 20 minutes, drain the water and keep aside. In a pressure cooker, pour clarified butter and bring to a medium-low heat. Sauté the spices until they start to release the flavor. Add onion and sauté until it turns to golden. Put in the ginger paste and stir fry until it starts to produce the aroma. Add the biriyani masala, tomatoes, ground red chili, curd, coriander, mint, turmeric powder, and salt. Sauté until the tomatoes become tender and turn to pulpy. Now pour water, gently stir and check the salt level. Put in the rice, cover the cooker, and cook on a medium-low heat for 1 whistle. After the whistle, put off the stove and let it settle the pressure naturally. Open the lid, fluff the rice, and serve hot.

Mango Rice

Cooking Time: 25 minutes |Serves: 4 |Per Serving: Calories 450, Carbs 81g, Fat 10g, Protein 10g

Ingredients
- Rice - 2 cups.
- Raw mango – 1 medium size.

- Curry leaves - 2 sprigs.
- Green chilies – 3.
- Red chilies – 2.
- Salt – 1 tsp.
- Turmeric - ¼ tsp.
- Peanuts - 3 tbsps.
- Split chickpeas - 1 tbsp.
- Black lentil - 1 tbsp.
- Mustard seeds - 1 tsp.
- Ginger - 1 inch.
- Hing - ¼ tsp.
- Oil - 3 tbsps.

Directions
Rinse rice in a bowl until the water turns clear. Pour 4 cups of water in the pressure cooker and put in the rice. Cover the lid, lock the vent and cook on a medium-high heat for 3 whistles. Let the pressure release naturally. After that, open the lid and transfer the rice to a flat plate to cool. Rinse, peel, and finely chop the mango and keep it ready.

Pour half of the oil in a saucepan on a medium-low heat and half roast the peanuts. Add split chickpeas, and black lentils followed by the mustard. When they start to splutter, add ginger, red chilies, green chiles, and curry leaves. Add hing, when the curry leaves become crisp. Remove this to a small bowl. In the same pan, pour the remaining oil, add chopped mango, turmeric, and salt. Sauté and cover to cook until the mango becomes tender and mushy. Add back the seasoning mix and keep covered for about 3 minutes. Finally, add the cooked rice to the saucepan and mix gently. Serve warm.

Spinach Paratha
Cooking Time: 20 minutes |Serves: 7 |Per Serving: Calories 130, Carbs 20g, Fat 4.4g, Protein 5g

Ingredients:
- Whole wheat flour - 1½ cups.
- Spinach, coarsely chopped - 1½ cups.
- Ginger, minced – 1 tsp.
- Garam masala - ¼ tsp.
- Salt - ¾ tsp.
- Water for blending spinach - 2 tbsps.
- Oil for kneading - 1 tbsp.
- Clarified butter for toasting - 2 tbsps.

Directions
Rinse and drain spinach. Make a puree blending spinach with ginger, and water in a mixer grinder. Combine the puree with the flour along with salt and spice powders. Knead well by adding oil and keep it aside for 20-30 minutes for foaming. After 30 minutes, make 7 balls out of the dough. Spread some flour on the worktable and flatten the dough using a roller to make a thick spinach

paratha. Place a thick pan on the stove and regulate the heat to medium-high. Place the spinach paratha on the heated pan. Flip to the other side when the bubble forms. Spread a little clarified butter over the paratha. Cook until it is golden. Place a parchment paper on a plate and stack the paratha on it so that it will remain soft. Serve with lentil curry or chutney.

Mix Vegetable Paratha

Cooking Time: 20 minutes |Serves: 6 |Per Serving: Calories 79, Carbs 10g, Fat 4.2g, Protein 2g

Ingredients:
- Whole wheat flour - 1 cup.
- Salt - ½ tsp.
- Ginger, minced - ½ tsp.
- Ground red chili - ½ tsp.
- Garam masala - ¼ tsp.
- Carom seeds - ½ tsp.
- Clarified butter – 2 tbsps.
- Potatoes, cubed - ½ cup.
- Carrots, cubed - ½ cup.
- Cauliflower, cut into florets - ¼ cup.
- Green peas - ¼ cup.
- Spinach - ¼ cup.
- Cilantro leaves - ¼ cup.

Directions:
Steam the vegetables and mash them well when they are still hot. Combine all the other ingredients into the mashed vegetable except the wheat flour and mix well. Add the flour into it, add water if required and knead thoroughly to make a tender dough. Make 6 balls out of the dough. Sprinkle some flour on the working table and flatten the rolls to make the paratha. Heat a thick pan on the stove and cook the paratha on it for about a minute. Flip the sides when bubbles appear on the paratha. Spread some clarified ghee on it and cook until a golden spot appears on the paratha. Repeat the process to make the remaining parathas.

Corn Pulao

Cooking Time: 20 minutes |Serves: 2 |Per Serving: Calories 358, Carbs 80g, Fat 1.6g, Protein 9g

Ingredients:
- Basmati rice - 1 cup.
- Water – 1½ cups.
- Sweet corn - 1 cup.
- Green peas - ½ cup.
- Bay leaf – 1 small.
- Green cardamom – 3.
- Cinnamon stick - 1 inch.
- Cloves – 4.
- Cumin - ¾ tsp.

- Lemon juice – 1 tbsp.
- Turmeric powder - ⅛ tbsp.
- Ground red chili - ½ tsp.
- Garam masala - ¾ tsp.
- Salt - ¾ tsp.
- Onion - 1 medium.
- Ginger – 1-inch length.
- Mint leaves - ½ cup.
- Green chili – 1.
- Garlic cloves, minced – 1 tbsp.

Directions:
Rinse the rice until the water turns clear and soak it for 30 minutes. Chop onion, garlic, ginger, mint leaves, chili, and put them in a mixer grinder without adding water for making a paste. Heat oil in a pressure cooker and sauté bay leaf, cloves, cumin, and cinnamon until it splutters. Stir in the onion-mint paste, turmeric, red chili powder, garam masala and sauté for about 3 minutes. Add corn, peas and fry for another 3 minutes. Drain the rice and put it in the cooker. At medium-high heat stir gently for 2 minutes. Pour water, add salt, close the lid and cook for 1 whistle at a medium-high heat. After the whistle, allow it to settle down the pressure. After that, open the cooker and fluff the pulao with a fork. Allow the pulao to cool down for some time. Before serving, sprinkle lemon juice and scatter chopped cilantro leaves.

Sweet Corn Fried Rice

Cooking Time: 25 minutes |Serves: 2 |Per Serving: Calories 507, Carbs 103g, Fat 6.9g, Protein 10g

Ingredients
- Rice - 1 cup.
- Water - 2 cups.
- Clarified butter - 1 tbsps.
- Garlic cloves – 2.
- Onion - 1 medium.
- Green chili - 1 to 2 tsps.
- Sweet corn – ½ cup.
- Bell pepper - ½ cup.
- Herbs – 2 sprigs.
- Ground pepper - ¼ tsp.

Directions
Rinse the rice until the water turns clear and soak for 20 minutes. In a rice cooking bowl, pour 2 cups of water and cook the rice. The rice must be tender but firm. Drain the rice and spread it on a plate for cooling. In a large skillet, heat oil and fry garlic until it starts to emanate the fragrance. After that, add chili and onions. Sauté until the onion becomes golden. Stir in corn and add all the vegetables into the skillet. Now, transfer the cooked rice into the skillet and gently stir. Before serving, sprinkle salt, pepper powder, and sauté in low heat. Serve hot.

Poori

Cooking Time: 10 minutes | Serves: 2 | Per Serving: Calories 245, Carbs 49g, Fat 2.1g, Protein 7g

Ingredients
- Wheat flour - 1cup.
- Semolina - ¾ tsp.
- Oil - ¾ tsp.
- Water - ¼ cup
- Salt - ⅛ tsp.

Directions
In a large mixing bowl, combine flour, semolina, salt, and oil. Adding ¼ cup of water make a tight dough. Knead it lightly by adding ¼ teaspoon of oil and make it smooth. Excess kneading will be a reason to absorb more oil while frying. Keep it covered just for 3 to 5 minutes, and don't let it rest more than 5 minutes. After that, make 10 balls and flatten the balls to make round poori using a roller or chapati maker by applying some oil on the dough ball. Drizzle some oil on the rolling area. Don't make it too thick or too thin. Make all the pooris and start frying.

In a poori making pan, or deep skillet pour oil and bring to a medium-high heat. The oil must be hot enough, and when you place the poori in the hot oil, it should rise immediately without browning. So, regulate the heat as per the requirements. Slide the poori into the hot oil. Using a perforated ladle, press the poori so that it will puff very well. When puffed well, flip the other side and continue cooking until it becomes a golden crisp. Depending on cooking consistency, keep flipping the poori to get the required quality. Using a colander, remove the poori and start making the next poori. Continue the same process until you finish with the entire batch.

Coconut Milk Pulao

Cooking Time: 25 minutes | Serves: 5 | Per Serving: Calories 604, Carbs 80g, Fat 27.4g, Protein 12g

Ingredients
- Clarified butter - 1 tbsps.
- Bay leaf - 1 large.
- Star anise – 1.
- Cloves – 4.
- Cinnamon stick - 2 inch.
- Nutmeg – a small piece.
- Green cardamoms – 4.
- Cumin - ¾ tsp.
- Mace - 1 strand.
- Cashew nuts – 10.
- Soy chunks - ¼ cup.
- Rice – 2 cups.
- Ginger, minced - 2 tsps.

- Carrot, beans, peas, potato - 2 cups.
- Green chili, deseeded and chopped – 1.
- Mint leaves, coarsely chopped - ¼ cup.
- Coconut milk – 2 cups.
- Water – 1 cup
- Salt – 1 tsp.

Directions:
Rinse rice until the water turns clear and soak for 20 minutes. After 20 minutes, drain the rice and keep aside. Pour clarified butter in a saucepan and fry all the spices and nuts, except the powdered items in a medium-low heat until the fragrance emanates. Add ginger paste and continue sautéing until the raw smell disappears. Put in the ground pepper, fennel, and sauté for a moment. Add vegetables, and chopped chili immediately and stir fry for about 3 minutes. Now add mint leaves and sauté for another 1 minute.

In a cooking pan, boil coconut milk by adding water and salt. Add the soaked rice into the pan and cook till the coconut milk gets wholly absorbed on a medium-low heat. Cover the pan with a tight lid, when moisture remains to be absorbed. Reduce the heat and continue cooking until the rice is cooked well. In a small pan roast cashew nuts and soya chunks and scatter on top of the rice and fluff it.

Paneer Pulao

Cooking Time: 20 minutes |Serves: 4 |Per Serving: Calories 544, Carbs 77g, Fat 19.2g, Protein 16g

Ingredients:
- Basmati rice - 1½ cups .
- Water - 2½ cups.
- Clarified butter - 2 tbsps.
- Large onion, sliced – 1.
- Green chilies – 2.
- Green peas - ½ cup.
- Carrots, sliced - ½ cup.
- Ginger garlic paste - 1 tbsp.
- Coriander leaves, coarsely chopped – 2 tbsps.
- Mint leaves, coarsely chopped - 1 tbsp.
- Salt - ¾ tsp.

For whole spices
- Bay leaf – 1.
- Star anise – 1.
- Cumin - ½ tsp.
- Ground green cardamoms – 3.
- Cloves – 6.
- Strand mace - ¼ tsp.
- Cinnamon, stick - 1 inch.

For Paneer marinating:
- Paneer cheese cubes - 1½ cups.
- Clarified butter - 1½ tbsps.
- Ginger garlic paste - ¾ tsp.
- Red chili powder - ¼ tsp.
- Garam masala - ½ tsp.
- Salt - ½ tsp.
- Gram flour - 1 tbsp.
- Dried fenugreek leaves - ½ tsp.

Directions:

Making Paneer Pulao:
Rinse the rice until the water turns clear and soak for 20 minutes. After 20 minutes, drain the rice and keep it aside. Put all the marinating ingredients in a medium bowl by adding some water and mixing them well. In a pressure cooker, add some ghee and start frying all the dry spices. When it starts sizzling, stir in sliced onion and sauté until it becomes golden brown. Add the ginger-garlic paste and roast until the raw smell disappears. Now add all the chopped veggies into the pan and keep frying for a couple of minutes. Add the mint leaves and coriander. When it smells good, add salt and water into the pan and let it boil. Add soaked rice and pressure cook at a medium-low heat for 1 whistle. Stop cooking and allow the pressure to settle naturally. Open the cooker lid and fluff the rice with a fork.

Frying Paneer to mix in pulao:
Put paneer cheese in a pan and bring to a medium-low heat and fry them with the listed marinade items, until they become golden. Top the rice with paneer. Serve the pulao hot.

Skillet Pulao

Cooking Time: 25 minutes |Serves: 1 |Per Serving: Calories 602, Carbs 109g, Fat 13.3g, Protein 12g

Ingredients:
- Rice - ½ cup.
- Clarified butter - 1 tbsp.
- Cumin - ½ tsp.
- Onion, sliced – 1 medium size.
- Ginger garlic paste -1 tsp.
- Tomato, chopped - ⅓ cup.
- Salt - ¼ tsp.
- Pav bhaji masala - 1 tbsp.
- Red chili paste - ½ tsp.
- Bell pepper, chopped - ¼ cup.
- Boiled vegetables (carrot, peas, beans, potato) - ¾ cup.
- Water - 2 tbsps.
- Coriander leaves, finely chopped – 2 tbsps.

Directions:

Rinse and soak the rice for 20 minutes. After that, drain the rice and cook it for some time until it is half cooked. When the rice is half cooked, keep it aside for cooling. Now wash other veggies like capsicum, tomatoes, beans, carrots, and chop them. Boil them until they become tender, but not too soft.

Heat clarified butter in a pan and put in cumin seeds. When they splutter, stir in onions and keep sautéing until they become transparent. Put the ginger-garlic paste into the pan and cook until the raw smell disappears. Now add red chili powder along with pav bhaji masala. You can add the bell pepper now and fry it for a couple of minutes. Pour in water and let the masala cook well. When the water starts to evaporate, add all the boiled vegetables. At this point, put in the half-cooked rice and cook for some time until the rice gets cooked well. Garnish with fresh coriander leaves and serve hot.

Green Peas Pulao

Cooking Time: 25 minutes |Serves: 3 |Per Serving: Calories 435, Carbs 77g, Fat 10g, Protein 11g

Ingredients:
- Basmati rice - 1½ cups.
- Green peas – 1 cup.
- Water - 2½ cups.
- Garlic, minced -1 tbsp.
- Chilies, julienned – 2.
- Cilantro leaves, chopped – 2 tbsps.
- Clarified butter - 2 tbsps.
- Onion, sliced – 1 medium size.
- Cashews - ¼ cup.
- Salt - ¾ tsp.

Whole spices:
- Cumin - 1 tsp.
- Bay leaf – 1.
- Cloves – 6.
- Ground green cardamoms - ¼ tsp.
- Cinnamon stick – 2 inches.
- Nutmeg, small piece – 1.
- Mace - 2 strands.
- Star anise – 1.

Directions:
Wash and drain rice until the water becomes clear. Soak it for 20 minutes and after soaking drain the rice and keep aside. In a pressure cooker, heat clarified butter and fry the cashews until they become golden. Keep them aside. Now add all the whole spices. Put cardamoms, cumin, nutmeg, mace, cinnamon, cloves, star anise, and bay leaf into it one by one and sauté for 1 minute. Put the onions, green chilies, and sauté until the onion becomes golden brown. At this point, you can add minced garlic until it emanates the fragrance. When you get a pleasant smell from the sautéing ingredients, add chopped cilantro leaves and continuously stir for a minute. Now, add the soaked rice and peas at this stage. Add water, salt, and cook for 1 whistle at a medium-low heat. Let the

pressure settle down naturally, and after that, open the lid. If there is any water content, cook it open until the water absorbs completely. After that, fluff the rice with a fork and let it settle for 2-3 minutes. Garnish with roasted cashew and serve.

Carrot Pulao

Cooking Time: 25 minutes |Serves: 2 |Per Serving: Calories 514, Carbs 94g, Fat 11.2g, Protein 10g

Ingredients:
- Rice - 1 cup.
- Water – ¾ cup.
- Clarified butter - 1 tbsp.

Spices:
- Bay leaf – 1.
- Cumin – 1 tbsp.
- Ground cardamom - ½ tsp.
- Cinnamon stick – 1 inch.

Other ingredients:
- Onion, sliced – 1 medium size.
- Ginger garlic paste – 1 tsp.
- Carrots, grated - ½ cup.
- Coriander leaves, chopped – 2 tbsps.
- Chili powder - ¼ tsp.
- Roasted cashews – 12.
- Salt - ¾ tsp.

Direction:
Rinse rice until the water becomes clear and soak it for 20 minutes. In a pressure cooker, cook it for 1 whistle and allow the settle pressure naturally. Keep it aside to settle down the heat.

In a large skillet, pour clarified butter and bring to medium-low heat. Add the whole spices one by one, starting with cumin seeds. Sauté and let it splutter. Now add onions into the skillet and stir fry until it becomes transparent and add ginger garlic paste. Keep sautéing until you can smell the fragrance. Now mix the carrots into the skillet and add salt. Put in all the spices and coriander leaves into it and keep stirring for one minute. After that, add the cooked rice into the pan. Check the salt taste and, if required, add a bit more. Cover and cook for 2-3 minutes, and when the cooking is over, top it with roasted cashews.

Black Eyed Peas Pulao

Cooking Time: 25 minutes |Serves: 3 |Per Serving: Calories 557, Carbs 98g, Fat 13.5g, Protein 12g

Ingredients:
- Basmati rice - 1½ cups.
- Water – 2¾ cups.

- Black eyed peas - 1 cup.
- Ginger garlic paste - 1 tbsp.
- Green chilies, julienned – 2.
- Cilantro leaves, chopped - ¼ cup.
- Onion, sliced - ½ cup.
- Clarified butter - 2 tbsps.
- Cashew - ¼ cup.
- Salt – 1 tsp.

Whole spices:
- Cumin - 1 tsp.
- Star anise – 1.
- Ground green cardamoms - ½ tsp.
- Cloves – 6.
- Mace - 2 strands.
- Bay leaf – 1.
- Cinnamon stick - 2 inch.
- Nutmeg – 1 small piece.

Directions:
Rinse the rice until the water becomes clear and soak the rice for half an hour. After soaking, drain the rice and keep it aside.

In a pressure cooker, pour clarified butter and bring to a medium-low heat. Roast cashews and keep them aside. Now put cumin, nutmeg, cardamoms, and mace into the pan. Add cinnamon, star anise and bay leaf one by one into the pan. Let them fry for some time. Put the sliced onion in and sauté until it becomes golden brown. When onions are ready, put the ginger-garlic paste into the cooker and stir fry until its raw smell disappears. Now put chopped cilantro leaves in and sauté for 2 mins. Put the rice and peas in the pressure cooker, pour water, and salt. Stir gently once, close the pressure cooker and cook for 1 whistle. After the whistle, stop cooking and allow it to settle down the pressure. If the rice still has moisture, cook it for few minutes without covering until the water evaporates thoroughly. Fluff the rice with a fork and garnish with roasted cashew nuts.

Coconut Rice

Cooking Time: 15 minutes | Serves: 3 | Per Serving: Calories 553, Carbs 71g, Fat 26.9g, Protein 10g

Ingredients:
- Rice - 1 cup.
- Water - ¾ cup.
- Grated coconut - 1 cups.
- Green chilies – 2, julienned.
- Red chilies, broken -1.
- Clarified butter - 1½ tbsp.
- Bay leaf – 1.
- Mustard - ½ tsp.
- Cumin - ½ tsp.

- Hing - ⅛ tsp.
- Split chickpeas - 1 tbsp.
- Split black gram - ½ tbsp.
- Ginger, minced - 1 tsp.
- Cashew - ¼ cup
- Salt - ½ tsp.

Directions:

Rinse the rice 2 or 3 times until the water turns clear and soak it for 30 minutes. After soaking, drain it and keep aside. Now put the rice in a pressure cooker with ¾ cup water and pressure cook for 1 whistle. After the whistle, switch off the stove and allow the cooker to settle the pressure. Once the pressure has settled down, open the cooker and fluff the rice.

In a large thick skillet pour clarified butter and bring to medium-low heat. When the butter becomes hot, roast cashews until they becomes golden brown and keep them aside; in the same skillet, add mustard to splutter and add cumin. Put split chickpeas, split black gram and sauté until they become golden brown. Now add minced ginger, green chili, red chili, and a bay leaf. Sprinkle hing and continue sautéing. When the aroma starts to emanate, add grated coconut and keep stir-frying by adding salt until the coconut is cooked well for about 2 or 3 minutes. Transfer the cooked rice, fold the rice gently and turn off the stove. Garnish with roasted cashew nuts and serve hot.

Mint Rice

Cooking Time: 20 minutes | Serves: 4 |Per Serving: Calories 499, Carbs 79g, Fat 17.2g, Protein 10g

Ingredients:
- Basmati rice - 1½ cups.
- Water – 2½ cups.
- Mint leaves – 1 cup.
- Cilantro leaves – 2 tbsps.
- Green chilies – 2.
- Ginger - 1 inch.
- Garlic – 3 cloves.
- Coconut, chopped - ¼cup.
- Salt- 1 tsp.
- Clarified butter -2 tbsps.
- Lemon juice - 2 tbsps.
- Mix veggies - 1½ cups.
- Cashews - ¼ cup
- Lemon juice – 2 tbsps.

Spices for mint rice:
- Bay leaves – 1.
- Star anise – 1.
- Mace - 1 strand.
- Cumin seed - ½ tsp.
- Ground green cardamoms – 4.

- Cinnamon stick - 2 inch.
- Cloves – 6.

Directions:
Rinse the rice thoroughly until the water turns clear and soak for 20 minutes. Wash and dry the mint and cilantro leaves. Put the leaves in a grinder along with ginger, chilies, chopped coconut, and garlic and blitz to make a paste without water.

In a pressure cooker, add clarified butter and bring to a medium-low heat. Roast the cashew nuts without burning and keep them aside. In this same cooker add anise, mace and sauté. Add cumin, cinnamon, cloves, cardamoms and sauté until the aroma releases. Now add the mint-cilantro paste and stir fry for about 3 minutes at a medium-low heat. Add mixed vegetables and stir fry for another 2 minutes.

Pour water, salt and put the soaked rice in. Cook it open until the water almost gets evaporated. Close the cooker and cook for about 5 minutes at a medium-low heat and switch off the stove without letting the cooker blow the whistle. After that, allow the pressure to subsidize naturally and open the cover. Sprinkle with lemon juice and fluff the rice. Garnish with cashew nuts and serve hot.

Cabbage Rice

Cooking Time: 30 minutes | Serves: 2 | Per Serving: Calories 311, Carbs 54g, Fat 7.9g, Protein 7g

Ingredients:
- Rice - ½ cup.
- Water – 1 cup.
- Cabbage, coarsely chopped - 2 cups.
- Green peas - ¼ cup.
- Green chilies – 2, julienned.
- Veg oil - 1 tbsp.
- Garlic cloves, minced – 3.
- Vinegar - ¾ tsp.
- Pepper, crushed - ¼ tsp.
- Salt - ½ tsp.
- Star anise - ½.
- Mace – 1 strand.

Directions:
Rinse rice until the water turns clear and drain the water. In a rice cooker, cook the rice with 1 cup of water until the water evaporates. After cooking, allow it to cool. In a large, deep skillet pour cooking oil and bring to a medium-low heat. Put garlic, chilies, star anise, and strands of mace into the skillet and sauté for about 3 minutes, until the fragrance emanates. Now put peas and chopped cabbage into the skillet, and continue sautéing for about 3 minutes. When it becomes crunchy, add crushed pepper, rice, and salt. Mix them gently, without letting the rice become mushy for a couple of minutes. Serve hot.

Fenugreek Leaves Rice

Cooking Time: 20 minutes |Serves: 2 |Per Serving: Calories 499, Carbs 96g, Fat 8.4g, Protein 11g

Ingredients:
- Rice – 1 cup.
- Water - ¾ cup.
- Vegetable oil - 1 tbsp.
- Cumin dee - ½ tsp.
- Garlic cloves, minced – 2.
- Fenugreek leaves, coarsely chopped - 1¼ cups.
- Green peas - ½ cup.
- Green chili – 2, julienned.
- Bay leaf – 1.
- Cinnamon stick – 1 inch.
- Crushed cardamom – 2.
- Garam masala - ½ tsp.
- Turmeric powder - ¼ tsp.
- Lemon juice - 2 tbsps.
- Salt - ½ tsp.

Directions:
Rinse the rice 2 or 3 times until the water turns clear and soak it for 20 minutes. In the pressure cooker, pour vegetable oil and bring to a medium-low heat. Put in cumin seeds and when they sizzle, add garlic, green chili and sauté for 2 minutes. Add bay leaves, cinnamon stick, crushed cardamom, and continue sautéing for another 2 minutes. Now add fenugreek leaves and sauté for about 4 minutes until it starts to wilt. Add turmeric powder, garam masala and stir fry for 2 minutes.

Put the rice in the pressure cooker with ¾ cup of water and salt, and gently stir once. Close the cooker and cook for 1 whistle. Allow the pressure to settle down naturally, and after that, open the cooker and fluff the rice. Sprinkle with lemon juice and serve hot.

Potato-Fenugreek Leaves Paratha

Cooking Time: 15 minutes |Serves: 4 |Per Serving: Calories 90, Carbs 17g, Fat 1.8g, Protein 3g

Ingredients:
- Potato, cubed - 2 cups.
- Garlic, minced - 2 cloves.
- Fenugreek leaves, coarsely chopped - 1½ cups.
- Cumin seeds - ¾ tsp.
- Clarified butter - 1½ tbsps.
- Green chili, julienned – 2.
- Turmeric powder - ¼ tsp.
- Hing - ⅛ tsp.

- Garam masala powder - ¾ tsp.
- Salt - ½ tsp.

Preparation:
Soak fenugreek leaves for 10 minutes in a large bowl by adding some salt. The salt will neutralize the pesticide residue and clean the leaves. After that, dry the leaves and coarsely chop.

Peel and rinse the potatoes, then cube the potatoes. Soak them in water for some time to retain their color. In a thick saucepan, pour clarified butter and bring to a medium-low heat. Put some cumin in to sizzle and stir in minced garlic. When the garlic starts to produce the aroma, add hing, and continue sautéing for 1 minute. Drain potatoes and put them in the pan. Add salt, turmeric, garam masala and fry them for a couple of minutes. To get the desired softness, cover the pan and let it cook for some time at a medium-low heat stirring occasionally. If the ingredients look too dry, add some water to maintain the moisture. Now put the chopped fenugreek into the pan. Keep frying until it wilts, and it becomes fork soft. Serve hot.

Potato Rice

Cooking Time: 23 minutes |Serves: 3 |Per Serving: Calories 465, Carbs 85g, Fat 11g, Protein 9g

Ingredients:
- Potatoes, cubed - 2 cups.
- Rice – 1 cup.
- Water - ¾ cup.
- Mint leaves, chopped – 12.
- Onion, sliced – 1 medium.
- Garlic, minced – 2.
- Green chili – 1, julienned.
- Garam masala - ½ tsp.
- Turmeric powder - ⅛ tsp.
- Vegetable oil – 2 tbsps.
- Salt - ¾ tsp.

Spices:
- Bay leaf – 1.
- Crushed cardamoms – 3.
- Cloves – 6.
- Cinnamon stick – 1 inch.
- Star anise – 1.
- Mace strand – 1.

Directions:
Rinse the rice 2 or 3 times and soak it for 20 minutes. After 20 minutes, drain the rice. In a pressure cooker, pour ¾ cup of water and cook the rice for 1 whistle. After the whistle, stop cooking and allow the pressure to settle down naturally. Then, open the cooker and fluff the rice.

Peel and wash the potatoes in running water. Cut into cubes and keep it aside. In a thick saucepan, pour vegetable oil and fry the spices until they start to produce the aroma. Now, put sliced onion, ginger and garlic into the pan, and stir fry for some time until the onion becomes soft. Put red chili powder, turmeric garam masala, mint and salt into the pan, and stir fry for about 3 minutes. Add potato pieces and cook until the potato cubes become fork soft. You can add little water for cooking the potato if required. Now transfer the cooked rice into the pan and gently fold mix. Turn off the stove and garnish with chopped mint leaves. Serve hot.

Yogurt Rice

Cooking Time: 25 minutes |Serves: 3 |Per Serving: Calories 243, Carbs 35g, Fat 4.1g, Protein 16g

Ingredients:
- Rice - ½ cup.
- Yogurt – 1½ cups.
- Water - 1½ cups.
- Full fat milk, boiled - ½ cup.

For seasoning:
- Vegetable oil - 1½ tsps.
- Mustard seeds - ½ tsp.
- Cumin - ½ tsp.
- Hing - ⅛ tsp.
- Split chickpeas - ¾ tbsp.
- Curry leaves - 1 sprig.
- Crushed pepper - ½ tsp.
- Split black gram - ½ tbsp.

Directions:
Rinse rice 2 or 3 times until the water turns clear and soak it for 30 minutes. In a pressure cooker, pour 1½ cups of water and pressure cook the rice for 2 whistles. Turn off the stove and let the pressure settle down. Open the cooker and add the boiled milk. Keep it aside and let it cool down. After cooling down, combine yogurt, salt and mix it gently.

In a saucepan, pour oil and bring to medium-low heat. Put mustard to splutter and add cumin to sizzle. After that, put split chickpeas, split black gram and sauté until they become golden. At this point, add hing, pepper, and curry leaves. Turn off the stove and transfer it over the precooked yogurt rice. Mix very well to serve.

Sweet Rice Pulao

Cooking Time: 30 minutes |Serves: 5 |Per Serving: Calories 421, Carbs 71g, Fat 14.63g, Protein 6g

Ingredients:
- Basmati rice – 1 cup.
- Water – 5 cups.
- Saffron for coloring - ¼ tsp.

- Clarified butter – 4 tbsps.
- Crushed cloves – 4.
- Crushed cardamoms – 4.

To make sugar syrup:
- Sugar - ¾ cup.
- Water – 4 tbsps.

Nuts and fruits:
- Almonds, chopped – 8.
- Cashew, halved – 8.
- Raisins – 10.
- Pistachios – 10.

Directions:
Rinse rice until the water turns clear and soak for 30 minutes. In a large bowl, pour 5 cups of water and bring to a rolling boil and add saffron. Drain the rice and put it into the boiling water. Stop cooking when the rice gets cooked by 95%. The rice should not be too hard or too mushy too. Drain the rice and spread on a colander. Let it cool down.

In a large saucepan, pour clarified butter and bring to a medium-low heat. Roast cashew nuts until they become golden brown and remove them to a plate. Sauté raisins and transfer to the plate. After that, add the crushed cardamoms, cloves, and stir fry for about 1 minute until the fragrance emanates. Add sugar, 4 tablespoons of water and stir until it dissolves. When the syrup develops a string consistency, add the cooked rice, and mix gently. Garnish with roasted cashew nuts and raisins. Serve hot.

South Indian Sour Cream Rice

Cooking Time: 30 minutes | Serves: 2 | Per Serving: Calories 419, Carbs 58g, Fat 16.2g, Protein 11g

Ingredients:
- Basmati rice - ½ cup.
- Water – 1½ cups.
- Sour cream - 1 cup, fresh.
- Milk - ¼ cup.
- Salt - ½ tsp.

Veggies:
- Carrot, finely chopped – 2 tbsps.
- Cucumber, finely grated – 2 tbsps.
- Cilantro leaves, coarsely chopped – 1 tbsp.

For tempering:
- Vegetable oil – 1 tsp.
- Cumin seeds - ½ tsp.
- Mustard - ½ tsp.

- Split chickpeas – 1 tsp.
- Split black gram – 1 tsp.
- Red chili – 1 broken.
- Curry leaves – 1 twig.
- Hing - ⅛ tsp.
- Ginger, finely grated - ½ tsp.
- Green chili, julienned – 1.
- Full cream milk -¼ cup.

Directions:
Rinse rice until the water turns clear. In a pressure cooker pour water, salt and pressure cook for 2 whistles. Turn off the stove and allow the pressure to settle naturally. After that, open the cooker and fluff the rice. Pour milk, stir and allow it to cool down. Add sour cream to the rice and combine well to mix. Add the chopped cilantro, grated cucumbers, and salt.

Pour oil in a saucepan and bring to medium-low heat. Put in mustard seed and when it splutters, add cumin seed. When the cumin seed sizzles add chili powder, split black gram and chickpeas. Sauté until it becomes golden. Now add curry leaves, green chili, and ginger. Add hing when the curry leaves turn crisp. Put off the stove and transfer the tempering onto the sour cream rice.

Split Chickpeas Pulao

Cooking Time: 20 minutes |Serves: 3 |Per Serving: Calories 463, Carbs 90g, Fat 6g, Protein 14g

Ingredients:
- Rice - 1 cup.
- Split chickpeas - ½ cup.
- Water – 2¼ cups.
- Carrot, cut into cubes - 1 large.
- Onion, sliced - 1 medium.
- Green chili, julienned – 1.
- Ginger garlic paste - 1 tsp.
- Mint leaves, chopped – 2 tbsps.
- Bay leaf – 1.
- Cumin - ½ tsp.
- Star anise – 1.
- Mace - 1 strand.
- Green cardamoms – 2.
- Cinnamon stick - 1 inch.
- Oil - ½ tbsp.
- Salt - ¾ tsp.
- Lemon juice - 1 tsp.
- Cilantro leaves, chopped – 2 tbsps.

Directions:

Sort, rinse, and soak split chickpeas for about 6 hours. Similarly, rinse rice until the water turns clear and soak it for 20 minutes. Drain both items before cooking and keep ready to use them. In a pressure cooker, pour oil and bring to medium-low heat. Sauté the spices until they start to splutter without letting it burn. Add onions and stir fry until it becomes tender, and after that, add ginger garlic paste. Fry for some time until it gets rid of its raw smell. Add vegetables, mint, and stir fry for 2 minutes.

Transfer the soaked rice and chickpeas to the cooker and fry again for about 3 minutes. Pour water, sprinkle salt and give a gentle stir. Wait for the rice to cook. When the water is almost absorbed, cover the lid, select the heat to a medium-low, and continue cooking for about 5 minutes. Let the pressure get settled naturally and open the lid. Fluff the food with a fork and scatter cilantro leaves and sprinkle lemon juice before serving the pulao.

Lemon Millet

Cooking Time: 25 minutes |Serves: 2 |Per Serving: Calories 362, Carbs 53g, Fat 12.4g, Protein 13g

Ingredients:
- Kodo millet - ½ cup.
- Water – 1½ cups.
- Salt - ½ tsp.
- Oil - 1½ tbsps.
- Mustard - ½ tsp.
- Split chickpeas - 1½ tbsps.
- Skinned black gram - 1½ tbsps.
- Peanuts – ¼ cup.
- Asafetida - ⅛ tsp.
- Green chili – 1.
- Broken red chili – 1.
- Turmeric powder - ⅛ tsp.
- Ginger, minced - 1 tsp.
- Curry leaves - 1 sprig
- Lemon – 1 medium size.

Directions:
Rinse and drain the millet. In a bowl, pour 1½ cups of water, salt, and soak it for 6 hours. After that, cook the soaked millet on a medium-low heat by closing the lid and until the water gets entirely absorbed. Fluff the cooked millet and keep aside for cooling.

Pour oil in a saucepan at a medium-low heat and splutter mustard seed. After that, add chickpeas, black gram, peanuts, red chili, and green chili. Wait until the chickpeas turn golden and add curry leaves and ginger. Stop sautéing when the curry leaves become crispy and add turmeric and asafetida. Transfer the seasoned ingredients into the cooked millet, squeeze lemon juice, and gently mix. Serve warm.

Pineapple Fried Rice

Cooking Time: 25 minutes |Serves: 1 |Per Serving: Calories 620, Carbs 95g, Fat 22.8g, Protein 9g

Ingredients:
- Rice - ½ cup.
- Clarified butter - ½ tbsp.
- Garlic, minced - ½ tbsp.
- Cashews – 5.
- Raisins – 10.
- Spring onions, chopped - ¼ cup.
- Green chili - ½, julienned.
- Curry powder - ½ tsp.
- Soya sauce - 1 tsp.
- Vinegar - 1 tsp.
- Salt - ½ tsp.
- Pineapple, cubes - ½ cup.
- Cilantro leaves, coarsely chopped - 1 tbsp.
- Oil – 1 tbsp.

Directions:
Wash the rice until the water turns clear and soak it for 15 minutes. Cook the rice in 2½ cups of water until al dente. After cooking, drain and keep it for cooling. In a saucepan, pour clarified butter and sauté cashews on medium-low heat until it turns golden. At this point, add raisins and garlic until the garlic starts to produce the fragrance. Remove it from the pan and keep it aside. Now, in the same pan, sauté chili, bell peppers, and spring onions, until they become slightly crunchy. Stir in curry powder, salt, vinegar and soya sauce. Put pineapple chunks and stir for about 2 minutes. Transfer the mix and roasted cashew nut-raisin mixture to the cooked rice. Scatter chopped cilantro leaves over it and gently mix and serve warm.

Curry Leaves Rice

Cooking Time: 30 minutes |Serves: 4 |Per Serving: Calories 227, Carbs 24g, Fat 15.3g, Protein 8g

Ingredients:

For the powder:
- Split chickpeas - 1 tbsp.
- Split black gram - 1 tbsp.
- Ground sesame seeds - 1 tbsp.
- Dry coconut, shredded - 1 tbsp.
- Red chilies – 3.
- Cumin - 1 tsp.
- Garlic – 3.
- Curry leaves - 1 cup.

- Oil - 1 tbsp.

For curry leaves rice:
- Rice - 1½ cups.
- Water - 2¾ cups.
- Ground curry leaves - 2 tbsps.
- Salt – 1 tsp.
- Peanuts - ¼ cup.
- Oil - 2 tbsps.
- Lemon juice - 1 tbsp.

Directions:
Clean and rinse the curry leaves in running water, and pat dry thoroughly. In a saucepan, roast chickpeas and split black gram until it becomes half roasted and stir in red chilies until the lentils become golden. Transfer them to a plate and allow them to cool. Now put shredded coconut, sesame seeds, and cumin into the pan sauté for a moment and transfer to another plate and allow to cool down. Pour 2 tablespoons of oil into the pan and sizzle curry leaves to crisp and let them cool down. Put all the ingredients in a mixer grinder and make a dry powder.

For making the curry leaves rice, cook the rice in a pressure cooker with 2¾ cups of water for 1 whistle. After that, allow it to settle down the heat and open and fluff the rice. Drizzle 2½ tablespoons of curry leaves power and crushed roasted peanuts over the rice. Drizzle lemon juice and sprinkle some clarified butter over it and mix gently. Serve hot.

Carrot Rice

Cooking Time: 25 minutes |Serves: 3 |Per Serving: Calories 341, Carbs 63g, Fat 7.6g, Protein 6g

Ingredients:
- Rice - 1 cup.
- Clarified butter - 1 tbsp.
- Bay leaf – 1.
- Cumin - ½ tsp.
- Green cardamoms – 2.
- Cinnamon stick - 1 inch.
- Onion, sliced – 1 medium.
- Ginger garlic paste - 1 tsp.
- Carrots, grated – 2.
- Cilantro leaves, chopped – 2 tbsps.
- Garam masala - ¾ tsp.
- Red chili powder - ½ tsp.
- Cashews – 12.
- Lemon juice – 1 tbsp.
- Salt - ¾ tsp.

Directions:

Rinse rice until the water turns clear and soak it for about 20 minutes. Cook it until al dente, by adding 2 cups of water in the pressure cooker for 1 whistle. After 1 whistle, allow it to settle down the pressure, open it, and fluff the rice. Keep aside to cool.

Meanwhile, fry the dry spices in a saucepan under a medium-low heat until they start to splutter. Now, put in the sliced onion and sauté until it becomes golden. Add ginger-garlic paste and stir-fry until the raw smell disappears. Transfer the grated carrots and add some salt into the saucepan and fry for 2 minutes. Add chili powder, garam masala, cilantro leaves, and continue sautéing for 2-3 minutes. Transfer the entire saucepan mix onto the cooked rice and sprinkle on some salt for taste. Toast cashews and spread on the rice. Finally, you can drizzle lemon juice and gently mix before serving.

Lentil Khichdi

Cooking Time: 25 minutes |Serves: 2 |Per Serving: Calories 490, Carbs 87g, Fat 9.9g, Protein 14g

Ingredients:
- Clarified butter - 1½ tbsp, divided.
- Cumin - ½ tsp.
- Bay leaf – 1.
- Ginger, grated - ½ tsp.
- Onion, sliced - 1 small.
- Green chili, julienned – 1.
- Tomato, chopped - 1 small.
- Turmeric, powder - ⅛ tsp.
- Salt - ½ tsp.
- Rice - ½ cup.
- Split green gram - ¼ cup.
- Water - 4 cups
- Asafetida - ¼ tsp.

Vegetables:
- Carrot, chopped - 1 medium size.
- French beans, chopped – 8.
- Potato, cubed – 1 small.

Directions:
Rinse split green gram and rice in a bowl until the water turns clear. Drain and keep it ready to cook. In a pressure cooker, pour clarified butter on a medium-low heat and put in a bay leaf. Sauté for 1 minute and add grated ginger and hing. Stir fry it until the fragrance emanates. Put sliced onions, green chilies, and sauté until the onion becomes translucent. Add the chopped tomatoes, all the vegetables, turmeric powder, salt and sauté for about 5 minutes.

Add the soaked split green gram, rice, and pressure cook for 2 whistles on a medium-low heat. 2 whistles are okay for a fluffy kichadi, and if you like to have a more liquid consistency dish, then cook for 4 whistles at a medium-low heat. Allow it to settle the pressure naturally. Open the cooker, drop ½ tablespoon of clarified butter and whisk gently. Serve warm.

Khichdi with Tapioca Pearls

Cooking Time: 10 minutes |Serves: 2 |Per Serving: Calories 553, Carbs 85g, Fat 21.3g, Protein 9g

Ingredients:
- Tapioca pearls - 1 cup.
- Peanuts - 2 tbsps.
- Clarified butter - 2 tbsps.
- Cumin- ½ tsp.
- Curry leaves - 1 sprig.
- Green chili, chopped – 2.
- Potato, boiled and cubed – 1 small.
- Salt - ½ tsp.
- Cilantro leaves, coarsely chopped - 2 tbsps.
- Lemon juice - 1 tbsp.
- Ginger, grated - 1 tsp.
- Peanuts, powder - 2 tbsps.
- Coconut, shredded - 2 tbsps.

Directions:
Put tapioca pearls in a large bowl and pour about 3 cups of water in. Rinse by rubbing it with fingers and drain water. Repeat the process 3 times. Soak it in freshwater for about 6 hours until it becomes tender. After 6 hours, drain and mash the tapioca pearls.

Roast peanuts in a saucepan and make a powder with half the portion and keep the roasted peanuts separately aside. Pour clarified butter in the pan and bring to medium-low heat. Now add, curry leaves, cumin, ginger, green chilies and sauté for about 2 minutes. Put the boiled potato cubes in and stir fry for 2 minutes. Add salt and peanut powder into the mashed tapioca pearls along with shredded coconut and transfer the mix into the saucepan. Stir fry the mix for about 3 minutes. Scatter roasted peanuts and sprinkle lemon juice over the dish. Garnish with chopped cilantro and serve hot.

Kashmiri Pulao

Cooking Time: 20 minutes |Serves: 2 |Per Serving: Calories 536, Carbs 104g, Fat 9.4g, Protein 10g

Ingredients:
- Clarified butter - 2 tbsps.
- Basmati rice - 1 cup.
- Onion, sliced - 1 small.
- Saffron - ¼ tsp.
- Milk - 3 tbsps.
- Cashew nuts – 8.
- Walnuts – 6.
- Almonds – 6.
- Raisins- 1 tbsp.

- Water - 1½ cups.
- Sugar - 1 tbsps.
- Rose water – 2 tbsp.

Spices section:
- Fennel seeds - ½ tsp.
- Bay leaf – 1.
- Cumin seeds - ½ tsp.
- Black cardamom - 1 small.
- Cinnamon, stick – 1 inch.
- Green cardamoms – 3.
- Cloves – 4.
- Dry ginger powder - ½ tsp.

Fruit section:
- Pomegranate - 2 tbsps.
- Apple - ¼ cup.
- Pineapple - ¼ cup.

Directions

Soak saffron in hot milk and keep aside. Crush fennel seeds and keep ready to use them. Rinse rice until the water becomes clear and soak for 15 minutes. After 15 minutes, drain it and keep aside. In a saucepan, heat ½ tablespoon of clarified butter. In the pan, roast raisins and nuts on a low heat and transfer onto a plate. In the same pan, add chopped onions and sauté until they becomes golden brown. Remove them from the pan and keep aside for garnishing.

Fry all the dry spices in a pressure cooker until they start to produce the fragrance. Transfer the rice to the cooker, add the remaining ½ tablespoon of clarified ghee, and sprinkle salt. Stir fry it for about 3 minutes. Now, pour in saffron milk and water. Check the salt level and, if required, add salt accordingly. Close the cooker and cook for 1 whistle. Allow it to settle the pressure naturally, and after that, open the cooker. Make sure to absorb the water thoroughly. Add rose water, close the pressure cooker, and cook for 5 minutes under a low heat. After 5 minutes, open the cooker and fluff the rice. Garnish with raisins, nuts, fried onions, and fruits.

Beetroot Rice

Cooking Time: 25 minutes |Serves: 4 |Per Serving: Calories 456, Carbs 92g, Fat 5.5g, Protein 9g

Ingredients:
- Basmati rice - 2 cups.
- Water - 3½ cups.
- Clarified butter - 1½ tbsp.
- Onion, sliced – 1 small.
- Green chilies – 1.
- Ginger garlic paste - 1 tbsp.
- Turmeric powder - ⅛ tsp.
- Green peas - ¼ cup.

- Beetroot, cubed - 1 medium.
- Potato, cubed - ½ cup.
- Coriander leaves, chopped - 2 tbsp.
- Mint leaves, coarsely chopped - 2 tbsp.
- Salt – 1 tsp.

Spices section:
- Bay leaf - 1 small.
- Cumin seed - ¾ tsp.
- Star anise - 1 small.
- Cinnamon stick - 1 inch.
- Cloves – 6.
- Cardamoms – 2.
- Mace - 1 strand.

Directions:
Rinse rice until the water becomes clear and soak it for 20 minutes. In a pressure cooker, pour in clarified butter and sauté spices on a medium-low heat. Add green chili, onions, and sauté until onions become golden brown. Finally, add ginger paste and stir fry until the raw smell disappears.

In the same pressure cooker, sauté beetroot cubes, green peas, and potato cubes. Pour in 3½ cups of water and add salt. Add the drained rice. Simmer until the water gets evaporated completely. Close the pressure cooker when the water is about to disappear entirely and cook under a low heat for about 5 minutes for 1 whistle. Allow it to settle the pressure. Open the cooker and fluff the rice with a fork.

Cabbage Paratha

Cooking Time: 15 minutes |Serves: 10 |Per Serving: Calories 121, Carbs 20g, Fat 3.3g, Protein 3g

Ingredients:
- Cabbage, finely chopped - 2 cups.
- Wheat flour - 2 cups+¼ cup for rolling.
- Garam masala - ½ tsp.
- Coriander leaves, coarsely chopped – 3 tbsps.
- Turmeric - ¼ tsp.
- Salt – 1 tsp.
- Oil - 1½ tsps.
- Clarified butter – 2 tbsps.

Directions:
Rinse the cabbage and cut it into pieces. Soak the pieces in warm salt water for 10 minutes. After 10 minutes, drain the cabbage and coarsely chop it. To make the dough, put all ingredients into a bowl and shredded cabbage except for the clarified butter and oil. Knead the wheat flour combining the grated cabbage, water, salt, garam masala, turmeric, and coriander leaves. Add oil to make the dough softer. Keep aside the dough covering it for 20 minutes.

After 20 minutes, make 10 equal balls out of the dough. Spread some flour on the working table for flattening the balls. Place a thick pan on the stove and set to a medium-high heat. Place the paratha on the hot pan and flip sides when small bubbles appear on the paratha. When it shows golden brown spots, remove the paratha from the pan, and apply ghee. Stack it in a plate covered with a kitchen towel. Repeat the same process for the remaining parathas.

Coconut Milk Rice

Cooking Time: 15 minutes |Serves: 4 |Per Serving: Calories 481, Carbs 75g, Fat 17.2g, Protein 8g

Ingredients:
- Rice – 2 cups.
- Coconut milk - 1 cup.
- Water – 2¼ cups.
- Ginger, finely minced - 2 tsp.
- Green chili, julienned – 1.
- Carrots, chopped – 1 medium size.
- Green peas – ½ cup.
- Beans, chopped – 6.
- Clarified butter – 2 tbsps.
- Salt – 1 tsp.

Spices:
- Bay leaf – 1.
- Cardamoms – 4.
- Cloves – 6.
- Cinnamon stick – 2 inches.
- Cumin – 1 tsp.

For garnishing:
- Cashew nuts – 10.
- Grated coconut flakes – 4 tbsps.

Directions:
Rinse rice until the water becomes clear and soak for 15 minutes. After soaking, drain the rice and keep it aside. Pour clarified butter in a pressure cooker and bring to a medium-low heat. Sauté the cashew nuts until golden brown and keep them aside. Add spices and sauté until the fragrance starts to emanate. At this point, add ginger, green chili, and sauté for 2-3 minutes. Now add the vegetables and stir fry for about 3 minutes.

Pour coconut milk and water into the cooker. Add salt and bring the liquid to a rolling boil. Into the boiling water, put in the drained rice and mix gently. Close the cooker and cook for 1 whistle. After 1 whistle, turn off the stove and allow the pressure to settle down naturally. Open the cooker, and if there is still liquid, heat it until the water evaporates. After that, fluff the rice. Now in a pan toast the coconut flakes. Garnish the rice with toasted coconut flakes and cashew nuts while serving.

Chapter 6 Rice & Grains

Jeera (Cumin) Rice

Cooking Time: 12 minutes |Serves: 2 | Per Serving: Calories 151, Carbs 19g, Fat 10.6g, Protein 5g

Ingredients:
- Washed drained rice - 1 cup.
- Clarified butter -2 tbsps.
- Bay leaves-2.
- Cumin seeds-1 tsp.
- Turmeric powder-1 tsp.
- Ground cumin seed - ½ tsp.
- Ground pepper -1 tsp.
- Water -2 cups
- Salt – ¾ tsp.

Directions:
Put the pressure cooker on a medium-high temperature and place the butter into the base of the cooker. Add bay leaves and cumin seeds. Stir it for two minutes. Now put ground cumin seed, ground pepper, and stir once. Add drained rice into it and sauté for three minutes. Pour in 2 cups of water and salt. Stir it once and close the cooker with weight. Within 10 minutes after two whistles, switch off the cooker and allow to settle down the pressure. When the pressure declined completely, open the cooker and transfer it to plates.

Yogurt Rice

Cooking Time: 12 minutes |Serves: 2 | Per Serving: Calories 433, Carbs 42g, Fat 23.3g, Protein 25g

Ingredients:
- Washed drained rice - 1 cup.
- Curd - 2 cups.
- Curry leaves – 10 leaves.
- Green chilies - 2, cut into three pieces each.
- Ginger - ½ inch piece coarsely chopped.
- Coriander leaves- 3 stems with leaves.
- Broken black gram - 2 tsps.
- Mustard seeds - 1 tsp.
- Asafetida - ½ tsp.
- Dry red chilies – 4.
- Cooking oil - 2 tbsps.
- Water -2 cups.
- Salt - 1 tsp.

Directions:

Add drained rice into the pressure cooker. Pour 2 cups of water. Stir it once and close the cooker with its weight on it. Within 10 minutes after two whistles, switch off the cooker and allow to depressure the cooker naturally. When the pressure has declined thoroughly, open the cooker and leave it for a while.

Put oil in a frying pan. Add black gram and dry chili pieces. Add mustard seeds and when it splutters add asafetida, curry leaves, ginger pieces, and cut green chilies. Switch off the cooker and add the content into the cooked rice. Add curd, salt and stir it.

Garnish it with chopped coriander leaves while serving.

Lemon Rice

Cooking Time: 12 minutes | Serves: 2 | Per Serving: Calories 337, Carbs 47g, Fat 14.2g, Protein 16g

Ingredients:
- Washed drained rice - 1 cup.
- Squeezed fresh lemon juice - 2 tbsps.
- Curry leaves – 10.
- Green chilies - 2, julienned.
- Coriander leaves- 3 stems with leaves.
- Mustard seeds - 1 tsp.
- Asafetida - ½ tsp.
- Dry red chilies-4.
- Cooking oil – 2 tbsps.
- Water -2 cups.
- Salt - ¾ tsp.

Directions:
Put drained rice into the pressure cooker. Add 2 cups of water. Stir it once and close the cooker with its weight on it. Within 10 minutes after two whistles, switch off the stove and allow the pressure to decline naturally. After that, open the cooker and leave it for 2-3 minutes to settle heat.

Now heat the frying pan on low-medium temperature, and when the pan becomes hot, pour in 2 tablespoons of oil. Put in dry chili pieces, mustard seeds and let them splutter. When they splutter, add asafetida, curry leaves, and the julienned chilies. Switch off the stove and add the content on to the already cooked rice. Drizzle lemon juice, salt, and stir it.

Garnish it with cut coriander leaves while serving.

Onion Rice

Cooking Time: 12 minutes |Serves: 2 |Per Serving: Calories 305, Carbs 41g, Fat 15.6g, Protein 11g

Ingredients:
- Washed drained rice - 1 cup.
- Medium-sized onion- 2, finely chopped.

- Curry leaves – 10-15.
- Green chilies – 2, julienned.
- Mustard seeds - 1 tsp.
- Asafetida - ½ tsp.
- Dry red chilies – 4.
- Cooking oil - 2 tbsps.
- Butter - 1 tbsp.
- Salt - ¾ tsp.
- Water - 2 cups.

Directions:
Put the drained rice into the pressure cooker. Pour in 2 cups of water. Stir it once and close the cooker and pressure valve. After two whistles, switch off the cooker and allow it to settle the pressure naturally. After that, open the cooker and leave it for a while.

Heat a frying pan on a medium-high temperature. Pour in oil, and when the oil becomes hot, put in mustard seeds. When they splutter add asafetida, curry leaves, cut green chilies and grated onion. Stir them frequently until the onion turns brown. At this point, add butter. Switch off the stove and transfer the content onto the cooked rice. Add salt and stir it.

Garlic Rice

Cooking Time: 12 minutes |Serves: 2 | Per Serving: Calories 287, Carbs 36g, Fat 15.5g, Protein 11g

Ingredients:
- Washed drained rice - 1 cup.
- Garlic flakes, split lengthwise - ½ cup.
- Curry leaves – 10 – 15.
- Green chilies, julienned – 2.
- Mustard seeds - 1 tsp.
- Asafetida - ½ tsp.
- Dry red chilies – 4.
- Cooking oil - 2 tbsps.
- Butter - 1 tbsp.
- Salt - ¾ tsp.
- Water - 2 cups.

Directions:
Put drained rice into the pressure cooker. Pour in 2 cups of water. Add salt and stir it once and close the cooker with the weight on it. Turn off the cooker after blowing two whistles. Allow the pressure to subside naturally and open the cooker. Leave it for a while.

Heat the frying pan to a medium-high temperature. Pour in oil when the pan becomes hot. Put mustard seeds in to splutter. Add asafetida, curry leaves, julienned green chilies, and split garlic. Stir it continuously till the garlic turns pale. At this time, add butter. Switch off the stove and transfer the content into the cooking pot. Stir gently and serve.

Tomato Rice

Cooking Time: 12 minutes | Serves: 2 |Per Serving: Calories 291, Carbs 41g, Fat 14.1g, Protein 12g

Ingredients:
- Washed drained rice - 1 cup.
- Tomato cut into pieces - 1 cup.
- Onion grated - 1 cup.
- Garlic flakes, split into lengthwise – 2.
- Curry leaves – 10.
- Coriander - 3 stems with leaves.
- Green chilies, julienned -2.
- Ground turmeric - 1 tsp.
- Ground chili - ½ tsp.
- Ground pepper - ½ tsp.
- Mustard seeds - 1 tsp.
- Asafetida - ½ tsp.
- Dry red chilies – 4.
- Cooking oil - 2 tbsps.
- Water -2 cups.
- Salt - ¾ tsp.

Directions:
Put the drained rice into the pressure cooker. Pour in 2 cups of water. Put in salt and stir it once and close the cooker keeping the weight on it. Turn off the cooker after two whistles. Allow the cooker to settle down the pressure for some time. Once the pressure has settled, open the cooker and leave it for a while.

Bring the frying pan to a medium-high temperature. When the pan becomes hot, pour in the oil. Put dry chili pieces and mustard seeds into the frying pan when the oil becomes hot. When the mustard splutters, add asafetida, curry leaves, julienned green chilies, cut tomatoes, grated onion, and split garlic. Stir in turmeric, chili, and ground pepper powder. Stir it frequently and cover it with a lid for 5 minutes on a low heat. Open and stir it once again. Turn off the cooker and transfer the condiments into the cooker. Garnish it with coriander leaves while serving.

Lentil Rice (Khichdi)

Cooking Time: 12 minutes | Serves: 4 |Per Serving: Calories 120, Carbs 18g, Fat 5.7g, Protein 4g

Ingredients:
- Washed & drained rice - ½ cup.
- Split green gram - ½ cup.
- Tomato cut into pieces - 1 cup.
- Grated carrot – 1.
- Green chili, coarsely chopped -2.
- Green peas - ¼ cup.
- Ginger, finely chopped - 1 tsp.
- Bay leaves – 2.

- Cinnamon bark – 1 inch.
- Coriander - 3 stems with leaves.
- Ground turmeric - 1 tsp.
- Ground chili - 1 tsp.
- Ground cumin - ½ tsp.
- Ground pepper - ½ tsp.
- Cumin seeds - 1 tsp.
- Asafetida - ½ tsp.
- Dry red chilies – 2.
- Cooking oil - 2 tbsps.
- Water - 3 cups
- Salt - 1 tsp.

Directions:
Set the pressure cooker to a low-medium heat and pour in cooking oil when it becomes hot. Put in bay leaves, red chilies, and cinnamon pieces. Stir and add cumin seeds, followed by asafetida. When it splutters, stir and add green chili, carrot, green peas tomato, and coarsely chopped ginger. Stir in ground spices of chili, turmeric, cumin seed, and pepper. Sauté for three minutes and add the drained rice and split green gram. Stir for a while and add 3 cups of water and salt. Cover the pressure cooker with the pressure valve locked. Continue cooking at a medium-high temperature. After 3 whistles, put off the cooker and allow the pressure to settle naturally. Once the pressure declines, transfer it into a bowl and garnish it with coriander leaves.

Veg Spicy Khichdi

Cooking Time: 15 minutes | Serves: 3 | Per Serving: Calories 321, Carbs 58g, Fat 8.1g, Protein 11g

Ingredients:
- Washed & drained rice - ½ cup.
- Split pigeon peas - ½ cup.
- Medium size tomato – 1.
- Medium size potato – 1.
- Medium size onion – 1.
- Medium size carrot – 1.
- French beans – 5.
- Bell pepper – 1.
- Green peas - ¼ cup.
- Green chilli-2.
- Ginger piece -1 inch.
- Garlic cloves -4.
- Bay leaves- 2.
- Cinnamon bark—1 inch.
- Coriander - 3 stems with leaves.
- Ground turmeric - 1 tsp.
- Ground chili - 1 tsp.
- Ground cumin seed - ½ tsp.

- Ground pepper - ½ tsp.
- Ground garam masala - ½ tsp.
- Cumin seeds - 1 tsp.
- Mustard seeds - 1 tsp.
- Asafetida - ½ tsp.
- Dry red chilies – 2.
- Cooking oil - 2 tbsps.
- Water - 3 cups.
- Salt - 1 tsp.

Directions:

Cut tomato, potato, onion, carrot, French beans, and capsicum into small pieces. Using a pestle, grind green chili, ginger, and garlic cloves. Pour cooking oil in the pressure cooker on a low-medium temperature. Put bay leaves, red chilies, and cinnamon pieces in. Stir it and put cumin seeds, mustard seeds followed by asafetida. When it splutters, stir in the chopped onion and continue sautéing until it softens. Now put all the cut vegetables and green peas in. Stir well and add ginger-garlic-green chilies mortar. Stir in ground spices of chili, turmeric, cumin seed, garam masala, and pepper. After three minutes, add the drained rice and pigeon peas. Stir for a while and add 3 cups of water and salt. Mix well and cover the pressure cooker locking the vent in a medium-high temperature. After 3 whistles, turn off the cooker and allow the pressure to settle naturally. Open the cooker and transfer the dish into a bowl and garnish with coriander leaves before serving.

Oats Lentil Khichdi

Cooking Time: 16 minutes | Serves: 3 | Per Serving: Calories 131, Carbs 18g, Fat 5.6g, Protein 4g

Ingredients:
- Quick-cooking oats - ½ cup.
- Split green gram - ½ cup.
- Finely chopped onion - ½ cup.
- Tomato cut into pieces - 1 cup.
- Grated carrot – 1.
- Finely chopped green chili – 2.
- Green peas - ¼ cup
- Ginger, finely chopped – 1 teaspoon.
- Lemon - ½ piece.
- Bay leaves- 2.
- Cinnamon bark – 1 inch.
- Coriander - 3 stems with leaves.
- Ground turmeric - 1 teaspoon.
- Ground chili - 1 teaspoon.
- Ground cumin seed - ½ teaspoon.
- Pepper powder - ½ teaspoon.
- Cumin seeds - 1 teaspoon.
- Asafetida - ½ teaspoon.
- Dry red chilies – 2.
- Cooking oil - 2 tablespoons.

- Water – 3 cups.
- Salt - 1 teaspoon.

Directions:
Pour cooking oil in the pressure cooker, keeping on a low-medium temperature. Put in bay leaves, red chilies, and cinnamon pieces. Stir well and add cumin seeds, followed by asafetida. When it splutters, put in the onion and keep stirring. Once the onion becomes soft, put in all the chopped vegetables. Continue stirring and add ground spices of chili, turmeric, and pepper. Sauté and continue cooking for three more minutes and add the drained split green gram. Stir for a while and add oats to it. Keep sautéing and add 3 cups of water and salt. Cover the pressure cooker keeping the vent locked. Change the temperature to medium-high. After 3 whistles, turn off the cooker and allow the pressure to settle naturally. When the pressure has settled down, open the cooker and transfer the cooked dish onto a serving plate. Squeeze the half lemon over it and garnish with coriander leaves before serving.

Rasam Rice

Cooking Time: 25 minutes | Serves: 3 |Per Serving: Calories 227, Carbs 27g, Fat 12.3g, Protein 4g

Ingredients:
- Washed & drained rice – 1 cup.
- Tomato – 1 cup, grated.
- Green chili – 2, julienned to 1 inch.
- Curry leaves – 1 twig.
- Asafetida – ⅛ tsp.
- Mustard seeds – 1 tsp.
- Pepper – 1 tsp.
- Dried red chili – 1 cut into pieces.
- Cooking oil – 2 tbsps.
- Cilantro – 3 stems with leaves - chopped.
- Ground turmeric – 1 tsp.
- Ground chili - 1 tsp.
- Rasam powder – 1 tsp.
- Ground pepper - ½ tsp.
- Butter – 1 tbsp.
- Water – 5 cups divided.
- Salt – 1 tsp.

Directions:
Pour 2 cups of water into the pressure cooker and add washed and drained rice into it. Cover the cooker and lock the pressure vents. Cook at a low-medium temperature until it blows 2 whistles. Put off the cooker and allow it to settle the pressure.

Pour oil in a pan and bring to a low-medium temperature. Add butter to it. When the oil becomes hot, put mustard seed in to splutter. After that, put pepper and red chili pieces. Once it is seasoned, add asafetida and curry leaves. Stir well.

Add grated tomato, green chilies, and continue stirring. Put all ground spices, salt, and 3 cups of water. Cook until it starts to boil for about 10 minutes. Add chopped coriander leaves. Now, add the cooked rice to the hot water. It is best when served hot with a roasted papad.

Eggplant Rice

Cooking Time: 30 minutes | Serves: 2 | Per Serving: Calories 445, Carbs 61g, Fat 26.8g, Protein 14g

Ingredients:
- Washed & drained rice – 1 cup.
- Medium size eggplant, cut into 16 pieces – 2.
- Green chili, julienned – 2.
- Curry leaves – 1 twig.
- Asafetida – ⅛ tsp.
- Mustard seeds – 1 tsp.
- Split black gram – 1 tsp.
- Split chickpea – 1 tsp.
- Dried red chili, in pieces – 2.
- Peanuts – 20.
- Tamarind pulp - ¼ cup.
- Ground brown sugar – 1 tsp.
- Cooking oil - 3 tbsps.
- Cilantro – 3 stems with leaves, chopped.
- Turmeric powder – 1 tsp.
- Ground chili - 1 tsp.
- Vegetable masala powder – 1 tsp.
- Ground pepper - ½ tsp.
- Water – 2 cups.
- Salt - 1 tsp.

Directions:
Cut Eggplant and keep it in water to remove the bitterness and to retain the color. Cook rice in the pressure cooker in 2 cups of water. After 2 whistles, put off the cooker and keep aside to settle the pressure.

In a pan pour oil and bring to a low-medium temperature. When the oil becomes hot, stir in black gram, chickpea, and dried red chili. Now put mustard and asafetida to it. When it splutters, put in curry leaves, green chilies, and eggplant pieces. Add peanuts and continue stirring. Add tamarind extract and give a gentle stir. Put powdered spices, turmeric, chili and vegetable masala, ground pepper, ground brown sugar, and salt. Keep stirring until the tamarind extract becomes thick. Stop cooking and mix it with cooked rice and garnish with cilantro leaves.

Veg Biriyani

Cooking Time: 45 minutes | Serve: 5 | Per Serving: Calories 357, Carbs 67g, Fat 4.7g, Protein 12g

Ingredients:

- Basmati rice - 1½ cups.
- Bay leaves – 2.
- Green cardamoms – 4.
- Cloves – 4.
- Black cardamom -2.
- Cinnamon- 2 (1-inch pieces).
- Mace -2 strands.
- Cumin seeds -1 tsp.
- Turmeric powder -1 tsp.
- Red chili powder – 1 tsp.
- Split cashews - 5 (cashews).
- Raisins – 10.
- Almonds – 5 broken.
- Clarified butter -2 tbsps.
- Fresh curd -1 cup beaten.
- Milk – 4 tbsps.
- Saffron – ¼ strands
- Rosewater - 2 tsps.
- Green peas - ½ cup.
- Tomato - ½ cup.
- Cauliflower - ½ cup.
- French beans - ½ cup.
- Carrot – ½ cup.
- Onion, finely sliced – 1 cup.
- Ginger, finely chopped – ½ tsp.
- Garlic, minced – 1 tbsp.
- Green chilies, finely chopped -2.
- Coriander leaves, coarsely chopped – ⅓ cup.
- Mint leaves, coarsely chopped – ⅓ cup.

Directions:

For cooking rice:
Rinse the rice until it is free of starch and soak for 30 minutes. After 30 minutes, drain the rice and keep it ready to cook. In a deep cooking bowl, pour 5 cups of water and bring to boil on a high heat. Add 1 bay leaf (Indian bay leaf), 2 green cardamoms, 2 cloves, 1 black cardamom, cinnamon, mace, and put in the rice. Give a gentle stir and continue boiling until 75% of the rice is cooked. The rice should be in an almost cooked stage and not fully cooked. Strain the rice using a sieve, fluff, and keep it aside. To stop the rice from further cooking, pour 2 cups of water before straining.

Making gravy for biriyani:
In a pressure cooker, add 2 tablespoons of clarified butter. Put the following spices –cumin, 1 bay leaf, 2 green cardamoms, 2 cloves, 1 black cardamom, and 1 cinnamon. Stir until it crackles. Add sliced onion and stir on low heat. You can add ⅛ teaspoon salt for easy cooking of the onion.

When the onion turns golden, add finely sliced ginger, garlic, and green chilies. Sauté until the aroma starts to emanate. Add turmeric and chili powder and mix well. Stir in the vegetables and sauté for 2 minutes. Transfer the beaten curd by adding ½ cup water, and salt. Close the pressure cooker and cook on a medium heat. Wait for 1 whistle and switch of the cooker. Allow the pressure to settle naturally and open the lid and simmer for a few minutes until the gravy reaches the required constituency. If it is watery, heat it without the top until the sauce becomes thick. Add raisins, almonds, and cashews to the gravy and stir.

Warm 4 tablespoons of milk in a small pan and add ¼ teaspoon of saffron strands and stir.

The layering of biriyani:
Place half of the gravy into a thick bottomed pan and layer half of the cooked rice. Drizzle saffron milk, shredded mint leaves and half a portion of shredded cilantro leaves over the rice layer. Sprinkle the remaining coriander, mint leaves, and saffron milk over it. Finally, drizzle rose water over it and cover the pan with a tight-fitting lid.

Note: The first layer should be gravy, and the top layer should be cooked rice. Based on the quantity, you can make 2 or 4 layers.

Dum cooking the biriyani:
For making traditional biriyani, you need to dum (indirect or direct heating from bottom) it. Use an aluminum foil seal and secure the pot. Then cover the pot with the lid. Heat a griddle pan on high temperature, and when it becomes hot, place the sealed container on it for 25 to 30 minutes at low heat. Alternatively, you can dum the biriyani directly on low heat for 7 to 10 minutes.

Vegetable Fried Rice

Cooking Time: 1 hour |Serve: 3 |Per Serving: Calories 433, Carbs 80g, Fat 8.6g, Protein 10g

Ingredients:
- Basmati rice – 1 cup.
- French beans – 5.
- Garlic - 2 cloves.
- Ginger -1 piece (1inch size).
- Spring onion – 1 cup.
- Corn grains – ¼ cup.
- Green peas – ¼ cup.
- Green chili, finely chopped – 2.
- Celery leaves, finely chopped – 1 tbsp.
- Bay leaves – 2.
- Star anise – 1.
- Ground pepper – ½ tsp.
- Salt - 3 tsps.
- Cooking oil - 3 tbsps.
- Water – 5 cups.
- Soya sauce – 3 tsp.
- Chili sauce – 2 tsps.
- Vinegar – 1 tsp.

Directions:
Rinse basmati rice until the starch color disappears and soak for 30 mins. After 30 minutes, drain it. Add 5 cups of water in a cooking pot and add ½ teaspoon of salt, 3 drops of cooking oil and bring to boil. Once it boils, add drained rice to the boiling water. Simmer on low heat and just cook the rice 75 to 80%. Drain the water, fluff it and keep aside for cooling.

Finely cut the vegetables such as French beans, garlic, ginger, green chilies, and spring onions. Heat oil in a pan. When the oil becomes hot, start adding star anise and fry for some seconds or until the fragrance emanate. Now put the chopped beans, followed by garlic, ginger, and sauté for a few minutes. Add 2 tablespoons of chopped spring onions and sauté for 2 minutes.

Add all the remaining vegetables, including the shredded celery. Maintain the heat to medium-high and stir to fry the vegetables by frequently tossing. Stir and see that the vegetables retain their crunch. Add 3 teaspoon of soya sauce, salt, and ½ teaspoon of ground black pepper. Keep stirring and add chili sauce and stir and add to the rice. Stir it continuously for 3 minutes until the sauce gets coated with the rice well. Fry the rice in low heat. Add 1 teaspoon of vinegar and mix well. Garnish the rice with the remaining chopped spring onions.

Note: Total cooking time will be 1 hour (20 minutes for rice cooking+40 minutes for veg cooking)

Peanut Rice

Cooking Time: 30 minutes |Serves: 4 |Per Serving: Calories 338, Carbs 51g, Fat 32.8g, Protein 10g

Ingredients:
- White rice – 1 cup.
- Water – 2 cups.
- Peanuts - ½ cup.
- Split chickpeas – 1 tbsp.
- Split black gram – 1 tbsp.
- Dry red chili – 3.
- Grated coconut – 3 tbsps.
- Turmeric powder - ¼ tsp.
- Sesame seed (white) - 2 tbsps.
- Salt – 1½ tsps.
- Mustard seeds - ½ tsp.
- Sesame oil - 1 tbsp.
- Asafetida - ⅛ tsp.
- Curry leaves -8.

Directions:
Rinse the rice and soak in water for 30 minutes. For brown rice, soak it for 40 minutes. Drain the water, put the rice into the pressure cooker, pour 1¾ to 2 cups of water, and add ½ teaspoon of salt. Give a gentle stir to mix the salt. Close the pressure cooker and also the pressure vent. Start cooking at medium heat or as per the setting in the cooker. After 2 whistles, stop cooking and allow the pressure to settle down naturally. If you are using brown rice, you need to cook until it blows 10-12 whistles in medium heat.

Heat a thick bottomed pan at medium-low temperature. Put ½ cup peanuts into it and stir gently to roast the peanuts crisp. Keep the roasted peanuts aside. Add 1 tablespoon of split chickpeas to the pan on low heat and sauté until they become golden and aromatic. Place them aside.

Add 1 tablespoon of split black grams to the pan on a low heat and sauté. Keep them aside. Put 3 dry red chilies and 3 tablespoons of grated coconut. Sauté continuously until the coconut becomes light brown. Stop sautéing and add ¼ teaspoon of turmeric powder and sesame seeds. Stir the ingredients and allow them to cool.

Using a blender, grind the coconut mixture with the already made roasted chickpeas and black gram. Keep it aside. Grind the roasted peanuts to a semi-fine powder. Add the ground coconut mixture and the ground peanut to the cooked rice and add 1½ teaspoons of salt and mix well.

Heat 1 tablespoon of sesame oil in a pan. Splutter mustard seed in ½ teaspoon of oil and season curry leaves and asafetida. Turn off the cooker. Transfer the seasoning to the Peanut rice. Mix the contents well and serve hot.

Red Kidney Beans rice

Cooking Time: 30 minutes | Serves: 2 | Per Serving: Calories 695, Carbs 108g, Fat 22.5g, Protein 16g

Ingredients:
- Red kidney beans -1 cup.
- Basmati rice - 1 cup.
- Onion, thinly sliced - 1 large.
- Tomato -1 sliced.
- Ginger, grated – 1-inch piece.
- Green chilies, chopped – 3.
- Cumin seeds - ½ tsp.
- Cinnamon powder – ½ tsp.
- Turmeric powder - ½ tsp.
- Cilantro leaves, coarsely chopped – 1 tbsp.
- Dried mango powder - ½ tsp.
- Chaat masala - 1 tsp.
- Oil – 2 tbsps.
- Salt -1 tsp.
- Water – 6 cups, divided.
- Yogurt – 1 cup

Directions:
Sort and soak kidney beans for 8 hours or overnight. Pressure cook with 1 cup of water for 4 whistles and let it the pressure settle down naturally. Keep them aside.

Rinse and soak the rice for 20 minutes. Drain the rice after the soaking period and keep it aside. Pour 5 cups of water in a cooking pot and put in the rice. Add ½ teaspoon of salt, 3 drops of cooking oil and bring to a rolling boil. After it starts to boil, bring down the heat to medium-low. Cook the rice al dente and drain the water. After draining, open the lid and fluff the rice to avoid lumping.

Add oil in a pan and bring to a medium-low heat. Add cumin seeds and stir. When it sizzles, add sliced onion and sauté until the onion becomes tender. Add powdered cinnamon, minced ginger, chopped green chilies and stir fry for 2 minutes.

Add chopped cilantro leaves, dry mango powder, and turmeric powder. Stir and cook for another 4 minutes. Now, add the cooked red kidneys along with the stock. Stir in sliced tomato and simmer for 5 minutes. When the gravy becomes thick, add chaat masala and salt. Mix well and bring to boil and turn off the stove. Add cooked rice to the mixture and combine gently. Garnish with chopped cilantro leaves and serve hot with yogurt.

Collard Green Lemon Rice

Cooking Time: 30 minutes | Serve: 2 | Per Serving: Calories 348, Carbs 43g, Fat 17.1g, Protein 11g

Ingredients:
- Basmati rice – 1 cup.
- Water -5 cups.
- Clarified butter – 2 tbsps.

Required spices:
- Cumin seeds – ½ tsp.
- Cardamom, crushed – 2.
- Cinnamon stick – ½ inch piece.
- Dried red chilies – 2.
- Green chilies, julienned – 2.
- Cashew nuts – 2 tbsps.
- Garlic, minced – ½ tsp.
- Collard green, coarsely chopped – 2 cups.
- Salt – 1 tsp.
- Fresh lemon juice – 3 tsps.

Directions:
Wash the rice 2 or 3 times until the water turns clear and drain it. Add 5 cups of water in a cooking pot, ½ teaspoon of salt and 3 drops of cooking oil and bring it to a rolling boil. Once it boils, add the drained rice. Simmer on a low heat and cook the rice al dente. Strain and remove the water.

Heat clarified butter in a frying pan over a medium-high temperature. Add whole spices. sauté until the aroma starts to release. Then, add dried red chilies, cashews, and stir for 2 minutes. Add garlic and stir for a few seconds. Add spinach and mix the contents. Stir for a while until it begins to dry. Add pre-cooked rice and salt. Stir gently and fry for 2 minutes and switch off the flame. Sprinkle with fresh lemon juice and mix well. Serve hot.

Mixed Vegetable Rice

Cooking Time: 30 minutes | Serve: 2 | Per Serving: Calories 569, Carbs 100g, Fat 14.9g, Protein 10g

Ingredients:

- Basmati rice – 1 cup.
- Water – 1¾ cups.
- Clarified butter – 1 tbsp.

Spices:
- Cardamom, crushed – 3.
- Cloves, crushed – 4.
- Cinnamon stick – ½ inch.
- Bay leaf – 1.
- Fresh ground pepper – 1 tsp.

Other ingredients:
- Onion, finely sliced – ½ cup.
- Salt – 1 tsp.
- Coconut oil - 1 tbsps.
- Potato, cut into cubes – ¼ cup.
- Beans, cut into pieces – ¼ cup.
- Carrot, sliced into thin pieces – ¼ cup.
- Green bell pepper, thinly sliced - ¼ cup.
- Red bell pepper, finely chopped – ¼ cup.
- Fresh green peas – ¼ cup.
- Fresh corn – ¼ cup.
- Cashews -4 .
- Raisins – 1 tbsp.

Directions:
Soak rinsed rice for 15 minutes. Drain and keep the rice aside. Rinse the vegetables, drain, chop into pieces, and keep aside. Add clarified butter in a pressure cooker and bring to a medium-low heat. Put the whole spices, fresh ground pepper, and stir until the aroma comes. Add sliced onion and sauté until it softens. Put the drained rice in the cooker and give a gentle mix. Pour water into pressure cooker at medium-high for 1 whistle. After the first whistle, switch off the stove and allow it to de-pressure naturally.

Pour coconut oil into a thick pan and bring to a medium-low heat. Roast cashew nuts and raisins separately and keep aside. In the same pan, add potato, beans, carrot, capsicum, green peas, corn, and stir for about 2 minutes. Add salt to taste and stir well. Finally, add the cooked rice and ground pepper powder. Mix well. Garnish it with roasted cashew and raisins.

Saffron Rice

Cooking Time: 40 minutes |Serves: 2 |Per Serving: Calories 440, Carbs 84g, Fat 8g, Protein 7g

Ingredients:
- Basmati rice – 1 cup.
- Saffron - ¼ tsp, divided.

Spices:

- Black cumin seeds - ½ tsp.
- Green cardamoms, crushed -2.
- Bay leaf – 1.
- Cinnamon, stick – 1.
- Cloves – 2.
- Mace strand – 1.

Other ingredients:
- Water - 2¼ cups.
- Turmeric powder - ⅛ tsp.
- Cooking oil – 1 tbsp.
- Cilantro leaves, coarsely chopped – 1 tbsp.
- Salt - 1 tsp.

Directions:
Rinse until the water becomes clear and soak the rice for 20 minutes. After 20 minutes, drain the rice and keep aside. In a thick deep pan, pour oil and bring to medium-low heat. Sauté all the ingredients until they splutter and then add the drained rice. Combine it gently for 2 minutes. Add crushed saffron, turmeric powder, salt, and water and stir well. Cover the pan and cook the rice until the liquid absorbs entirely. After the water has evaporated well, fluff the rice. Garnish it with cilantro leaves and serve hot.

Masala Rice

Cooking Time: 20 minutes |Serves: 2 |Per Serving: Calories 306, Carbs 47g, Fat 11g, Protein 5g

Ingredients:
- Steamed rice – 2 cups.
- Green chili, chopped – 1.
- Tomato, finely chopped – 1 medium size.
- Onion, finely chopped – 1 medium size.
- Turmeric powder - ¼ tsp.
- Chili powder - ¼ tsp.
- Mustard seeds - ½ tsp.
- Cumin seeds - ½ tsp.
- Garam masala powder - ¼ tsp.
- Ground coriander - ½ tsp.
- Ground fennel powder - ½ tsp.
- Hing - ⅛ tsp.
- Curry leaves – 1 twig.
- Cilantro leaves, chopped (for garnishing) – 2 tbsps.
- Salt - ½ tsp.
- Cooking oil – 1½ tbsps.
- Water – 5 cups.

Directions:

In a thick skillet, pour oil and bring to a low-medium heat. When the oil becomes hot, put mustard seeds in to splutter. Put cumin seeds in and sauté until they become brown. Put sliced onion in and sauté until it becomes soft and brown. Now add chopped green chilies and curry leaves and sauté for 1 minute. Put the chopped tomatoes in and continue cooking until they becomes soft by stirring frequently. Now add all the remaining spices, and hing and stir to mix well. Finally, add the steamed rice and gently stir to mix the masala with the rice. Sauté the mix for about 3 minutes. Garnish with cilantro leaves before serving.

Bell Pepper Rice

Cooking Time: 40 minutes |Serve: 2 |Per Serving: Calories 214, Carbs 26g, Fat 14.2g, Protein 7g

Ingredients:
- Basmati rice - 1 cup.
- Bell peppers (green, red and yellow) cut into small cubes – 1 cup.
- Water – 5 cups.
- Vegetable oil -2 tbsps.
- Cloves – 2.
- Bay leaf – 1.
- Green cardamom – 2.
- Cinnamon stick -1piece (1 inch).
- Black cardamom-1.
- Peppercorns small – 3.
- Cumin seeds - 1 tsp.
- Ginger garlic paste – 1½ tsp., divided.
- Green chili, chopped – 2.
- Onion, finely chopped – 1 medium size.
- Tomato, chopped – 1 large size.
- Garam masala - ¼ tsp.
- Salt - 2 tsps.
- Chopped cilantro leaves for garnishing – 1 tbsp.
- Lemon juice -1 tsp.
- Curd – 1 tbsp.

Directions:
Wash and drain the rice. Pour 5 cups of water in a cooking bowl and add ½ teaspoon of salt and 3 drops of cooking oil and bring to boil. Add rice to the boiling water. Simmer on a low heat until the rice is cooked. Drain the rice and keep it aside. You can also pressure cook the rice in 3½ cups of water and put off after 1 whistle. Release the pressure manually, open the lid, and allow the rice to settle down.

Heat oil in a pan and add green cardamom, black cardamom, cinnamon stick, bay leaf, cloves, and peppercorn. Sauté for 30 seconds till you get the aroma of the spices. Add cumin seeds and let them splutter. Then add chopped green chili and stir until it becomes golden brown. Add onions and continue stirring until they become translucent and emanate the flavor. Now you can put the ginger garlic paste and cook for 2 minutes. Add cut tomatoes, salt, and continue stirring.

Continue cooking for 5 minutes until they become soft and nicely cooked. Add bell pepper cubes and cook for 3 minutes. Stir in curd and mix well until it gets well incorporated with the vegetables and spices. Continue cooking the dish for about 4 minutes on a medium heat.

Towards the final process, transfer the cooked rice into the vegetable mixture pan and mix thoroughly. Sprinkle with garam masala and cook further for 2 more minutes. Squeeze with lemon juice and stir. Transfer the content into a bowl and garnish with coriander leaves.

Steamed Rice

Cooking Time: 27 minutes |Serve: 8 |Per Serving: Calories 207, Carbs 45.3g, Fat 0.4g, Protein 4g

Ingredients:
- Jasmine rice – 1 pound.
- Water – 3¾ cups.
- Salt - 1½ tsp.

Directions:
Rinse the rice in running water until the starch disappears and drain it. In a 4 quart pot, pour water, put the rice, salt, and gently stir once and bring to boil for about 7 minutes without covering the lid and until the steam holes appear on top of the rice level. When you see the steam holes, reduce the heat, cover the lid and simmer for about 15 minutes. Stop cooking and let it remain there for another 5 minutes. After that, before serving, gently fluff the rice with a fork and serve hot.

Clarified Butter Rice with Shallots

Cooking Time: 30 minutes |Serve: 2 |Per Serving: Calories 884, Carbs 98g, Fat 51.7g, Protein 10g

Ingredients:
- Basmati rice – 1 cup.
- Shallots – ½ cup, divided.
- Clarified butter – 8 tbsps.

Spices:
- Cinnamon stick – 1 inch.
- Cardamom, crushed – 2.
- Cloves – 4.
- Cumin seeds - ⅛ tsp.
- Bay leaf – 1.

Other ingredients:
- Cashew nuts – 2 tbsps.
- Raisins – 2 tbsps.
- Water – 1¾ cups.

Directions:

Rinse the rice until the water becomes clear and soak for 15 minutes. After soaking, drain the rice and keep aside. In a thick pan, pour 4 tablespoons of clarified butter and bring to a medium-low heat. Roast cashew nuts and raisins separately and keep aside. In the same pan, put ¼ cup sliced onion with ⅛ teaspoon of salt and sauté until the onion becomes golden brown. Remove it on to a tissue paper and keep aside.

In a pressure cooker, pour the remaining clarified butter and bring to medium-low heat. Add the whole spices and sauté for about 2 minutes until it starts to produce the aroma. Put the drained rice and stir fry for 2 minutes. Pour water and give a gentle stir. Cover and pressure cook for 1 whistle. Allow the pressure to settle down naturally, and after that, open the cooker and fluff the rice. If moisture is there in the cooker, cook under a medium-low heat until the water absorbs entirely. Garnish it with roasted cashew nuts, raisins, and sliced fried onion.

Mushroom Biriyani

Cooking Time: 25 minutes |Serve: 3 |Per Serving: Calories 324, Carbs 114g, Fat 12g, Protein 13g

Ingredients for mushroom biriyani:
- Mushrooms, sliced – 2½ cups.
- Basmati rice – 2 cups.
- Onion – 1 large, sliced.
- Yogurt - ¼ cup.
- Tomatoes, chopped - ½ cup.
- Mint leaves, chopped – 3 tbsps.
- Cilantro leaves, chopped – 3tbsps, divided.
- Ginger, minced - ¾ tbsp.
- Garlic, minced - ¾ tbsp.
- Green chilies – 2, julienned.
- Clarified butter – 2 tbsps.
- Red chili powder - ½ tsp.
- Water - 3½ cups.

Spices for tempering:
- Bay leaf – 1.
- Star anise – 1.
- Carom seeds - ½ tsp.
- Cardamom – 2, crushed.
- Cinnamon – 2-inch piece.
- Cloves – 4.

For the biriyani masala:
- 1 strand mace – 1 small.
- Green cardamoms – 4.
- Cinnamon – 1 inch.
- Cloves – 6.
- Nutmeg – 1 pinch.
- Fennel seeds - ½ tsp.

Directions:
Rinse and soak the rice for 15 minutes. After 15 minutes, drain the rice and keep ready to use it. Put all the biriyani masala in a dry grinder and make smooth masala powder.

Pour oil in the pressure cooker and add bay leaf, cloves, cinnamon, star anise, carom seeds, and crushed cardamoms. Let them sizzle for 1 minute under medium-low heat. Then, add chilies and onions until the onions become tender and golden. Now add minced garlic, ginger, and sauté until the raw smell of ginger and garlic disappears. Then, add powdered masala, red chili powder, 2½ tablespoons of chopped coriander leaves, mint leaves, and sauté for about 2 minutes until the aroma starts to release. Now, add chopped tomatoes, salt, and turmeric powder until tomatoes begin to secrete the juice. Pour in yogurt and salt, and stir well to mix.

Add the sliced mushrooms and sauté for about 3 minutes. Put the drained rice into the cooker and pour 3½ cups of water. Stir gently and check the salt level and, if required, add more salt. Close the lid and cook for 1 whistle at a medium-low heat. After 1 whistle, allow it to settle down the pressure and open the cooker. Fluff the biriyani with a fork and before serving garnish with chopped coriander leaves.

Plain Biriyani

Cooking Time: 30 minutes |Serve: 4 |Per Serving: Calories 382, Carbs 80g, Fat 1g, Protein 9g

Ingredients:
- Basmati rice – 2 cups.
- Water – 3½ cups.
- Oil - 2½ tbsps.
- Onion, sliced - ½ cup.
- Ginger, grated - ½ tbsp.
- Garlic, minced - ½ tbsp.
- Tomato, chopped - ½ cup.
- Salt – 1 tsp.
- Cilantro leaves, chopped – 1 tbsp.
- Yogurt - ¼ cup

For the plain biriyani masala:
- Bay leaf – 1.
- Cloves – 6.
- Green cardamoms – 6, crushed.
- Star anise – 1.
- Carom seeds - ½ tsp.
- Mace strand – 1.
- Cinnamon – 2 inches.
- Turmeric powder - ¼ tsp.
- Red chili powder - ¾ tsp.
- Biriyani masala powder - 1½ tsps.

Directions:
Rinse the rice until the water turns clear and soak it for about 20 minutes. After soaking, drain the water and keep ready to use it.

In a pressure cooker, pour oil and bring to medium-low heat. Put all the biriyani masala spices in the given order when the oil becomes hot and sauté until it starts to emanate the aroma. Then, add sliced onions for about 3 minutes until they becomes tender and golden. Now add minced garlic, grated ginger, and sauté until the raw aroma disappears. After that, put red chili powder, coriander, turmeric, salt, and sauté for about 2 minutes until it is roasted. Now add chopped tomato, chopped cilantro leaves, and sauté for about 2 minutes until the tomato starts to secrete the juice, and it becomes mushy.

Pour 3½ cups of water in the cooker and stir the mix. Check the salt level and, if required, add more salt. Then add the soaked rice, stir gently and close the lid. Lock the vent and pressure cook under a medium-low heat for 1 whistle. Wait for the pressure to subsidize naturally. After that, open the cover and fluff the rice. Serve warm.

Tamarind Rice

Cooking Time: 30 minutes |Serve: 4 |Per Serving: Calories 493, Carbs 67g, Fat 22.2g, Protein 11g

Ingredients:
- Sona masoori rice – 1 cup.
- Salt - ⅓ tsp.
- Water - 2½ cups.
- Turmeric powder - ¼ tsp.
- Sesame oil – 1 tbsp.

Spices for tamarind rice:
- Red chilies – 4.
- Coriander seeds – 2 tsps.
- Split chickpeas – 1 tsp.
- Split black gram – 1 tsp.
- Fenugreek seeds - ¼ tsp.
- Whole black pepper - ¼ tsp.
- Sesame seeds - ½ tsp.
- Hing - ¼ tsp.

Tamarind pulp:
- Tamarind - ⅓ cup.
- Hot water – 2 cups.

For tempering:
- Sesame oil – 3 tbsps.
- Mustard seeds – 1 tsp.
- Split black gram – 1 tsp.
- Split chickpeas – 1 tsp.

- Peanuts - ¼ cup.
- Turmeric powder - ¼ tsp.
- Hing - ⅛ tsp.
- Curry leaves – 1 twig.
- Red chilies – 3.
- Brown sugar – 2 tsps.
- Salt - ½ tsp.

Directions:

Rinse the rice 2 or 3 times, until the water turns clear. Put the rice into the pressure cooker along and with 2½ cups of water, ⅓ teaspoon of salt for 3 or 4 whistles. The rice should not be overcooked. Depending on the quality of the rice, you can increase or decrease the pressure-cooking time/whistles. Allow the pressure to settle down. Open the cooker and fluff the rice with a fork. Transfer the rice to a flat plate and allow it to cool down. Add 1 tablespoon of sesame oil and ¼ teaspoon turmeric powder to the rice when it is warm. In doing so, it can stop the rice from breaking.

Put the tamarind in a small bowl with 2 cups of hot water and soak it for about 40 minutes. After soaking, squeeze and extract the pulp. Keep it ready for use.

Heat a pan at a medium-low temperature and put all the spices mentioned in the 'spices for tamarind rice,' sauté until they start to produce the fragrance. Then, put in the split chickpeas and split black gram, and roast until it becomes golden brown. Turn off the stove and add hing. Stir it with the spices and let the spices cool down. Put all the spices and roasted lentils in a grinder and make a dry spice powder. Keep the spice powder handy.

In a pan, pour 3 tablespoons of sesame oil and bring to a medium-low heat. When the oil becomes hot, add mustard seeds to splutter. Then, add split black gram, ¼ cup peanuts, and 1 teaspoon of split chickpeas. Stir fry until the lentils become golden brown. The peanuts also will be well roasted by this time. Now add 3 dry chilies, 1 twig of curry leaves, and ¼ teaspoon turmeric powder. Add ⅛ teaspoon of hing, mix well and turn off the stove. Now pour the tamarind pulp into the tempering by straining and stir to combine. Then, add brown sugar and salt. Reduce the heat and mix everything on low heat until the mixture becomes slightly thick. When the oil starts to flow on the top, add the ground spice mix. Combine it well and slow cook for 2 or 3 minutes by stirring until the mixture becomes a thick sauce. You can turn off the stove once the consistency of the sauce has reached the required level.

Add the tamarind sauce to the rice and mix gently. Allow it to infuse the flavors for about 5 minutes and serve hot.

Chapter 7 Pasta & Noodles

Masala Pasta

Cooking Time: 20 minutes |Serves: 3 |Per Serving: Calories 318, Carbs 56g, Fat 3g, Protein 12g

Ingredients:

For the pasta:
- Penne pasta - 1 cup.
- Water - 4 cups.
- Salt - ¼ tsp.

For the masala:
- Oil – 2 tbsps.
- Onion, thinly chopped - ⅓ cup
- Ginger, grated - ½ tsp.
- Garlic, minced - ½ tsp.
- Tomatoes, coarsely chopped – 1 cup.
- Turmeric powder - ¼ tsp.
- Ground cumin - ¼ tsp.
- Ground black pepper - ¼ tsp.
- Red chili powder - ¼ tsp.
- Ground coriander - ½ tsp.
- Carrots, thinly chopped - ⅓ cup.
- Green peas, fresh - ¼ cup.
- Bell pepper - ¼ cup.
- Water - ½ cup.
- Cilantro leaves, chopped – 2 tbsps.
- Spring onions, chopped, fresh – 2 tbsps.
- Salt - ½ tsp.
- Cheddar cheese, grated - ¼ cup, for garnishing.

Directions:
In a thick deep bottomed pan, pour 4 cups of water, ¼ teaspoon salt, and bring to a rolling boil. Now, put the pasta into the boiling water and cook until it becomes soft but firm. After that, turn off the stove and drain the water and keep it to use.

Pour 2 tablespoons of oil in a pan and bring to a medium-low heat. Put in the chopped onions and sauté until the onions become soft and brown. Add ginger, garlic, and sauté for about 2 minutes until the raw aroma of garlic and ginger disappears. Then, add the spice powder in the listed order and sauté for about 2-3 minutes. Now, add the chopped tomatoes and stir fry until the tomatoes become soft and pulpy. After that, add the vegetables, salt and sauté for 1 minute. Add ½ cup of water and stir gently to combine. Cover the pan and cook on a medium-low heat until the vegetables are cooked well. Add the cooked pasta into the pan after the vegetables are cooked thoroughly. After the vegetables are cooked well, add chopped coriander leaves, chopped spring onions, and mix very well. Finally, add the masala powder and mix to combine well. Turn off the stove. Garnish with shredded cheese, chopped coriander leaves and serve hot.

Indian Style Macaroni

Cooking Time: 10 minutes |Serves: 3 |Per Serving: Calories 412, Carbs 72g, Fat 7.6g, Protein 15g

Ingredients:
- Macaroni – 2 cups, cooked.
- Oil – 1 tbsp.
- Cumin seeds – 1 tsp.
- Garlic, minced – 2 tsps.
- Onions, thinly chopped - ½ cup.
- Bell pepper, finely chopped - ¼ cup.
- Tomatoes, chopped - ½ cup.
- Carrot, chopped & blanched - ¼ cup.
- French beans, chopped & blanched - ¼ cup.
- Green peas, boiled - ¼ cup.
- Salt - ¾ tsp.
- Chili powder - ½ tsp.
- Turmeric powder - ¼ tsp.
- Tomato ketchup – 2 tbsps.
- Garam masala - ½ tsp.
- Cheese, shredded – 1 tbsp for garnishing.

Directions:
In a large non-stick pan, sauté cumin seeds and garlic at a medium-low heat for ½ minute. Then, add chopped onion, bell pepper and stir fry for about 2 minutes, until the onion becomes translucent and bell pepper becomes soft. Now, add garam masala, turmeric powder, and chili powder and sauté for 1 minute. When the spices become dry, add 2 tablespoons of water. Add chopped tomatoes and mix thoroughly with the spices-onion mix. Continue sautéing for about 3 minutes, until the tomatoes become pulpy and start to produce the juice. At this point, add salt, chopped French beans, carrots, green peas, and cook for another 2 minutes by stirring frequently. Add the cooked macaroni and gently mix to coat. Remove it from the stove after cooking for 2 minutes. Serve hot by garnishing with shredded cheese.

White Sauce Pasta

Cooking Time: 8 minutes |Serves: 4 |Per Serving: Calories 371, Carbs 60g, Fat 12.4g, Protein 10g

Ingredients:

For White Sauce Pasta:
- Cooked fusilli – 2 cups.
- Milk – 2 cups.
- Plain flour – 2 tbsps.
- Salt - ¾ tsp.

- Clarified butter – 2 tbsps.
- Garlic, minced – 2 tsps.
- Yellow bell pepper, julienned - ¼ cup.
- Green bell pepper, julienned - ¼ cup.
- Red bell pepper, julienned - ¼ cup.
- Zucchini, sliced - ¼ cup.
- Broccoli florets, blanched and cut into size - ¼ cup.
- Baby corn, blanched and diagonal cuts - ¼ cup.
- Red chili flakes – 1 tsp.
- Mix herbs - 1½ tsps.
- Processed cheese, shredded - ¼ cup.

Directions:

Heat enough water in a large deep pan enough to cook fusilli and bring to a rolling boil. Put in the fusilli and cook uncovered, until it becomes tender. After it reaches the required tenderness, drain the water immediately, and pour some fresh cold water and drain again, which will help it to stop cooking further. Then drizzle in 1 tablespoon of oil and toss well so that the cooked fusilli won't stick together. Keep it aside for cooling.

For blanching the broccoli, rinse and trim the stalks and stem. Heat water in a stockpot, bring it to a rolling boil, put the florets, and allow them to blanch for a minute. After that, remove them and put them in cold water. Keep them ready to use.

For blanching the baby corn, put it in the boiling water for 15 seconds, after removing the husk and silk. After that, transfer it to cold water and keep it ready to use.

In a small bowl, mix plain flour, milk, salt, and mix well to form a smooth paste without any lumps. Keep it aside.

In a large and deep non-stick pan, pour clarified butter and bring to a medium-low heat. When the butter becomes hot, add the minced garlic and sauté for a few seconds. Then add all the julienned bell peppers, sliced zucchini, and stir fry under a medium-low heat for 2 minutes until the bell peppers become tender. Now add the blanched broccoli, baby corn, and sauté for 2 minutes by stirring continuously. To this, add the milk-plain flour mixture, mixed herbs, chili flakes, salt, cheese, and cook for about 2 minutes stirring frequently.

Add the cooked fusilli and combine gently using a fork or spoon. Cook it for another 2 minutes by combining gently. Serve the white sauce pasta hot.

Pasta Salad with Vegetables

Cooking Time: 30 minutes |Serves: 4 |Per Serving: Calories 123, Carbs 18g, Fat 4.6g, Protein 3g

Ingredients:
- Cooked fusilli – 1½ cups.
- Lettuce, chopped – 2 cups.
- Broccoli florets, blanched - ½ cup.
- Cherry tomatoes – 4, cut into halves.

For the dressing:
- Yogurt - ¼ cup.
- Cream, fresh – 5 tbsps.
- Spring onion greens, fresh, chopped – 2 tbsps.
- Celery, chopped – 1 tbsp.
- Salt - ¾ tsp.

Directions:
In a large, deep bowl, mix all the ingredients and refrigerate for about 1 hour. Before serving, mix all the dressing ingredients in a medium bowl. Pour it over the vegetables and toss gently. Serve fresh.

Creamy Mushroom Veg Pasta

Cooking Time: 12 minutes |Serves: 4 |Per Serving: Calories 310, Carbs 36g, Fat 13.7g, Protein 12g

Ingredients:
- Clarified butter – 2tbsps.
- Onions, sliced - ½ cup.
- Garlic, minced – 2 tbsps.
- Plain flour – 2 tbsps.
- Mushroom, sliced - 1½ cups.
- Milk – 2 cups.
- Cooked macaroni – 2 cups.
- Fresh cream - ¼ cup.
- Ground black pepper - ¾ tsp.
- Salt – 1 tsp.
- Cheese, shredded - ¼ cup for garnishing.

Directions:
Pour clarified butter in a large deep pan and bring to a medium-low heat. When the butter becomes hot, add the sliced onions, minced garlic, and stir fry for about 3 minutes until the onions become tender. Then add the plain flour, chopped mushrooms, and mix well. Continue cooking for about 3 minutes by stirring frequently. Now pour milk and cook for another 4 minutes. Keep stirring, add cooked macaroni, fresh cream, pepper, and salt. Cook the mixture for another 3 minutes and remove from the stove. Garnish with shredded cheese and serve hot.

Cheese Pasta with Vegetables

Cooking Time: 12 minutes |Serves: 3 |Per Serving: Calories 213, Carbs 26g, Fat 9g, Protein 9g

Ingredients:
- Processed cheese, grated – 2 tbsps.
- Oil – 1 tsp.
- Garlic, minced – 2 tsps.
- Onions, chopped - ½ cup.

- Corn kernels, boiled - ¼ cup.
- Bell pepper, finely sliced - ¼ cup.
- Broccoli florets, blanched & chopped - ¼ cup.
- Carrots, grated - ¼ cup.
- Corn flour – 1 tsp.
- Milk - ½ cup.
- Salt - ½ tsp.
- Ground black pepper - ½ tsp.

For the pasta:
- Cooked whole-wheat pasta - 1 cup.
- Oil - ½ tsp.
- Garlic, minced – 1 tsp.
- Red chili flakes - ¼ tsp.

Directions:
Heat oil in a large non-stick pan under a medium-low temperature. When the oil becomes hot, add the chopped onions, minced garlic, and sauté for about 2 minutes until the onions become soft. Now, add bell pepper, sweet corn, chopped carrots, blanched broccoli, and stir fry for 2 minutes. In a small bowl, mix corn flour with milk and pour it into the cooking pan. Add cheese, salt and cook for another 3 minutes by stirring continuously. Then, sprinkle in ground pepper, mix well and cook for 1 minute and keep aside.

In a large non-stick pan, pour ½ teaspoon oil and bring to medium-low heat. Put in chili flakes, minced garlic, and sauté for about 1 minute until the aroma starts to release. Now add the cooked pasta and stir fry for another 2 minutes. Remove it from the heat and keep aside.

Before serving, reheat the cooked sauce on a medium-low heat for about 2 minutes and combine the pasta mix in the pan. Cook pasta mix for another 2 minutes, by stirring frequently and serve hot.

Garlic Spaghetti Pasta

Cooking Time: 28 minutes |Serves: 4 |Per Serving: Calories 187, Carbs 28g, Fat 5.8g, Protein 7g

Ingredients:
- Cooked spaghetti – 2 cups.
- Garlic, minced – 2 tbsps.
- Onions, chopped – ½ cup.
- All-purpose flour – ¼ cup.
- Oil – 2 tsps.
- Ground black pepper - ½ tsp.
- Soy sauce – 1 tsp.
- Garlic sauce – 2 tsps.
- Salt - ¾ tsp.
- Processed cheese, shredded – ¼ cup.
- Cilantro leaves, coarsely chopped – 2 tbsps, for garnishing.

Directions:
Boil the spaghetti with ¼ teaspoon of salt in a large deep pan until it is cooked 80%, but soft and firm. After boiling to the required softness, drain water and pour some cold water to stop it from further cooking. Drizzle a few drops of oil and toss it well so that it won't stick together. Keep the cooked spaghetti aside.

In a large non-stick skillet pour oil and bring to a medium-low heat. When the oil becomes hot, add minced garlic and sauté for 1 minute until the raw smell of garlic disappears. Then add chopped onions and stir fry for 3 minutes until the onions become tender and brown. Keep it aside.

In a small pan roast the all-purpose flour for about 1 minute until it becomes slightly golden and remove to cool down. Then add the ingredients like soy sauce, ground black pepper, garlic sauce, salt, cooked onion, roasted all-purpose flour, cooked spaghetti, salt in a large bowl and mix well.

Preheat the oven to 200°C for 20 minutes. Line a baking dish with parchment paper and transfer the spaghetti mix onto it. Spread the mix evenly in the baking tray, scatter the shredded cheese on top and bake for 20 minutes. After baking, remove it from the oven, garnish with chopped cilantro leaves and serve hot.

Whole Wheat Spaghetti Pasta with Vegetables

Cooking Time: 5 minutes |Serves: 4 |Per Serving: Calories 192, Carbs 15.5g, Fat 10.5g, Protein 6.9g

Ingredients:
- Boiled whole wheat spaghetti - 1¼ cups.
- Onion, finely sliced - ½ cup.
- Bell pepper, sliced - ½ cup.
- Carrot, blanched and julienned - ½ cup.
- Broccoli florets, blanched and cut into pieces - ½ cup.
- Almonds - ¼ cup.
- Milk - ¾ cup.
- Olive oil – 2 tsps.
- Processed cheese, shredded – 3 tbsps.
- Dry red chili flakes – 1 tsp.
- Ground black pepper - ¾ tsp.
- Salt - ¾ tsp.

Directions:
Boil the whole-wheat spaghetti in a large deep pan until it is cooked well. After cooking, drain the water and pour some cold water to stop further cooking with the built-in heat and drain immediately. Drizzle a few drops of oil and toss it gently so that the cooked spaghetti won't stick together.

Soak the almonds in hot water for 20 minutes and after that peel the skin. Put them in an electric blender and add ½ cup of milk. Mix it until it blends with the milk thoroughly. Keep it aside.

Pour olive oil in a large deep non-stick pan and bring to medium-low heat. When the oil becomes hot, add onions and sauté for 2 minutes until they becomes tender. Then add the chopped bell pepper and stir fry for 2 minutes, until the bell pepper becomes soft. Now, add the almond-milk paste and cook for 1-minute stirring continuously. Add the cooked whole-wheat spaghetti, remaining milk, ground pepper, cheese, chili flakes, and continue cooking at medium-low heat by stirring frequently. Taste the salt and, if required, add more and serve hot.

Spring Onion and Bell Pepper Pasta

Cooking Time: 6 minutes | Serves: 3 | Per Serving: Calories 344, Carbs 48g, Fat 15.4g, Protein 10g

Ingredients:
- Spring onions whites, thinly chopped – 1 cup.
- Spring onions greens, thinly chopped – 1 cup.
- Red bell pepper, thinly sliced - ¾ cup.
- Cooked penne – 2 cups.
- Olive oil – 3 tbsps.
- Garlic, minced – 2 tsps.
- Sweet corn kernels, boiled - ½ cup.
- Dry red chili flakes – 2 tsps.
- Mixed herbs – 2 tsps.
- Salt – 1½ tsps., divided.

Directions:
Boil penne in a large deep pan by adding 1 teaspoon of oil and t teaspoon of salt. Cook it uncovered and stir occasionally and gently until the penne is cooked and tender. After reaching the required tenderness, drain the water and pour some fresh cold water to arrest further cooking with the in-built heat. Add a few drops of oil and toss it well so that it won't stick together. Keep it aside to use later.

For boiling the sweet corn kernels, heat water in a large bowl and bring to a rolling boil and place the corn with husks and silks removed. Tender corns required 30 seconds cooking and matured ones required about 3 minutes. After boiling, put it in cold water and drain the water. Release the kernels by scraping with a spoon.

In a large deep non-stick pan, pour oil and bring to medium-low heat. Add minced garlic and sauté for a few moments. Then add the chopped spring onion greens, spring onion whites, chopped red bell pepper, and sauté under a medium-low heat for 2 minutes until the bell pepper and spring onions become tender by stirring occasionally. Then add the boiled sweet corn kernels, mixed herbs, chili flakes, ½ teaspoon salt, and continue sautéing for 1 minute by stirring frequently.

To this, add the cooked penne and combine well and cook under medium-low heat for about 2 minutes. Serve hot.

Chickpea Pasta

Cooking Time: 20 minutes | Serves: 6 | Per Serving: Calories 363, Carbs 54g, Fat 11.2g, Protein 15g

Ingredients:
- Chickpeas - 2 cups.
- Pasta – 2 cups.
- Salt – 1 tsp.
- Red chili powder – ½ tsp.
- Cilantro leaves, chopped – 2 tbsps., for garnishing.

For chickpea masala:
- Onion, chopped – 1 large.
- Tomato, chopped – 1 medium.
- Ginger, grated – 1 tbsp.
- Garlic, minced – 1 tbsp.
- Green chili – 1, finely chopped.
- Coconut oil – 3 tbsps.
- Curry leaves – 1 twig.
- Chili powder – 1 tsp.
- Ground coriander – 1 tsp.
- Garam masala – 1 tsp.
- Turmeric powder - ½ tsp.
- Salt - ½ tsp.
- Water – 4 cups
- Cilantro leaves, chopped – 2 tbsps., divided.

Directions:

Cook the pasta in boiling water for about 15 minutes and drain the water. You can use any type of pasta, and the cooking time varies as per the size and shape. Check the instructions on the pasta packet. Keep the pasta aside for cooling.

Soak the chickpeas for 8 hours or overnight. After soaking, drain the chickpeas and keep ready to use them. For making the chickpea masala, pour oil in a pressure cooker and bring to a medium-low heat. When the oil becomes hot, put the chopped onions and sauté for about 3 minutes until they become soft. Then add minced garlic, grated ginger, and sauté for another 1 minute. Now add curry leaves, red chili powder, ground coriander, turmeric, garam masala and sauté until the aroma starts to release. After that, add the chopped tomato and sauté until the tomato becomes tender and mushy.

Pour 4 cups of water, stir to mix, and continue cooking for another 3 minutes. Now add the chickpeas, salt and pressure cook for 6 whistles. After the 6th whistle, turn off the stove and allow the pressure to settle naturally. After that, open the cooker and garnish with 1 tablespoon of cilantro leaves. The consistency of the gravy should be dry. If the sauce looks fluid, heat the cooker open until the moisture disappears.

Transfer the cooked pasta into the chickpea masala and combine gently. Garnish with the remaining 1 tablespoon of fresh cilantro leaves and serve hot.

Herb Pasta

Cooking Time: 9 minutes | Serves: 2 | Per Serving: Calories 93, Carbs 16g, Fat 2.9g, Protein 2g

Ingredients:
- Cooked pasta – 1 cup.
- Water – 4 cups.
- Oil – 2 tsps.
- Cilantro, leaves, chopped – ¼ cup.
- Basil leaves finely chopped – 2 tbsps.
- Lime juice – 1 tsp.
- Yogurt – 3 tsps.
- Mixed vegetables (Green beans, celery, asparagus, etc.) – 1 cup. Cut in lengthwise.
- Green chili – 1, finely chopped.
- Salt - ½ tsp.

Directions:

Heat water in a deep pan and bring to a rolling boil. Add pasta and cook for 3 minutes until it turns half cooked. Now, in the boiling water, put all the vegetables and continue cooking for about 5 minutes, until all the vegetables become tender, but not too soft. Drain the water and keep them aside for cooling.

Now grind basil and cilantro with yogurt to a smooth paste. In another pan, pour 2 teaspoons of oil and bring to medium-low heat. Add green chilies, lime juice, and sauté for a moment. Add the cooked pasta and herb paste. Remove it from the heat and toss to mix well. Sprinkle with some lemon juice and serve fresh.

Veg Hakka Noodles

Cooking Time: 10 minutes | Serve: 3 | Per Serving: Calories 291, Carbs 46g, Fat 9.6g, Protein 7g

Ingredients:
- Noodles – ¾ lbs.
- Sesame oil - 1 tbsp.
- Vegetable oil - 1 tbsp.
- Ginger, grated – 1 tsp.
- Garlic, minced – 1 tsp.
- Green chili – 1 sliced.
- Celery chopped - 1 tbsp.
- Onion – 1 medium size, chopped.
- Carrot – 1 large, chopped.
- Bell pepper, red – 1, sliced.
- Spring onion greens chopped – 1 cup, divided.
- Soya sauce - 1 tbsp.
- White vinegar - 1 tbsp.
- Hot sauce - 1 tsp.

- Ground black pepper - ¼ tsp.
- Sugar - 1 tsp.
- Ground white pepper - ¼ tsp.
- Chili powder - ½ tsp.
- Salt - ½ tsp.

Directions:

Rinse all the vegetables and cut as per the requirements. In a cooking pan, boil the noodles as per the package instructions. They should be ready in 2 minutes. Drain the water and pour on cold water and drain again. Pouring cold water can stop the noodles from cooking further. Drizzle ½ tablespoon of oil into the drained noodles and toss well. It will prevent the noodles from sticking together. Keep them aside, ready.

In a skillet pour 1 tablespoon of oil, 1 tablespoon sesame oil and bring to a medium-low heat. Add grated ginger and minced garlic to the pan when the oil becomes hot and sauté for 1 minute, until the color changes. Now add chopped onion and sauté until the onion becomes tender and turns to light brown. Then, add the chopped carrots, green onion, bell pepper, and cook on a medium-high heat so that the vegetables become crispy. Reduce the heat, move vegetables to one side of the pan. Now, pour soy sauce, sugar, hot sauce, and stir to mix with the vegetables. Add salt, black pepper, white pepper, and mix it well with the vegetables. Transfer the cooked noodles into the pan and combine them with the vegetable-sauce mixture. Finally, sprinkle salt chili powder and combine thoroughly. Garnish with spring onions and serve hot.

Noodles with Vegetables

Cooking Time: 10 minutes | Serves: 3 | Per Serving: Calories 392, Carbs 40g, Fat 24g, Protein 8g

Ingredients:

Curry sauce:
- Coconut milk – 1 cup,
- Red chili paste- 1 tbsp.
- Tamarind pulp - 1 tbsp.
- Sugar - 1 tbsp.
- Peanuts, roasted and chopped - 1 tbsp.
- Onions, chopped - ½ cup.
- Salt - ¼ tsp.

Other ingredients:
- Boiled noodles – 1½ cups.
- Bean sprouts – ½ cup.
- Broccoli florets, blanched – ¾ cup.
- Oil – 2 tsps.
- Salt - ¾ tsp.
- Ground black pepper - ¾ tsp.

Directions:

In a large non-stick pan, mix all the sauce ingredients and cook on a medium-low heat for about 8 minutes by stirring frequently. After cooking, keep it aside.

In another large non-stick pan, pour oil and bring to medium-low heat and put in the cooked noodles, blanched broccoli, bean sprouts, ground pepper, salt, and sauté for about 2 minutes. Pour the curry sauce on the noodles and serve hot.

Tangy Bell Pepper Noodles

Cooking Time: 6 minutes | Serves: 2 | Per Serving: Calories 540, Carbs 85g, Fat 16.2g, Protein 13.8g

Ingredients:
- Bell pepper, (yellow, red, green mix) chopped – 1 cup.
- Hakka noodles, boiled – 1 cup.
- Oil- 1 tbsp.
- Ginger, grated – ½ tbsp.
- Onions, sliced – ¼ cup.
- Salt - ½ tsp.
- Water – 3 cups.

For the tangy sauce:
- Soy sauce - 1 tbsp.
- Lemon juice - 1 tbsp.
- Sesame oil – 1½ tsps.
- Sugar, powdered – 1 tsp.
- Cilantro leaves, finely chopped – 1 tsp.

For garnishing:
- sesame seeds, roasted – 1 tsp.

Directions:
Pour 3 cups of water in a large deep pan, adding salt and few drops of oil. Bring the water to a rolling boil and put the Hakka noodles in until 75% done. After that, turn off the stove and drain the noodles. Add some cold water and drain it again. Add a few drops of oil and toss it. So that the noodles won't stick together; then, keep the cooked noodles aside in a bowl for use.

For making the tangy sauce, in a medium bowl, pour in the soy sauce and add lemon juice into it and mix well. Then add sesame oil, powdered sugar, and cilantro leaves and combine well. Keep the tangy sauce aside to use.

In a pan, dry roast the sesame seeds at a low heat and keep aside. After that, add oil and bring to a medium-high heat. Sauté grated ginger for a minute and add the sliced onions. Sauté them for 1 minute until they become tender. Then, add the chopped bell pepper and stir fry for 2 minutes. Now add the prepared tangy sauce, salt, and mix well. Finally, add the boiled Hakka noodles. Cook the Hakka noodles under a medium heat for 2 minutes, while combining them with two forks or two spoons. Garnish with roasted sesame seeds and serve hot.

Quick Masala Noodles

Cooking Time: 8 minutes |Serves: 4 |Per Serving: Calories 455, Carbs 36g, Fat 30.8g, Protein 12g

Ingredients:
- Boiled flat noodles – 4 cups.
- Oil – 1 tsp.
- Clarified butter- 2 tbsps.
- Onions, thinly chopped – 1 cup.
- Celery, finely chopped – 2 tbsps.
- Tomatoes, deseeded and chopped – ½ cup.
- Bell pepper mix colors, chopped – 1 cup.
- Mushrooms, chopped – ½ cup.
- Tomato ketchup – ¼ cup.
- Chili sauce- 1 tbsp.
- Fresh cream – ¼ cup
- Salt – 1 tsp.
- Lemon juice – ½ tbsp.
- Processed cheese, shredded - ½ cup for garnishing.

Directions:

In a deep pan, boil flat noodles with ½ teaspoon salt and cook 80%. When the cooking is over, drain the water and add cold water and drain again. Pouring cold water on the cooked noodles will stop them from further cooking. Drop 1 teaspoon oil on the cooked noodles and toss well so that they won't stick together. Keep them aside.

In a large deep pan, add butter and bring to a low heat. When the butter becomes hot, add the chopped onions and sauté for about 3 minutes, until the onions become translucent and brown. Now add celery and cook for 2-3 minutes. Now, add the chopped colored bell peppers, tomatoes, mushrooms, and sauté for about 4 minutes. Stir in chili sauce and tomato ketchup, salt, fresh cream and cook for 2 minutes.

Now it is time to add the cooked flat noodles and lemon juice. Keep cooking on a low heat and in the meantime combine the noodles with a spoon until they get the right mix. Before serving, garnish with shredded processed cheese.

Broccoli and Baby Corn Noodles

Cooking Time: 7 minutes |Serves: 4 |Per Serving: Calories 317, Carbs 57g, Fat 6.5g, Protein 8g

Ingredients:
- Boiled noodles – 3 cups.
- Broccoli florets, blanched - ½ cup.
- Baby corn in diagonal cuts - ½ cup.
- Oil – 1½ tbsps, divided.
- Ginger, grated – 2 tbsps.

- Garlic, minced – 1 tbsp.
- Celery, thinly chopped – 2 tbsps.
- Onions, chopped – ½ cup.
- Carrots, julienned - ½ cup.
- Bell pepper, chopped - ½ cup.
- Ground black pepper - ½ tsp.
- Salt - 1 tsp, divided.

Directions:

In a large deep pan, boil noodles after pouring enough water, and ½ teaspoon of salt until they are cooked 80%. The noodles should be cooked well but firm. After cooking, drain the water. Pour some cold water on the cooked noodles and drain the water again so that the noodles will stop cooking further on the built-up heat. Now add 3 or 4 drops of oil and toss it well, which shall prevent it from sticking together. Keep the cooked noodles aside.

Now in a large deep non-stick pan, pour 1 tablespoon of oil and heat on a high temperature. When the oil becomes hot, put in the minced garlic, grated ginger, chopped onions, chopped celery, and stir fry for about 3 minutes until the onion becomes translucent. Then add chopped bell pepper, carrots and sauté under a medium-low heat for about 2 minutes. Now, add the blanched broccoli, baby corn, and continue cooking for another 1 minute.

Put the cooked noodles in the pan with ground pepper, salt, soy sauce and mix well while cooking for about 2 minutes on a medium-low heat by stirring frequently. Serve the baby corn and broccoli noodles hot.

Noodle Basket with Veg Stir Fry

Cooking Time: 30 minutes |Serves: 4 |Per Serving: Calories 452, Carbs 79g, Fat 10.4g, Protein 11g

Ingredients:

For the noodle basket:
- Boiled Hakka noodles – 4 cups.
- Corn flour – 4 tsps.

For the vegetable stir fry:
- Oil – 2 tbsps., divided.
- Oil – 12 tbsps. for frying the noodle basket.
- Garlic, minced – 2 tbsps.
- Ginger, grated – 2 tbsps.
- Green chilies, thinly chopped – 1 tsp.
- Onion, cubed – ½ cup.
- Bell pepper, cubed - ½ cup.
- Cabbage, cubed - ½ cup.
- Parboiled baby corn in diagonal cuts - ½ cup.
- Parboiled carrot in julienne cuts - ½ cup.
- Parboiled French beans in lengthwise cuts - ½ cup.

- Schezwan sauce – 2 tbsps.
- Tomato ketchup – 2 tbsps.
- Salt – 1 tsp.
- Spring onion greens, thinly chopped – 2 tbsps., for garnishing.

Directions:
Boil Hakka noodles in a large deep pan with enough water adding ½ teaspoon salt until they become 80% cooked. After cooking, drain the water and pour some cold water into them. Drain the water and drizzle 4 or 5 drops of oil and toss the cooked noodles. Dropping oil can prevent the noodles from sticking together. Toss the noodles and keep them aside on a flat plate to cool down.

After cooling, transfer the cooked noodles into a large bowl. Add salt, corn flour, and toss gently to mix. Now, make 4 equal division of noodles. Place one portion of the noodles along with the mesh in the strainer to form like a basket. Pour little more oil in a deep pan and bring to medium-high heat. Then, place the sieve with the noodles in the hot oil and pour the hot oils all over the noodles. Dip the strainer in the hot oil and deep fry the noodles until it turns to golden color from all sides. After browning, remove the noodle basket into a shallow plate lined with tissue paper to absorb the excess oil. Make a total of 4 baskets like this and keep ready to use them.

In a large non-stick pan, pour 1½ tablespoons of oil and bring to a medium-low heat. When the oil becomes hot, add grated ginger, minced garlic, chopped green chilies and sauté for about 2 minutes. Then add chopped onions and stir fry for about 2 minutes until they becomes tender and golden brown. Add cubed cabbage, bell pepper, and sauté until they become soft for about 2 minutes. Now add all the chopped vegetables like baby corn, French beans, carrot and continue cooking for 1 minute. Pour tomato ketchup, Schezwan sauce, salt, and mix well while stir-cooking on a low heat for 1 minute. Stop cooking and keep it aside.

Now divide the stir-fried vegetables into 4 equal parts and place each portion in the noodle baskets. Garnish with spring onion greens and serve hot.

Veg Thai Pad, Indian Style Noodles

Cooking Time: 10 minutes | Serves: 3 | Per Serving: Calories 446, Carbs 43g, Fat 25.7g, Protein 15g

Ingredients:
- Boiled flat rice noodles – 1½ cups.
- Oil – 4 tbsps.
- Garlic, minced – ½ cup.
- Bean sprouts – 1 cup.
- Peanuts, roughly chopped roasted – 1 tbsp.
- Paneer cheese, cubed – ¾ cup.
- Soy sauce – 1 tbsp.
- Sugar- 1 tbsp.
- Chili powder – 1 tsp.
- Lemon juice – 1 tbsp.
- Salt – 1 tsp.
- Spring onion greens, coarsely chopped – ¼ cup.

For garnishing:
- Peanuts, chopped and roasted – 1 tbsp.
- Spring onion greens, coarsely chopped – 1 tbsp.
- Cilantro leaves, chopped – 1 tbsp.

Directions:
Boil the flat rice noodles in a large deep pan with enough water and ¼ teaspoon salt. When the noodles get cooked 80%, stop cooking and drain the water. The noodles should be cooked well but firm in texture. After draining, pour some cold water on to arrest the cooking from the built-up heat and drain them again. Add a few drops of oil and toss the noodles, so that noodles won't stick together. Transfer the noodles to a flat plate and allow them to cool down.

In a large skillet, pour oil and bring it to a medium-low heat and sauté garlic for 1 minute. Then, add the cooked noodles, beans sprouts, roasted peanuts, and stir fry on medium-high heat for about 3 minutes. Then add soy sauce, chili powder, cubed paneer cheese, chopped spring onion greens, salt, lemon juice, and continue stir-cooking for about 3 minutes. Garnish with roasted peanuts, chopped cilantro leaves, spring onion greens and serve hot.

Baked Noodles with Spinach and Yogurt

Cooking Time: 6 minutes | Serves: 4 | Per Serving: Calories 320, Carbs 37g, Fat 13.6g, Protein 15g

Ingredients:
- Cooked spaghetti – 2½ cups.
- Spinach, blanched and chopped – 2 cups.
- Yogurt – ½ cup.
- Onions, chopped – ½ cup.
- All-purpose flour – ¼ cup.
- Processed cheese, shredded – ¾ cup.
- Oil – 2 tsps.
- Ground black pepper - ½ tsp.
- Salt - ¾ tsp.

Directions:
Boil spaghetti in a large deep pan with enough water by adding ½ teaspoon salt. Drain the water when the spaghetti is cooked to 80%. The spaghetti should be cooked well and firm in texture. To stop overcooking, pour cold water on the spaghetti and drain it immediately. After that, keep it aside for cooling.

Heat oil in a large skillet, and when the oil becomes hot, put the chopped onions in until they become soft and brown. Remove the onion from the pan and keep aside. In a large bowl, mix all the ingredients, like the cooked spaghetti, yogurt, flour, spinach, cheese, onions, pepper, and salt.

Preheat the oven to 200°C for 20 minutes. Line a baking dish with parchment paper and pour the spaghetti-yogurt-flour-spinach mixture onto the baking tray. Scatter shredded cheese on top and bake the noodle mix for 20 minutes. After baking, serve it hot.

Crispy Fried Noodles

Cooking Time: 25 minutes |Serves: 3 |Per Serving: Calories 540, Carbs 85g, Fat 16.2g, Protein 13.8g

Ingredients:
- Hakka noodles – ½ lb.
- Oil – 2 tsps.
- Salt - ¾ tsp.
- Oil – 12 tbsps. for frying.

Directions:

In a large deep non-stick frying pan, add salt and few drops of oil with enough water and bring to a rolling boil. Add noodles to the boiling water and continue cooking for about 4 minutes by stirring under a medium-high heat. After cooking, drain the water. Allow them to cool and dry completely for about 15 minutes.

In a deep-frying pan, pour 12 tablespoons oil and bring to a medium-high heat. Deep fry the noodles in batches until they becomes golden brown and cook the whole noodles in the given process. Serve fresh.

Indian Rice Noodles

Cooking Time: 10 minutes | Serves: 4 |Per Serving: Calories 363, Carbs 47g, Fat 16.9g, Protein 8.1g

Ingredients:
- Boiled rice noodles – 1 cup.
- Oil - 2 tbsps.

For the baby corn and paneer cheese mixture:
- Paneer cheese, cubed – ½ cup.
- Baby corn, 1-inch cuts – 1 cup.
- Spring onion whites, chopped – ¼ cup.
- Celery, chopped - ½ tsp.
- Green chilies, chopped - ½ tsp.
- Garlic, minced - ½ tsp.
- Ginger, grated- ½ tsp.
- Bell pepper, chopped – ½ cup.
- Spring onion greens, chopped - ½ cup.
- Oil- 2 tbsps.

For soy sauce mixture:
- Soya sauce - 1 tsp.
- Corn flour - 1 tsp.
- Sugar - ½ tsp.
- Ground black pepper - ½ tsp.
- Salt - ¾ tsp.

Directions:
Boil the rice noodles in a large deep pan with enough water and drain the water when the noodles are cooked to 80%. Add some freshwater and drain to stop further cooking due to built-in heat. Drizzle a few drops of oil and toss so that the noodles will not stick together. Keep the cooked noodles on a shallow plate for cooling.

In another large deep pan, heat oil at a medium-low temperature and add chopped spring onion whites and stir fry for about 2 minutes, until the onion becomes tender. Then add chopped green chilies, minced garlic, chopped celery, grated ginger, and sauté for another 2 minutes. Add soy sauce, paneer cheese cubes, chopped bell pepper, baby corn and continue to stir-cook for about 3 minutes, until the sauce turns thick and coat on the cottage cheese and vegetables. To this, add chopped spring onion greens and keep aside.

Pour oil in a large skillet and bring to medium-low heat. When the oil becomes hot transfer the chili paneer cheese-baby corn mixture into the pan and cook for one minute. Add the cooked noodles and toss the mixture to combine well. Stop cooking and serve hot.

Chapati Masala Noodles

Cooking Time: 20 minutes |Serves: 4 |Per Serving: Calories 299, Carbs 49.2g, Fat 8.7g, Protein 8.3g

Ingredients:
- Chapatis/leftover chapatis – 10, cut into long strips.
- Clarified butter – 2 tbsps.
- Onions, sliced – ½ cup.
- Bell pepper, sliced – ½ cup.
- Garlic, minced – 3 cloves.
- Tomatoes, chopped – ½ cup.
- Turmeric powder – ½ tsp.
- Red chili powder - ½ tsp.
- Salt - ½ tsp.
- Cilantro leaves, coarsely chopped - 2 tbsps., for garnishing.
- Lemon – 1, cut into wedges for serving.

Directions:
Heat clarified butter in a pan at a medium-low temperature. When the butter becomes hot, add onions, capsicum and sauté for about 3 minutes until the onions become tender and golden brown. Then add minced garlic, grated ginger, and stir fry for about 2 minutes until the raw smell of garlic and ginger disappears. Add turmeric powder, red chili powder, salt and sauté for 3 minutes until the spices get roasted and dry. Then, add tomatoes and stir fry for about 3 minutes, until the tomatoes become tender and pulpy. To this mixture, add chapatti strips and toss gently. Serve hot garnished with coriander leaves and lemon wedges.

Garlic Noodles

Cooking Time: 3 minutes |Serves: 3 |Per Serving: Calories 246, Carbs 34g, Fat 9.9g, Protein 5g

Ingredients:
- Boiled Hakka noodles – 2 cups.
- Garlic, minced – 2 tsps.
- Oil – 2 tbsps.
- Red chili flakes – ½ tsp.
- Soy sauce – 1 tsp.
- Vinegar – 1 tsp.
- Salt – 1 tsp.
- Cilantro leaves, chopped – 1 tbsp

Directions:

In a large deep pan, boil Hakka noodles with enough water until they are cooked 80%. The noodles should be cooked well, but still firm. After cooking, drain the water. Pour some cold water on to stop them from cooking further and drain again. Then drizzle 3-4 drops of oil and toss the noodles, so that they will not stick together. Transfer them onto a plate to cool down and keep aside.

Heat oil in a large deep pan at a medium-low temperature, and when the oil becomes hot, add minced garlic and sauté for 2 minutes. Then add all the remaining ingredients except salt and sauté for 1 minute. Transfer the cooked Hakka noodles to the pan, sprinkle with salt, and toss them gently while cooking at a medium-low heat for about 3 minutes. Garnish with cilantro leaves and serve hot.

Hakka Mushroom and Rice Noodles

Cooking Time: 6 minutes |Serve: 2 |Per Serving: Calories 169, Carbs 26.1g, Fat 6.2g, Protein 3.8g

Ingredients:
- Hakka rice noodles, cooked - 1 cup.
- Mushrooms quartered - 1 cup.
- Oil - 2 tsps.
- Garlic, minced - 2 tsps.
- Spring onions whites, thinly chopped – ½ cup.
- Soy sauce – 2 tsps.
- Green chilies, thinly chopped – 1 tbsp.
- Corn flour- 1 tbsp.
- Water - 1½ tsps. for making corn flour mixture.
- Salt - ¾ tsp.
- Sugar – 1 tsp.
- Spring onions greens, coarsely chopped – 2 tbsps.

Directions:

Put the Hakka rice noodles in a pan and pour 2 cups boiled water over them. Cover and keep aside for 10 minutes until they become soft.

Pour oil in a large deep pan and bring to a medium-low heat. When the oil becomes hot, add garlic and spring onions whites and sauté them for 2 minutes at a medium-low heat until the onions become soft. Add mushrooms and soy sauce and again cook them for a minute. Now make corn flour slurry by mixing corn flour and lukewarm water in a small bowl. Add green chilies and corn flour slurry into the pan while the cooking is in progress. Then, add salt, ¼ cup of water, stir well and cook for about 2 minutes. Finally, add the cooked noodles and sugar. Toss gently and continue cooking for 1 or 2 minutes. Garnish with chopped spring onion greens and serve hot.

Chapter 8 Beans, Soy, Legumes

Black-Eyed Beans Sabzi

Cooking Time: 20 minutes | Serves: 3| Per Serving: Calories 349, Carbs 65g, Fat 1.6g, Protein 21g

Ingredients:
- Black-eyed beans - 1 ½ cups.
- Water – 4½ cups.
- Cumin seeds - ½ tsp.
- Hing - ¼ tsp.
- Turmeric powder - ¼ tsp.
- Chili powder - ½ tsp.
- Ground coriander-cumin seed - 1 tsp.
- Tamarind pulp - 2 tsps.
- Sugar brown - 1 tbsp.
- Cilantro leaves, coarsely chopped - 2 tbsps., divided.
- Salt - ¾ tsp.

Directions:
Sort and soak the black-eyed beans for 8 hours or overnight. After soaking, drain and pressure cook them in 4½ cups of water for 1 whistle by adding salt. Allow it to settle down the pressure. If you need more tender beans, add ½ cup more water and cook for 1 more whistle. Add hing and cumin seeds in a deep pan and sauté on a medium-low heat. Mix and sauté until the aroma emanates. To this, add the cooked black-eyed beans, chili powder, turmeric powder, ground coriander-cumin seed, tamarind pulp, brown sugar, some coriander leaves and cook for 10 minutes. Keep stirring until they blend and cook well. Garnish it with coriander leaves and serve hot.

Black-Eyed Mixed Vegetable Salad

Cooking Time: 25 minutes | Serves: 3| Per Serving: Calories 341, Carbs 63g, Fat 1.5g, Protein 21g

Ingredients:

- Black-eyed beans - 2 cups.
- Onions, thinly sliced - ¼ cup.
- Tomatoes, coarsely chopped - ¼ cup.
- Cucumber, chopped - ¼ cup.
- Bell pepper, thinly chopped - ¼ cup.
- Green chilies, chopped - ½ tsp.
- Cilantro leaves, coarsely chopped - 1 tbsp.
- Lettuce, coarsely chopped - ¼ cup.
- Lemon juice - 1½ tbsps.
- Ground black pepper – 1 tsp.

- Salt – 1 tsp.

Directions:
Sort and soak the black-eyed beans for 8 hours or overnight. After that, drain the beans and pressure cook with 6 cups of water for 2 whistles by adding salt After cooking, let it de-pressure naturally. Transfer the cooked beans into a bowl. Put all the vegetables in a bowl and combine well. Drizzle with lemon juice and sprinkle with ground black pepper before serving.

Soy Kurma

Cooking Time: 40 minutes | Serves: 4 | Per Serving: Calories 318, Carbs 42g, Fat 13.8g, Protein 8g

Ingredients:
- Soy chunks – 1 cup.
- Almond flakes - ½ cup.
- Rice – 1 cup.
- Coconut oil - 3 tbsps.
- Onions, thinly sliced – 1 large.
- Garlic - 2 cloves.
- Ginger, minced – 2 tbsps.
- Ground paprika - 1 tsp.
- Curry powder - 1½ tsps.
- Garam masala - 1 tsp.
- Ground cardamom - 1 tsp.
- Turmeric powder - 1 tsp.
- Tomato paste - 2 tbsps.
- Coconut milk, thick cream – 2 cups.
- Veg broth – 1¾ cups.
- Yogurt - ¾ cup.
- Cashew nuts - ¼ cup.
- Pepper - ½ tsp.
- Salt - ¾ tsp.

Directions:
Soak the soy chunks in a bowl for about 15 minutes. Boil the rice al dente, drain out the water and leave it aside. Add oil to a pan on a medium-low heat and fry the soy chunks for about 10 minutes until golden. Transfer them into a separate container. Pour oil into the same pan and fry the onion, garlic, and ginger until golden brown for about 3 minutes. Add all the spices and continue to sauté on a medium-low heat. Now add the tomato paste and continue sautéing for about 3 minutes. Add thick coconut cream, yogurt, vegetable broth, and the cashew nuts and let it simmer for 4 minutes. Garnish it with almond flakes and serve it hot with rice.

Mashed Green Gram Masala

Cooking Time: 25 minutes | Serves: 4| Per Serving: Calories 130, Carbs 18g, Fat 3.9g, Protein 6g

Ingredients:

- Green gram - ½ cup.
- Water - 1½ cups and 1 cup.
- Vegetable oil - 1 tbsp.
- Mustard seeds - 1 tsp.
- Red chili – 1.
- Green chili, julienned – 1.
- Curry leaves – 1 twig.
- Hing - ¼ tsp.
- Sambar powder - ½ tsp.
- Tamarind paste - 2 tsps.
- Salt - 1 tsp.
- Cilantro, chopped - ¼ cup.

Directions:
Sort and rinse the green gram. Soak it in a bowl for 1 hour. Put the tamarind paste in a cup of water and soak it until it becomes a liquid. Pour oil into the pressure cooker and bring to a medium-low heat. Add mustard seeds to splutter, and after that add green chili, red chili, hing, curry leaves, and sauté for 3 minutes. Now add the green gram, sambar powder, tamarind paste water, salt, and 1½ cups of water. Mix well and let it pressure cook on a medium-low heat for 1 whistle. Allow the pressure to settle naturally and open the lid. Add the cilantro leaves and give a gentle stir. Again, simmer it for about 5 minutes and serve hot.

French Beans and Carrot Soup

Cooking Time: 37 minutes | Serves: 6 | Per Serving: Calories 127, Carbs 19g, Fat 3.5g, Protein 6g

Ingredients:
- Black-eyed beans - 3 tbsps.
- Clarified butter - 1 tbsp.
- Onions, thinly sliced - ½ cup.
- Bay leaves – 2.
- Celery, chopped - 2 tbsps.
- French beans, chopped - ½ cup.
- Carrots, chopped - ½ cup.
- Potatoes, cubed - ½ cup.
- Cauliflower, chopped florets - ½ cup.
- Salt – 1 tsp.
- Water – 2 cups.
- Tomatoes, chopped - ½ cup.
- Cabbage, coarsely chopped - ½ cup.
- Ground black pepper - ½ tsp.
- Parsley, chopped - 2 tbsps.
- Cheese, grated - 2 tbsps.

Directions:
Rinse all vegetables before you chop them. Sort and soak black-eyed beans for 4 hours. After soaking, drain out the water and keep them aside. In a pan, pour clarified butter and bring to a

medium-low heat. Add the onions, bay leaves, celery, and sauté for 2-3 minutes until the onion becomes golden brown. At this point, add the French beans, soaked black-eyed beans, carrots, cauliflower, potatoes, salt and let it cook well for about 30 minutes in 2 cups of water until the vegetables become tender. Now add tomato and shredded cabbage and continue cooking for about 4 minutes. Sprinkle with pepper and garnish with grated cheese and parsley. Serve hot immediately.

South Indian Soy Curry

Cooking Time: 25 minutes | Serves: 4| Per Serving: Calories 142, Carbs 10g, Fat 11.2g, Protein 2g

Ingredients:

For marinating:
- Soybeans - ½ cup.
- Yogurt - 8 tsps.
- Tomato puree - 4 tsps.
- Turmeric powder - ⅛ tsp.
- Ground red chili - ⅛ tsp.
- Salt - ½ tsp.

For the curry:
- Vegetable oil – 1 tbsp.
- Mustard seeds - ⅛ tsp.
- Curry leaves – 1 twig, divided.
- Onion, thinly sliced – 1 medium size.
- Onion paste – 3 tbsps.
- Ginger paste – 1 tbsp.
- Garlic paste – 1 tbsp.
- Sambar powder - 2 tsps.
- Ground paprika - 1 tsp.
- Turmeric powder - ⅛ tsp.
- Ground red chili - ⅛ tsp.
- Water - ¼ cup
- Salt - ½ tsp.
- Sugar – ½ tbsp.
- Coconut milk - ½ cup.

Directions:
Boil the soybeans until they becomes tender and drain and squeeze out the water. In a medium bowl, beat the yogurt. Add tomato puree, salt, turmeric, and chili powder to the whipped yogurt, and mix well. Add this mixture to the boiled soya beans and leave it aside to marinate for about 90 minutes. After that, in a cooking pan, heat oil at medium temperature. When the oil becomes hot, put the mustard seeds and curry leaves in to splutter. Then, add the onions, onion paste, ginger-garlic paste, and sauté them for about 7 minutes, until the onion becomes tender. Add the turmeric powder, ground red chili, salt, and stir fry for about 3 minutes.

When the red chili powder and turmeric powder have sautéed well, pour in ¼ cup of water, without letting it burn and keep stirring it for a further 3 minutes. To this, add the marinated soya and combine well under a medium-low heat for about 2 minutes. Now add, sambar powder, ground paprika, sugar, and continue cooking for about 3 minutes by stirring until the oil comes out of the mixture. Finally, pour in the coconut milk, combine to mix, and cook for about 7 minutes, stirring continuously. Garnish with curry leaves and serve hot.

Vegan Red Kidney Beans Curry

Cooking Time: 25 minutes | Serves: 4| Per Serving: Calories 126, Carbs 16g, Fat 5.5g, Protein 5g

Ingredients:
- Red kidney beans - ½ cup.
- Onions, thinly sliced - 1 large.
- Red Kashmiri chili – 3.
- Coconut oil - 2 tsps.
- Curry leaves – 1 twig.
- Coconut milk - 1 cup.
- Grated coconut - ½ cup.
- Fresh cilantro, chopped - 1½ tbsps.
- Coriander seeds - 1 tsp.
- Peppercorns - 1 tsp.
- Cumin seeds - 1 tsp.
- Water - 2 cups, divided.
- Salt - ½ tsp.

Directions:
Soak the red kidney beans for 8 hours. After soaking, drain out the water. Put them in a cooker along with 1½ cups of water and pressure cook for 1 whistle. After cooking, allow it to settle down the pressure. If you need more tenderness for the beans, add ½ cup more water and cook for 1 more whistle. In a cooking pan, pour coconut oil and bring to a medium heat. Once it is hot enough, add the cumin seeds and curry leaves to sizzle. After that, add onions and sauté until it turns tender for about 3-4 minutes. In a dry grinder, put the coriander, peppercorns, red chilies, and blitz to make a smooth mixture. Add the ground masala to the cooked red kidney beans in the pressure cooker. Also, add coconut milk, salt, water, and combine well. Cook it open on a medium-low heat for 3 minutes. Garnish it with fresh cilantro and serve hot with rice or chapattis.

Black-Eyed Beans and Sprouted Green Gram Salad

Cooking Time: 25 minutes | Serves: 3| Per Serving: Calories 230, Carbs 42g, Fat 1.1g, Protein 14g

Ingredients:
- Black-eyed beans - 1 cup.
- Sprouted green gram - ¼ cup.
- Water - 3¾ cups of water.
- Spring onions, chopped - ¼ cup.
- Tomatoes, thinly chopped - ¼ cup.

- Cabbage, coarsely chopped - ¼ cup.
- Ground chili - ¼ tsp.
- Ground cumin seeds - ¼ tsp.
- Dried mango powder - ¼ tsp.
- Lemon juice - 1 tsp.
- Salt - ¾ tsp.

Directions:
Soak the black-eyed beans and sprouted green gram overnight. Drain the water and cook it in a pressure cooker with 3¾ cups of water for 1 whistle. Allow it to settle down the pressure. After that, open the lid and add the tomatoes, cabbage, spring onions, and mix well. Add the chili powder, cumin seed powder, dried mango powder, salt, and sprinkle with the lemon juice. Mix it well and serve immediately.

Soybean Sindh Style Curry

Cooking Time: 40 minutes | Serves: 2 | Per Serving: Calories 375, Carbs 43g, Fat 16.3g, Protein 21g

Ingredients:
- Soybeans - 1 cup.
- Water – 3½ cups, divided.
- Onions, thinly chopped – 2 large size.
- Tomatoes, finely chopped – 2 large size.
- Green chilies, finely chopped – 3.
- Ginger, minced – 1inch piece.
- Turmeric powder - ¼ tsp.
- Ground coriander - 1 tsp.
- Garam masala powder - ½ tsp.
- Oil - 1 tbsp.
- Salt - ½ tsp.

Directions:
Rinse soybeans and soak them for up to 8 hours. Drain out the water and rinse thoroughly twice. Put the soy beans with salt in a pressure cooker with 3 cups of water and pressure cook for 5 whistles. After cooking, allow it to settle down the pressure and transfer them into another bowl. Add oil to the same pressure cooker and fry onions at a medium-low heat until they become tender. Then add the tomatoes, ginger, green chilies, garam masala powder, turmeric powder, coriander powder, and continue sautéing for about 2 minutes. Increase the heat to medium-high and let the tomatoes cook until tender. Add ½ cup water to it and let it simmer till the raw tomato aroma goes away. To this mixture, transfer the cooked soya beans with the required salt and mix well. Let it pressure cook for 3 whistles. Garnish it with coriander leaves and serve with chapatis, rice, or bread.

Soy Chunks Curry

Cooking Time: 20 minutes | Serves: 4| Per Serving: Calories 218, Carbs 23g, Fat 9.8g, Protein 14g

Ingredients:
- Soy chunks - 2 cups.
- Onion, thinly chopped – 1 large.
- Garam masala - ¼ tsp.
- Cumin seeds - 1 tsp.
- Bay leaf – 1.
- Turmeric powder - ½ tsp.
- Cinnamon stick - 1 inch.
- Kashmiri chili powder - 1 tsp.
- Ground coriander - 1 tsp.
- Yogurt - ¼ cup.
- Dry fenugreek leaves - 1 tsp.
- Oil - 3 tsps.
- Water - ½ cup.

For the masala:
- Onion, finely sliced – 1 large.
- Ginger, minced - 1 tbsp.
- Garlic, minced – 1 tbsp.
- Tomatoes, finely chopped – 2.
- Cashew nuts – 8.
- Oil - 2 tsps.

Directions:
In a large bowl, boil soya chunks for about 8 minutes and transfer them to cold water. Once the soya chunks have cooled down, squeeze, and keep them aside. In a saucepan pour oil and bring to a medium-low heat. When the oil becomes hot, sauté onions, ginger, and garlic until the onions becomes tender and brown. At this point, add the tomatoes, cashew nuts, and cook until the tomatoes become tender. In a blender, mix the ingredients into a smooth masala paste and keep it aside.

In another deep cooking pan, add oil and sauté the cumin seeds, cinnamon stick and bay leaf until they start to release the aroma. After that, add onion, chili powder, turmeric powder and sauté them for 2-3 minutes, until the ingredients become tight. Now add the masala paste and continue sautéing for another 2 minutes until they combine well. After that, add ground coriander and salt. Stir fry continuously until they become a smooth think masala. Now add yogurt, ½ cup water, and combine well. Put the squeezed soya in and simmer for 10 minutes by covering the pan. Before serving, garnish with dry fenugreek leaves and sprinkle with garam masala.

Butter Beans Masala Curry

Cooking Time: 20 minutes | Serves: 4 | Per Serving: Calories 85, Carbs 10g, Fat 5.1g, Protein 2g

Ingredients:

- Butter beans - 1 cup.
- Water – 3¼ cups, divided.

- Onions, thinly sliced – 1 large.
- Fennel seeds - 2 tsps.
- Coconut, grated - ⅓ cup.
- Green chilies, chopped – 2.
- Turmeric powder - ⅛ cup.
- Mustard seeds – ½ tbsp.
- Curry leaves – 1 twig.
- Water – 3 cups.
- Oil - 1 tsp.
- Salt - 1¼ tsps.

Directions:

Rinse and soak the butter beans overnight or for 4 hours. Pressure cook them with 3 cups of water and some salt for 1 whistle. Check the tenderness, if you need more softness for the beans, then add ½ cup of water and cook for 1 more whistle. Allow it to settle the pressure naturally and drain the water. Let it cool and keep them aside. Put the coconut, fennel seeds, and green chilies in a grinder and grind to a smooth paste adding ¼ cup of water. Rinse the grinder with 1 or 2 tablespoons of water and keep it aside.

In a deep cooking pan, pour in oil and bring to a medium-low heat. Put mustard seed to splutter. After that, put curry leaves to sizzle and then put in the chopped onion. Stir fry the onion for about 3-4 minutes until it becomes translucent. Now transfer the coconut-fennel seed paste into the pan and the rinsed grinding jar water. Cook the gravy for about 3 minutes, under a medium-high heat until the ingredients' raw smell goes off. Add turmeric powder and cooked beans, and combine well. Cook for another 2 minutes by stirring occasionally and serve hot.

Instant Pot Lentils Fry

Cooking Time: 45 minutes | Serves: 4 | Per Serving: Calories 160, Carbs 26g, Fat 3g, Protein 9g

Ingredients:
- Red split lentils - 2 tbsps.
- Brown split lentils - 2 tbsps.
- Green gram - 2 tbsps.
- Pigeon peas - 2 tbsps.
- Split chickpeas - 2 tbsps.
- Cumin seeds – 1 tsp.
- Green cardamom – 1.
- Cloves – 2.
- Cinnamon - 1-inch piece.
- Hing - ½ tsp.
- Onion, thinly sliced – 1 large.
- Red chili powder - ½ tsp.
- Turmeric powder - ¼ tsp.
- Ground coriander - 1 tsp.
- Sugar - 1 tsp.
- Salt - 1½ tsps.

- Tomato, chopped – 1 large.
- Garlic clove, minced – 1 tsp.
- Ginger, minced – 1 tbsp.
- Bay leaf - 1
- Cilantro, coarsely chopped - ¼ cup
- Water - 4 cups.
- Oil - 2 tsps.
- Fenugreek, crushed - ½ tbsp.

Directions:

Rinse all the lentils thoroughly and soak them for about 10 minutes. Select the sauté mode on the instant pot and pour oil into it. When the oil becomes hot, add cumin seeds, cloves, green cardamom, bay leaf, cinnamon and sauté for 1 minute. Add the onions and stir fry until they become translucent. Into the same mix, add red chili, all the spices, turmeric powder, ground coriander, salt, and sauté until the ingredients become roasted. At that point, add the tomatoes and sauté until they become tender and watery. Combine the mixture thoroughly.

Pour 3 cups water into the mixture and add all the lentils. Give a gentle stir. Close the lid and the pressure vent; in the manual pressure cook mode, select timer for 5 minutes. After 5 minutes, the cooker will shut down automatically and allow it to settle the pressure for 5 minutes and do a quick release to depressurize the cooker. Open the lid, add 1 more cup of water and mash the lentils using a potato masher. After that, add sugar and stir well. Put in crushed fenugreek, and chopped cilantro leaves. Stir and simmer on sauté mode for 5 minutes, at a medium-low heat.

Goan Dry Peas Curry

Cooking Time: 35 minutes | Serves: 4| Per Serving: Calories 215, Carbs 44g, Fat 2.8g, Protein 6g

Ingredients:
- Dried white peas - ½ cup.
- Potatoes, peeled and diced – 2 large size.

For roasting and grinding:
- Oil – 2 tsps.
- Clove Garlic, minced – 2.
- Onion, thinly sliced – 1 large.
- Peppercorns, crushed - ¼ tsp.
- Red chilies halved – 2.
- Coriander seeds – 1 tsp.
- Cardamom, crushed – 1
- Fennel seeds - ½ tsp.
- Cinnamon stick – 1 inch.
- Coconut slices - ⅓ cup.
- Tamarind paste - ½ tsp.
- Turmeric powder - ¼ tsp.
- Sugar - ½ tsp.
- Salt - 1½ tsps.
- Water – 1¾ cups, divided.
- Cilantro leaves, chopped – 2 tbsps.

Directions:
Rinse and soak white peas for 5 hours or overnight. Wash all vegetables before using them. Add oil to a cooking pan and bring to a medium-low heat. When the oil becomes hot, add the chopped onions, garlic and sauté until the onion becomes translucent. Remove it to a plate and in the same pan put fennel seeds, cloves, cinnamon, peppercorns, coriander seeds, red chilies, cardamom, and stir fry for 2-3 minutes. At this point, add the coconut slices and sauté for another minute. Transfer them to a plate, and let it cool down. Now, put all the dry roasted ingredients, ¼ cup water, and sautéed garlic-onion mix, turmeric powder, tamarind paste to make a masala paste. Transfer it into a pressure cooker along with the soaked white peas, potatoes, and 1½ cups of water. Cook it for 2 whistles under a medium-high heat. After the whistle, turn off the stove and allow the pressure to subside naturally. Open the lid and garnish it with cilantro.

Yellow Cucumber and Lentils
Cooking Time: 20 minutes | Serves: 4| Per Serving: Calories 129, Carbs 21g, Fat 3.7g, Protein 5g

Ingredients:
- Split pigeon peas - 1 cup.
- Yellow cucumber, skinned and diced - 4 cups.
- Green chili, julienned – 2.
- Ginger, minced – 1 tbsp.
- Cumin seeds - 2 tsps.
- Mustard seeds - 1 tsp.
- Curry leaves – 1 twig.
- Hing - ½ tsp.
- Cilantro leaves, chopped - 2 tbsps.
- Turmeric powder - ½ tsp.
- Red chili powder - 1 tsp.
- Onion, thinly sliced – 1 large size.
- Tomato, chopped – 1 large size.
- Tamarind paste - ½ tsp.
- Oil - 2 tsps.
- Salt - 2 tsps.
- Water – 3 cups.

Directions:
Sort and rinse the split pigeon peas and leave them aside to soak until you chop the vegetables. Rinse all the vegetables before you cut them. Mix the tamarind paste in one cup of water. Select the instant pot cooking mode to sauté medium heat. Pour oil and when the oil becomes hot, add the mustard seeds. When it splutters, add cumin seeds and hing. Stir and let the cumin seeds sizzle and add sliced onions. Stir-fry it for about 3-4 minutes until the onions become translucent. After that, add minced ginger, chilies, and curry leaves. Sauté for about another 2 minutes until the raw smell of the ginger and garlic disappear. Add chili powder, turmeric powder and roast it without letting it burn.

Add tomatoes and yellow cucumber and mix well. Add the soaked split pigeon peas and mix well. Finally, add water, tamarind water and stir gently. Close the lid and pressure valve. Set the pressure manually for 12 minutes. When the timer is over, go for quick release to de-pressure the cooker.

Beans Masala Dry Fry

Cooking Time: 20 minutes | Serves: 4| Per Serving: Calories 403, Carbs 70g, Fat 6.3g, Protein 20g

Ingredients:
- Oil - 1 tbsp.
- Mustard seeds - 1 tsp.
- Black gram - 2 tsps.
- Curry leaves – 1 twig.
- Onions, thinly sliced - ½ cup.
- French beans, cut into 1-inch lengths - 2 cups.
- Turmeric powder - ⅛ tsp.
- Salt - ¼ tsp.
- Water 1¼ cups, divided.

For grinding:
- Shallots – 5.
- Garlic pods, minced – 4.
- Red chilies – 5.
- Coriander seeds - 1 tbsp.
- Coconut, grated - 3 tbsps.
- Black gram - 2 tsps.
- Black peppercorns - 2 tsps.
- Cumin seeds - 1 tsp.
- Coriander leaves, chopped - 2 tbsps.

Directions:
Rinse all the vegetables before cutting. Dry roast all the ingredients listed for grinding in a saucepan at a medium-low heat. After roasting, grind it well without water. Now, heat oil in a cooking pan at a medium-low temperature. When the oil becomes hot, add mustard seeds and wait to splutter. After that, add black gram, curry leaves, onions and sauté until the onions become translucent. Add the beans, turmeric powder, and salt and continue cooking on a medium-low heat for 3 minutes. Pour in 1 cup of water and let it cook well. Now add the ground masala and keep stirring and do not let it burn. Add ¼ cup water and continue cooking, occasionally stirring until the water evaporates, and curry becomes dry. Garnish with cilantro leaves and serve hot.

Potato Beans

Cooking Time: 20 minutes | Serves: 3| Per Serving: Calories 274, Carbs 39g, Fat 11g, Protein 8g

Ingredients:
- Green beans, chopped – 1 cup.
- Potatoes – 2 medium size.
- Onions, thinly sliced – 1.
- Vegetable oil - 1½ tsps.
- Cumin seeds - ¼ tsp.

- Mustard seeds - ¼ tsp.
- Curry leaves – 6.
- Red chili powder - ¼ tsp.
- Turmeric powder - ¼ tsp.
- Garam masala powder - ¼ tsp.
- Dried mango powder - ⅛ tsp.
- Salt – 1 tsp.
- Cilantro leaves, coarsely chopped – 2 tbsps.

Directions:
Rinse all vegetables before cutting. Peel and slice potatoes lengthwise. Pour oil into a cooking pan and bring to a medium-low heat. When the oil becomes hot, add the mustard and wait to splutter. After that, add cumin seeds and let them sizzle. Now, add the onion, curry leaves, and sauté for about 3-4 minutes until they turns translucent. Add the chili powder, turmeric powder, dry mango powder, and fry it well for up to 2 minutes on a low heat. Put the sliced potatoes in and mix them in the masala. Pour ½ cup of water, cover the pan, and cook for 4 minutes until it becomes tender. To this, put the green beans and pour ¼ cup of water and mix well. Cover the pan and cook for 4 minutes until the beans become tender. Finally, stir in the garam masala powder and cook for 1 more minute. Garnish it with coriander leaves and serve hot.

Sautéed Green Beans

Cooking Time: 30 minutes | Serves: 2 | Per Serving: Calories 82, Carbs 5g, Fat 7.1g, Protein 1g

Ingredients:
- Green beans - ½ cup.
- Coconut oil – 1 tbsp.
- Green bell pepper, de-seeded – 1.
- Garlic, minced – 1 tsp.
- Black pepper - 1 tsp.
- Salt - ½ tsp.

Directions:
Rinse all the vegetables and cut the beans into 1-inch length pieces. Boil the beans until they become tender and drain the water. Transfer the beans to a plate and let them cool down. In a cooking pan, pour coconut oil and bring to a medium heat. When the oil becomes hot, put the bell pepper in and roast it until its skin burns appropriately. After roasting, remove it into a plate and allow it to cool. After cooling, peel the skin and julienne it into thin pieces. Remove the seeds and core. In the same pan, sauté minced garlic until its fragrance starts to emanate. Now add black pepper and add the blanched green beans. Add salt to season and mix well. Serve hot.

Beans Patolli Vapid

Cooking Time: 30 minutes | Serves: 2 | Per Serving: Calories 440, Carbs 73g, Fat 9.4g, Protein 20g

Ingredients:
- French beans, chopped - 1 cup.
- Split yellow gram – 1 cup.

- Dried red chilies – 2.
- Cumin seeds - 1½ tsps., divided.
- Oil – 1 tbsp.
- Mustard seeds - ½ tsp.
- Black gram dal - 1 tsp.
- Onions, thinly sliced – 1 large.
- Green chilies, julienned – 2.
- Curry leaves – 1 twig.
- Ginger, minced – 1 tbsp.
- Turmeric powder - ⅛ tsp.
- Hing - ⅛ tsp.
- Salt - ¾ tsp.
- Water - ½ cup.

Directions:
Rinse all the vegetables before chopping and cooking. Cut the French beans into a 1-inch length and boil them. After blanching, drain the water and transfer the beans to a plate for cooling. Sort and soak the split yellow gram for 2 hours. Then grind it with the dry red chilies, and 1 teaspoon of cumin seeds. In a cooking pan, pour oil and bring to a medium-low heat. Put the mustard seeds until the oil becomes hot and let it crackle. After that, add cumin the seeds and wait to sizzle. Now, add black gram, hing, onions, green chilies, curry leaves, and stir fry them dry on a medium-high heat for about 4 minutes until the onions become tender. Add a pinch of turmeric powder and fry well. To this, add the blanched French beans and sauté fry for 3 minutes. Add the ground masala, ½ cup of water, salt and mix well. Stir occasionally and cook for 15 minutes until all the water evaporates. Stop cooking when the gravy becomes semi-dry and serve hot.

Beans Thoran

Cooking Time: 20 minutes | Serves: 3| Per Serving: Calories 460, Carbs 84g, Fat 4.4g, Protein 24g

Ingredients:
- French beans, chopped – 2 cups.
- Onions, coarsely chopped - ½ cup.
- Dried red chili – 1.
- Coconut, grated – ½ cup.
- Cumin seeds - ½ tsp, divided.
- Shallots – 4.
- Green chilies, chopped – 2.
- Coconut oil - 2 tsps.
- Turmeric powder - ¼ tsp.
- Mustard seeds - 1 tsp.
- Curry leaves – 1 twig.
- Water - ¼ cup.
- Salt – ¾ tsp.

Directions:

Rinse all vegetables before using them. Blanch the French beans and transfer them onto a plate for cooling. In a cooking pan, add grated coconut, red chili, ¼ teaspoon of cumin seeds, shallots, and stir fry until they become golden brown. Add turmeric powder and sauté for another 1 minute. Transfer them onto a plate and allow them to cool down. After that, put all the roasted ingredients into a grinder and blitz to make a coarse mixture.

In another cooking pan, pour coconut oil and bring to medium heat. When the oil becomes hot, put the mustard seeds to splutter, and after that, add ¼ teaspoon of cumin seeds to sizzle. Now add onions, green chilies, curry leaves, and sauté for 3 minutes until the onion becomes tender. Transfer the coarsely blended coconut mixture into it. Add the blanched French beans along with ¼ cup water and salt. Mix it gently and cook for 3 minutes until the water evaporates.

Ghar Ki Bhaji

Cooking Time: 30 minutes | Serves: 3| Per Serving: Calories 318, Carbs 42g, Fat 13.8g, Protein 8g

Ingredients:
- Chopped beans - 1 bowl.
- Mustard seeds - 1 tsp.
- Hing - ½ tsp.
- Onions, chopped – 2.
- Turmeric powder - ½ tsp.
- Chili powder - 1 tsp.
- Ground coriander - 1 tsp.
- Garam Masala - 1 tsp.
- White sugar - 1 tsp.
- Green chili, chopped - 1
- Peanut powder - 2 tsps.
- Oil - 2 tbsps.
- Water - 2 cups.
- Salt - ¾ tsp.

Directions:
Rinse all the vegetables. Pour oil in a cooking pan and bring to medium heat. Add mustard seeds when the oil becomes hot. Let it crackle, and then add the onions, green chili, and hing. Sauté them for about 3-4 minutes until they turn golden brown. Add the turmeric powder, chili powder, coriander powder, cumin powder, mix it well and fry the masala well for another 2 minutes. If the masala becomes too dry and about to burn, add ⅛ cup of water and deglaze. Now add the beans, salt, and 2 cups water and cook it for 10 minutes until the beans become tender. After that, add a bit of sugar with peanut powder. Mix them well and cook for 1 more minute. Serve hot.

Mixed Kathol

Cooking Time: 22 minutes | Serves: 4| Per Serving: Calories 193, Carbs 24g, Fat 8.3g, Protein 7g

Ingredients:
- Brown chickpeas - ¼ cup.

- Whole green gram - ¼ cup.
- Black-eyed gram - ¼ cup.
- Moth beans - ¼ cup.
- Dried green peas - ¼ cup.
- Mustard seeds - ½ tsp.
- Cumin seeds - 1 tsp.
- Hing - ¼ tsp.
- Red chilies – 4.
- Ginger and green chili paste - 1 tsp.
- Tamarind pulp - ½ tsp.
- Sugar - 1 tbsp.
- Chili powder - ½ tsp.
- Turmeric powder - ¼ tsp.
- Chickpea flour - 1 tsp.
- Oil - 2 tbsps.
- Water - 3¼ cups.
- Salt – 1¼ tsps.

Directions:
Rinse all the pulses and soak for 5 hours or overnight. Drain the water and pressure cook in 3¼ of water for 3 whistles. Allow it to settle down the pressure naturally.

Pour oil in a cooking pan and bring to a medium-low heat. Add mustard seeds when the oil becomes hot and let it splutter. After that, add cumin seeds to sizzle and hing. Now add the red chilies, ginger and green chili paste and stir fry for about 3 minutes. Add the cooked pulses, chili powder, turmeric powder, chickpea flour, salt, tamarind pulp 1 cup water, and some sugar. Mix well and cook it for about 7 minutes while stirring intermittently. Maintain the liquid consistency as per your choice. Serve it hot with chapati and rice.

Instant Pot Lentil Bafla

Cooking Time: 1 hour 5 minutes | Serves: 3| Per Serving: Calories 198, Carbs 29g, Fat 7g, Protein 5g

Ingredients:
- Wheat flour - ¾ cup.
- White millet flour - ¼ cup.
- Water - ½ cup and 1 tbsp.
- Water for boiling – 6 cups.
- Salt - ¾ tsp., divided.
- Turmeric powder - ¼ tsp.
- Cumin - ½ tsp.
- Clarified butter - 1 tbsp.

For the dal:
- Split pigeon peas - ½ cup.
- Salt - ¾ tsp.
- Turmeric powder - ½ tsp.

- Water - 1½ cups.

For tempering:
- Clarified butter – 1 tbsp.
- Red chili powder - ½ tsp.
- Mustard seeds - ½ tsp.
- Hing - ½ tsp.
- Cumin – 1 tsp.

Directions:
Select sauté mode in the instant pot and pour in 6 cups of water by adding ¼ teaspoon of salt, ¼ teaspoon of turmeric powder and bring to a rolling boil for about 10 minutes. Combine the flour in a mixing bowl along with cumin seeds, salt, clarified butter by adding ½ cup and 1 tablespoon of water gradually to make a smooth dough. Divide the dough into 4 equal sizes of balls, roll it in the palm to make it smooth. Put the balls into the boiling water and continue boiling for 8 minutes until they start to float. Remove the bafla to a plate and allow them to cool down.

Preheat the oven to 175°C for 10 minutes. Line the baking tray with baking paper and place the bafla on the baking dish. Bake it for about 35 minutes, until they become firm and crisp. While baking, turn it every 5 minutes to have an even baking. After baking, remove them to a cooling rack.

Before using the instant pot, clean it since we have used it for making the bafla. Rinse the split pigeon peas and put them in the instant pot along with 1½ cups of water, salt, and turmeric powder. Close the cooker and pressure vent. Set the cooking time for 12 minutes under pressure cook manual mode. When the timer goes off, allow the cooker to release the pressure naturally. After that, open the cooker and mash the split pigeon peas.

Now for the final stage, in a small cooking pan pour clarified butter and bring to a medium-low heat. When the butter becomes hot, add mustard seeds to splutter, followed by cumin seeds to sizzle. After that, add hing and chili powder and sauté on a low heat. Do not let the chili powder to burn. Transfer the tempering on the split pigeon peas and mix gently. While serving, crush bafla and drizzle some clarified butter over them and serve with dal.

Spinach and Lentil Gravy
Cooking Time: 30 minutes | Serves: 4| Per Serving: Calories 158, Carbs 24g, Fat 3g, Protein 9g

Ingredients:
- Split pigeon pea dal - ¼ cup.
- Split green gram - ¼ cup.
- Split chickpeas - ¼ cup.
- Split black gram - ¼ cup.
- Water - 3 cups.
- Oil - 2 tsps.
- Mustard seeds - 1 tsp.
- Cumin seeds - 1 tsp.
- Carom seeds - 1 tsp.

- Turmeric powder - ½ tsp.
- Hing - ¼ tsp.
- Red chili – 3.
- Spinach, coarsely chopped - 2 cups.
- Salt - ½ tsp.

Directions:
Rinse all the lentils and soak them for 15 minutes. Also, wash spinach in running water and pat dry. Add oil to the cooking pan and bring to a medium-low heat. Pour 3 cups of water in the pressure cooker, put in all the soaked lentils and cook for 3 whistles. After that, allow it to cool down the pressure. Open the cooker and mash the lentils.

In a cooking pan, pour in oil and bring to a medium-low heat. Add mustard seeds when the oil becomes hot. After spluttering the mustard seeds, add cumin seeds and carom seeds to sizzle. Now put in red chili, and hing and sauté for a minute. To this, add spinach, turmeric powder, salt and mix well. Cook it for 3 minutes. Then add the mashed lentils, salt and cook for about 5 minutes. Check the liquid consistency and, if required, add ¼ cup of water and cook for another 2 minutes until it boils. Serve hot with chapati or rice.

Indian Mixed Beans Curry

Cooking Time: 40 minutes | Serves: 5 | Per Serving: Calories 275, Carbs 44g, Fat 5g, Protein 16g

Ingredients:
- Whole black gram - ¾ cup.
- Kidney beans - ¼ cup.
- Chickpeas - ¼ cup.
- Whole black gram - ¼ cup.
- Black-eyed peas - ¼ cup.
- Onion, thinly sliced – 1 large
- Garlic, minced - ½ tsp.
- Ginger, minced - ½ tsp.
- Green chilies, julienned – 2.
- Tomatoes, coarsely chopped – 2 large size.
- Cilantro leaves, coarsely chopped - ¼ cup.
- Lime juice - ½ tsp.
- Cumin seeds - ½ tsp.
- Black peppercorns, crushed – 4.
- Cloves – 2.
- Bay leaf – 1.
- Cinnamon stick - 1 small piece.
- Ground coriander - ½ tbsp.
- Turmeric powder - ¼ tsp.
- Garam masala - ¼ tsp.
- Red chili powder - ½ tsp.
- Cooking oil - 1 tsp.
- Salt - 1½ tsp.

- Water - 6 cups.

Directions:
Rinse and soak all the pulses for 8 hours or overnight. Put them in the pressure cooker along with 6 cups of water, salt and pressure cook for 6 whistles under a medium heat until the beans become tender. Grind onion, ginger, and garlic into a fine paste and keep it aside. Then grind tomatoes and green chilies into a fine paste and keep it in a small bowl.

Heat cooking oil in a pan. Add the bay leaf, cumin seeds, and let the cumin seeds sizzle. After sizzling the cumin seeds, put peppercorns, cloves, cinnamon sticks, and sauté for about 2 minutes until it releases the aroma. Now add the onion paste to the spice mixture and sauté for another 3 or 4 minutes until it becomes golden brown. Add the tomato paste and cook for about 12 minutes until the raw aroma goes away.

Now transfer the cooked beans into the cooking pan mixture along with water in the cooker, combine well and cook for 10 minutes. Sprinkle with some garam masala and garnish it with coriander leaves as it simmers on a low heat for about 5 minutes. Squeeze with fresh lime and give a gentle stir. Serve the curry with rice or roti.

Instant Pot Green Coriander and Chickpeas Masala

Cooking Time: 25 minutes | Serves: 4| Per Serving: Calories 196, Carbs 32g, Fat 5g, Protein 9g

Ingredients:
- Green chickpeas – 12 ounces.
- Onions, thinly chopped – 1 cup.
- Tomatoes, coarsely chopped – 2 large size.
- Ground coriander - 1 tsp.
- Red chili powder - ¾ tsp.
- Garam Masala - ½ tsp.
- Ground cumin powder - ½ tsp.
- Turmeric powder - ¼ tsp.
- Cilantro, coarsely chopped - 1 cup.
- Cumin seeds - ½ cup.
- Green chili – 1.
- Ginger garlic paste - 1 tsp.
- Water - 2 cups.
- Oil - 2 tsps.
- Sugar - ½ tsp.
- Salt - 2 tsps.

Directions:
Rinse all vegetables before using them. Pressure cook green chickpeas for one whistle by adding 2 cups of water. Let the pressure drop naturally and keep it aside. Keep the water too, as we can use it later.

In a cooking pan, pour oil and bring to a medium heat. Put cumin seeds in the pan and let it sizzle. After sizzling, add hing and green chili. Sauté it for about 2 minutes and stir in chopped onion until it becomes translucent for about 3-4 minutes. Now add ginger garlic paste and sauté for about 3 minutes until its raw smell disappears. After that, put the chopped tomatoes, salt, sugar and cook it till it becomes tender. Using a ladle, mash the vegetables. Add the red chili powder, cumin powder, coriander powder, turmeric powder, and garam masala and stir to combine for about 3-4 minutes.

Put the cooked green chickpeas into this masala with the chickpeas' cooked water from earlier and simmer it for 3 minutes. Garnish with chopped cilantro leaves and simmer for another 2 minutes. Serve warm with your favorite food.

Chapter 9 Drinks

Lemonade

Cooking Time: 30 minutes |Serves: 3 |Per Serving: Calories 118, Carbs 29g, Fat 1.3g, Protein 1g

Ingredients:
- Water, normal or icy – 3½ cups.
- Fresh lemons -2 medium-size.
- Chia seeds - ½ tbsp.
- Brown sugar – 6 tbsps.
- Salt - ¼ tsp.
- Ground black pepper powder - ¼ tsp.
- Ground cumin, roasted - ½ tsp.
- Chaat masala powder (mix masala) - ½ tsp.
- Fresh mint leaves, coarsely chopped – 1 tbsp.
- Ice cubes – 6 tbsps.

Directions:
Soak chia seeds in ¾ cup of water for about 25 minutes. In a glass jar, take 3½ cups of water. Cut the lemons into halves and squeeze to the jar. Now add chaat masala powder, cumin, black pepper, and salt into it along with brown sugar. Add mint leaves and stir to mix well. Put ice cubes in the serving glasses and pour the lemonade onto it. Serve chilled for a better taste.

Cumin Drink

Cooking Time: 20 minutes |Serves: 3 |Per Serving: Calories 72, Carbs 17g, Fat 0.7g, Protein 1g

Ingredients:

For soaking tamarind:
- Hot water - ¼ cup.
- Tamarind – 1 tsp.

For making cumin chutney:
- Mint leaves, coarsely chopped - ½ cup.
- Cumin seeds -1½ tsps.
- Fennel seeds - 1 tsp.
- Whole black pepper - ½ tsp.
- Asafetida - ⅛ tsp.
- Black cardamom deseeded – 1.
- Dry mango powder - 1 tsp.
- Chaat masala powder - 1 tsp.
- Salt - ¼ tsp.

For cumin drink:
- Water - 1½ cups.
- Boondi - 2 tbsps.
- Mint leaves, coarsely chopped – 1 tbsp.

Directions:
Soak 1 tsp. of tamarind in ¼ cup of hot water for about 20 minutes. Rinse mint leaves, remove the stems and pat dry. Put the dried mint leaves in the grinder and add the tamarind along with the soaked water without the seeds. Add fennel seeds, cumin seeds, black pepper, and black cardamom into the blender. After that, add dry mango powder, asafetida, chaat masala, salt, and grind to make a smooth paste. Put the cumin paste into a bowl and pour in 1½ cupsof water. Combine well to make the drink. Add chaat masala, boondi, and garnish with mint before serving.

Lassie

Cooking Time: 10 minutes |Serves: 2 |Per Serving: Calories 272, Carbs 28g, Fat 14.9g, Protein 10g

Ingredients:
- Chilled yogurt - 2 cups.
- Chilled water - 2 cups.
- Sugar - 12 tbsps.
- Cardamom powder - 1 tsp.
- Saffron stands – ⅛ tsp.
- Ice cubes – 8.

Directions:
Pour 2 cups of chilled yogurt in a bowl and smoothen it with a hand blender. After that, add all ingredients and blend well. Now add sugar and chilled water into the mixture. Maintain the consistency of the Lassi at a moderate level and continue blitzing the liquid until foam starts to develop. After that, add cardamom powder along with some saffron strands. Serve with ice cubes.

Buttermilk

Cooking Time: 10 minutes |Serves: 3 |Per Serving: Calories 443, Carbs 87g, Fat 8g, Protein 10g

Ingredients:
- Yogurt - 1½ cups.
- Ground cumin roasted - ½ tsp.
- Water - 1 cup .
- Ice cubes – 6.
- Salt – ¼ tsp.
- Cilantro leaves, coarsely chopped – 1 tbsp.

Directions:
Put all the ingredients in a big blender jar, including ice cubes and except the cilantro leaves. Blitz the mixture until it becomes frothy. Pour the mixture in the serving glasses. Garnish with coriander leaves to serve immediately.

Rooh Afza

Cooking Time: 30 minutes |Serves: 3 |Per Serving: Calories 159, Carbs 42g, Fat 0.1g, Protein 0g

Ingredients:
- Chilled water - 3½ cups.
- Rooh Afza syrup – 3 tbsps.
- Basil seeds - ½ tbsp.
- Sugar – 6 tbsps.
- Ice cubes - 8

Directions:
In a small bowl, soak the basil seeds for 30 mins. Pour 3½ cups of chilled water in a glass jar. Add Rooh Afza syrup in the water. Add the soaked basil seeds, sugar, and ice cubes. Stir all the ingredients and serve immediately.

Cardamom Saffron Drinks

Cooking Time: 5 minutes |Serves: 3 |Per Serving: Calories 200, Carbs 28g, Fat 6.8g, Protein 8g

Ingredients:
- Shrikhand cardamom-saffron flavored - ¾ cup.
- Yogurt - 1½ cups.
- Milk – 1 cup.
- Sugar - 3 tbsps.
- Ground green cardamom - ½ tsp.
- Nutmeg powder - ¼ tsp.
- Sliced pistachios – 6.
- Saffron - ¼ tsp.

Directions:
In a large bowl, combine shrikhand, milk, yogurt, cardamom powder, sugar, and nutmeg powder using a hand blender until they become creamy and smooth. Refrigerate it for two hours. Add sugar into it and stir well. Serve the drinks topped with sliced pistachio, pistachio, and saffron.

Mango Drinks

Cooking Time: 5 minutes |Serve: 12 |Per Serving: Calories 98, Carbs 25g, Fat 0.1g, Protein 0g

Ingredients:

For cooking mangoes:
- Raw mangoes - 2 medium size.
- Water - 2 cups.

Other ingredients:
- Sugar - 1½ cups.
- Ground cardamom - 1 tsp.

- Roasted cumin powder - 1 tsp.
- Ground black pepper - ¼ tsp.
- Salt -2 tsps.
- Chilled water - 4¼ cups.
- Mint leaves, coarsely chopped – 2 tbsps.

Directions:
Rinse mangoes and pressure cook for 2 whistles. Let the pressure settle naturally and open the cooker. With a sharp knife, remove mango pulp into a bowl. Scrape the flesh from the skin too and discard the peels. Add sugar to the pulp. As a rule of thumb, add twice the amount of sugar to the quantity of pulp. After that, add cumin powder, cardamom powder, and pepper into the mango pulp. Also, add 2 teaspoons of salt into the pulp and mix them well using a blender. Pour the mango pulp into a large glass jar and mix with 4¼ cups of water and ice cubes. Serve chilled.

Lemon Squash

Cooking Time: 10 minutes | Serves: 3 |Per Serving: Calories 66, Carbs 17g, Fat 0.3g, Protein 1g

Ingredients:
- Lemon juice - 1 cup. Approx. 12 fresh lemons.
- Water – 1 cup.
- Sugar - 17½ ounces.
- Saffron, crushed - ½ tsp.
- Ground green cardamoms - ½ tsp.

Directions:
In a medium cooking bowl, pour 1 cup of water and the sugar and bring to a medium-low heat until the sugar dissolves. When the sugar liquid forms a sticky consistency, put off the stove. Strain the liquid into another bowl and let the temperature reduceto room level. For making lemon juice, you need to use about 12 lemons. Rinse the lemons, cut into halves, and squeeze into a bowl. Strain the juice to remove the seeds. Transfer the lemon juice into the sugar syrup and stir well. Add ground cardamom, saffron and mix well. Keep the squash refrigerated and for making the drink use 4 tablespoons of lemon syrup for 1 glass squash. Serve chilled.

Vetiver Syrup

Cooking Time: 25 minutes |Serve: 4|Per Serving: Calories 222, Carbs 56g, Fat 0.1g, Protein 1g

Ingredients:
- Vetiver - 2½ ounces.
- Water -1 liter.
- Sugar - 4 cups.

Directions:
Rinse, dry, and remove the grassroots. Coarsely chop the vetiver and soak it for 12 hours. Strain and collect the extract in a medium bowl. Stir in sugar and bring to medium-low heat until it dissolves. Let it boil for a few minutes until the liquid turns sticky. Allow it to cool down to room

temperature and transfer to a glass jar. For making the drink, mix add 3 tablespoons of syrup to a glass of water. Serve chilled for a better taste.

Jackfruit Milkshake

Cooking Time: 15 minute |Serves: 2 |Per Serving: Calories 451, Carbs 50g, Fat 29.4g, Protein 5g

Ingredients:
- Jackfruit, sliced - 1¼ cups sliced.
- Coconut milk thick – 1 cup.
- Brown sugar powder - 3 tbsps.
- Water - ½ cup.
- Ice cubes – 8.
- Jackfruit Finely chopped - 2 tbsps.
- Cashews – 8.

Directions:
Transfer the sliced jackfruits into a blender and blitz. Add brown sugar, water, coconut milk and blend it thoroughly. Add ice cubes. Serve chilled by garnishing with chopped jackfruits and cashews.

Chapter 10 Desserts

Burfi with Chickpea Flour

Cooking Time: 1 hour 30 minutes |Serve: 8 |Per Serving: Calories 388, Carbs 49g, Fat 19.7g, Protein 8g

Ingredients:
- Split chickpeas – 1 cup.
- Almond milk – 3 cups, divided.
- Cashews - ½ cup.
- Water - ½ cup.
- Ground green cardamom - ½ tsp.
- Coconut, grated - ¼ cup
- Coconut oil - ¼ cup
- Sugar - ¾ cup.
- Pumpkin seeds - ¼ cup.

Directions:
Sort and soak the split chickpeas for about 4 hours. Similarly, soak cashew nuts for 30 minutes in ½ cup of water. Boil 2 cups of almond milk and place drained split chickpeas in a saucepan for 30 minutes or until the split chickpeas become tender. After that, turn off the stove and allow the mixture to cool. Grind the chickpeas and almond milk in a wet grinder to make a thick paste.

In a large skillet, pour oil and bring to a medium-low heat. Put the chickpeas paste and sugar in the skillet and cook the mixture until the paste becomes dry. Then add the remaining 1 cup of almond milk, cardamom powder, pumpkin seeds, and continue cooking on a medium-low heat until the mixture becomes dry and turns opaque..

Spread baking oil on a rectangular 8-inch cake pan and transfer the hot split chickpea mixture onto it. Spread the batter evenly in the cake pan using a spatula or spoon. Then, scatter some pumpkin seeds and press them on the dough. Allow it to cool and become hard. Cut evenly and serve.

Dairy Free Rasmalai

Cooking Time: 15 minutes |Serve: 7 |Per Serving: Calories 548, Carbs 54g, Fat 35g, Protein 12g

Ingredients:

For cheese balls:
- Cashew nuts - 1½ cup.
- Lemon cheese – 3 tbsps.
- Maple syrup – 5 tbsps.
- Hot water - ½ cup.
- Salt - ⅛ tsp.

Sauce for rabri:
- Boiled water – 1 cup.
- Saffron - ⅛ tsp.
- Cashew nuts – 2 cups.
- Maple syrup - ¾ cup.
- Water - ⅔ cup.
- Rosewater – 1 tbsp.
- Green cardamom – 2.
- Cardamom powder - ⅛ tsp.

For garnishing:
- Pistachios, chopped - ¼ cup.
- Rose petals – 1 tbsp. Dried and edible.

Directions:
Soak the cashew nuts for about 30 minutes. After soaking, drain the cashews and keep ready in two batches. In an electric blender, grind all the 'cheese ball' ingredients into a smooth paste. Transfer the mixture into a nut-milk bag and place the milk bag onto a strainer, keeping the filter over a bowl. Close the nut milk bag and refrigerate it for about 10 hours or overnight.

Preheat the oven to 175°C for 15 minutes. Place a parchment paper liner in the baking tray. Scoop out 2 tablespoons of cheese precipitated in the nut milk bag and make balls with your hands and place it in the baking dish. Scoop out all cheese collected in the nut milk bag and place it in the baking tray by making balls. The quantity is enough to make 7 balls. Bake the balls for 15 minutes, and after that, move them to the cooling rack.

Now, let us make the 'rabri' sauce. Put the saffron in the boiled water and let it steep for some time, which will enable it to infuse the color and flavor. Put this saffron water along with the strands in a blender. Put all the remaining 'rabri' ingredients in the blender and make a smooth, creamy sauce.

Place the cheese balls in a serving bowl and pour the 'rabri' sauce over them. Garnish with chopped pistachios, rose petals and serve.

Chickpea Flour Ladoo

Cooking Time: 18 minutes | Serves: 15 | Per Serving: Calories 142, Carbs 16g, Fat 7g, Protein 2g

Ingredients:
- Chickpea flour – 2 cups.
- Clarified butter - ⅔ cup.
- Sugar, powdered – 1 cup.
- Green cardamoms – 4, powdered.
- Golden raisins – 2 tbsps.

Directions:
In a frying pan, roast the chickpea flour for about 12 minutes, stirring continuously. The powder should not be burned and must brown evenly. Melt the clarified butter in another pan and keep

ready to use it. Pour the melted ghee in the roasted chickpea flour and stir continuously for about 6 minutes. Turn off the stove when you get the fragrance of the roasted chickpea flour, and the clarified butter starts to release. Add the sugar powder and stir continuously without letting it form any lumps. Add dry fruits, cardamom powder and combine well. After mixing, allow the ladoo mixture to cool down. Scoop out the mixture and make ladoo balls with your hands.

Cheese Cake

Cooking Time: 18 minutes |Serve: 15 |Per Serving: Calories 347, Carbs 38g, Fat 19.6g, Protein 6g

Ingredients:
- Digestive biscuits – 12.
- Clarified butter – 1 tbsp.
- Cream cheese – 3 cups.
- Sugar powder - ¾ cup
- Corn starch – 1 tbsp.
- Vanilla extract – 1 tsp.
- Cream - ½ cup
- Lemon juice – 1 tbsp.

For the chocolate sauce:
- Milk - ½ cup.
- Sweet chocolate, chopped – 1 cup.
- Berries, cut into pieces - ½ cup. (Use any fruit of your choice)

Directions:
Break the digestive biscuits into pieces and put them in the blender jar. Then, blitz to make a fine powder and transfer it into a mixing bowl. After that, add the melted clarified butter into it and combine well with a spoon. Coat some butter on the baking tray and place the biscuit paste into the pan. With your fingers or using the back of the glass, press the biscuit-butter mix on the pan get a flat shape. Refrigerate the pan for 30 minutes.

Preheat the oven at 180°C for about 20 minutes by keeping the top and bottom elements on. Combine cream cheese, corn starch, sugar powder, vanilla extract, and lemon juice in a medium bowl. Using an electric beater, blend the mixture to a smooth paste. Do not beat the dough too much. Add ½ cream and continue beating until it forms to a smooth batter. Take out the refrigerated biscuit-butter mix and pour the whipped cream cheese mixture onto the biscuit-butter blend and spread it evenly.

Place the tray in the middle of the oven rack and bake for about 40 minutes. Check the doneness of the cheesecake by inserting a toothpick at the center of the cake, and if it comes out clean, the cake is ready. You can also find that the center of the cake will rise and it becomes soft when it is ready. The sides of the cake will get disengaged from the pan. Place the cake onto the cooling rack. After cooling, cover it with aluminum foil and refrigerate for 4 hours.

For making the chocolate sauce, heat ½ cup of milk and pour it into a medium bowl. Add the sweet chocolate and stir to mix until it dissolves. If the sweetness is not enough, add some sugar as per your taste. Allow it to cool down.

Remove the cheesecake from the pan using a butter knife gently running between the edges of the cake and pan. Push the pan from the bottom and gently remove the cake to a serving plate. Pour the chocolate sauce on the cake and serve. Do some toping with your favorite fruits.

Creamy Rice Dessert

Cooking Time: 30 minutes | Serves: 5 | Per Serving: Calories 254, Carbs 36g, Fat 9.4g, Protein 8g

Ingredients:
- Basmati rice – ¼ cup.
- Full fat milk – 4 cups.
- Sugar – 6 tbsps.
- Ground cardamom - ½ tsp.
- Saffron strands – ⅛ tsp.
- Almonds, blanched – 1 tbsp.
- Cashews, broken – 1 tbsp.
- Pistachios, sliced – 1 tbsp.
- Raisins – 1 tbsp.
- Rose water – 1 tbsp.

Directions:
Rinse basmati rice until the water turns clear and soak it for 20 minutes. Blanch the almonds by soaking them in hot water for 30 minutes. After 30 minutes, peel the almond skin. Pour full-fat milk in a saucepan and boil it on a medium flame. During the process, stir the milk continuously so that the milk does not stick in the bottom. Add a few saffron stands to the milk and keep it aside. Drain water from the rice and add to boiling milk and mix well. Cook and simmer on a low flame. Add sugar and stir intermittently until the rice is half cooked. Add pistachios, almonds, and cardamoms. Cook until the rice thickens. On cooling scrape milk solids from the sides. Add golden raisins, cardamom powder, and rose water. Serve warm.

Vermicelli Dessert

Cooking Time: 15 minutes | Serves: 4 | Per Serving: Calories 389, Carbs 59g, Fat 14.1g, Protein 8g

Ingredients
- Clarified butter – 1½ tbsps.
- Cashews – 12.
- Raisins – 2 tbsps.
- Vermicelli – 1 cup
- Full fat milk – 3½ cups.
- Sugar – 4 tbsps.
- Cardamom powder – ½ tsp.

Directions
Pour clarified butter in a thick skillet and melt it on medium-low heat. Fry cashews until they become golden brown and keep them aside. Similarly, fry the raisins until golden brown and

keep them aside. Add broken vermicelli to the same skillet and stir fry until they becomes brown. Add milk and continue cooking on a medium-low heat by stirring frequently. Add sugar and cardamom powder for about 4 minutes until the milk starts to boil. Turn off the stove and add roasted cashews and raisins. Serve hot.

Tapioca Pearls Dessert

Cooking Time: 20 minutes |Serves: 2 |Per Serving: Calories 477, Carbs 81g, Fat 13.5g, Protein 11g

Ingredients:
- Tapioca pearls – ½ cup.
- Milk – 2 cups.
- Water – 2 cups.
- Sugar – 4 tbsps.
- Ground green cardamoms – ½ tsp.
- Cashews – 2 tbsps.
- Raisins - ½ tsp.
- Saffron strands – 5.

Directions:
Rinse the tapioca pearls rubbing with fingers until the water becomes clear. Put the rinsed tapioca pearls in a deep skillet and pour over 2 cups of water. Cover and soak them in water for about 20 minutes. While they soak, you can roast the cashew nuts in a small saucepan and keep aside. Similarly, roast the raisins until they become brown and keep aside. Cook the tapioca pearls on a medium-low heat. Meantime cook the milk until it becomes warm, no need to boil. Add the hot milk and after 4 minutes of cooking the tapioca pearls put sugar and cardamom in and let it simmer for about 20 minutes on a low heat by stirring frequently. Switch off the stove and scatter roasted cashews and raisins. Garnish with saffron and serve hot.

Whole Wheat Vermicelli Dessert

Cooking Time: 18 minutes |Serves: 3 |Per Serving: Calories 272, Carbs 28g, Fat 14.9g, Protein 10g

Ingredients:
- Full fat organic milk – 2 cups.
- Clarified butter - 1 tbsp.
- Sugar – 1 tbsp.
- Broken whole wheat vermicelli – ½ cup.
- Cashews, broken – 8.
- Almonds – 9 sliced.
- Pistachios, raw – 8.
- Green cardamom, powder – ½ tsp.
- Chironji – 1 tbsp.
- Golden raisins – 1 tbsp.
- Rosewater – ½ tsp.

Directions:

In a deep saucepan, roast the broken whole wheat vermicelli until it becomes golden brown and keep aside. Pour 1 tablespoon of clarified butter and sauté cashews, almonds, pistachios, chironji, golden raisins on a medium-low heat, and keep it aside. Boil milk in a saucepan and simmer it to become thick by stirring continuously. Add sugar and roasted whole wheat vermicelli to the milk and cook on a medium-low heat. While cooking, the milk will thicken and reduce in volume. If you like to have a thin consistency, add the required amount of water, and add sugar as per the taste requirement. Now put all the roasted dry fruits into the dessert. Pour rose water and gently stir. Switch off the stove and serve warm.

Milk Dessert

Cooking Time: 50 minutes |Serves: 4 |Per Serving: Calories 317, Carbs 34g, Fat 15.8g, Protein 10g

Ingredients:
- Basmati rice – 3 tbsps.
- Full cream milk – 4¼ cups
- Sugar – 4 tbsps.
- Clarified butter – 1 tbsp.
- Mix dry fruits, roasted - ¼ cup
- Saffron strands - ¼ tsp.

Directions:
Rinse basmati rice until the water comes clear. Drain and keep aside. In a deep thick saucepan, heat clarified butter. Add basmati rice and cook on a medium-low heat until the aroma of the rice starts to release. Now, pour milk into the rice and stir. Bring the milk to boil on a medium-high heat by continually stirring so that the bottom does not stick. Continue cooking it on a medium-low heat until it gets cooked properly. Close the lid for faster cooking but beware of spillage. In the case of frothing, just open the cover, and reduce the heat, so that it can stop frothing. Add sugar, mash the rice while stirring. Simmer for about 10 minutes until the milk becomes thick. The consistency of the dessert may become more viscous when it cools down. So, you can manage the thickness according to the required consistency. Garnish with saffron and roasted dry fruits. Serve warm.

Badam Milk Dessert

Cooking Time: 20 minutes |Serves: 4 |Per Serving: Calories 210, Carbs 27g, Fat 8.2g, Protein 8g

Ingredients
- Almonds – ¼ cup.
- Water – ⅓ cup.
- Milk – 3 cups, divided.
- Sugar – 5 tbsps.
- Green cardamoms – 5.
- Saffron strands – 5 Nos.

Directions
Place the almonds in a bowl after rinsing. Boil ⅓ cup of water and pour it over the almonds. Keep them covered for 30 minutes. After 30 minutes, drain the water and peel the skin off almonds.

Slice 4 or 5 blanched almonds very thinly and keep ready. In a blending jar, put all the remaining blanched almonds, 5 tablespoons of sugar, and 5 cardamoms. Pour ½ cup of milk into the blender and mix it thoroughly until it becomes smooth without any chunks. In a large deep pan, pour the remaining 2½ cups of milk and bring to boil at a medium-low heat, frequently stirring so that it doesn't froth or stick to the pan. Add the saffron strands and keep stirring. Transfer the almond paste into the pan and mix gently. Let the badam dessert start to boil, and after boiling, turn off the stove. Garnish with the sliced almonds and serve warm or chilled.

Split Green Gram Coconut Milk Dessert

Cooking Time: 5 minutes |Serves: 4 |Per Serving: Calories 357, Carbs 67g, Fat 4.7g, Protein 12g

Ingredients:
- Split green gram – ½ cup.
- Water – 1½ cups.
- Thin coconut milk – ½ cup.
- Sugar powder (Jaggery)– ¾ cup.
- Thick coconut milk – 1 cup.
- Coconut oil – 2 tbsps.
- Cardamom powder – 1 tsp.
- Cashews – 15.
- Raisins – 1 tbsp.

Directions:
Sort, rinse, and drain split green gram. Put it in a pressure cooker with 1½ cups of water and for 6 whistles on a medium-high heat. Turn off the stove and transfer the lentils into a deep pan. Mash them with a spoon. Add thin coconut milk and mix well. Add jaggery powder for a sweet taste and cook the mixture on a low heat by continually stirring to dissolve the jaggery. After dissolving jaggery, pour in thick coconut milk. Mix well and heat for 2 minutes. In a small pan, pour oil and fry cashew nuts followed by raisins. Transfer the contents into the dessert. Mix well and serve warm or chilled.

Classic Creamy Pudding

Cooking Time: 25 minutes |Serves: 4 |Per Serving: Calories 406, Carbs 74g, Fat 8.3g, Protein 11g

Ingredients:
- Basmati rice – ¼ cup.
- Milk- 4¼ cups.
- Sugar- 1 cup.
- Almonds – 20.
- Ground green cardamoms – 8.
- Saffron – 6 strands.

Directions:
Put all the almonds in boiled water for 30 minutes covered. After 30 minutes, drain the water and peel the skin to blanch the almonds. Slice the almonds and keep aside. Rinse the rice until the

water turns clear and drain it. Keep it aside. Now put the completely drained rice into a dry grinder and grind it to make semolina like ground. Cook the milk in a thick saucepan at medium-high heat and add saffron strands to the boiling milk. Reduce the heat once boiled, keep stirring, and add sugar. Put the ground rice in the milk and cook under a medium-high heat. After the ground rice is cooked well, add cardamom, part of the sliced almonds. Cook until the cream becomes thick. Garnish with remaining sliced almonds. Serve warm or chilled.

Split Chickpea Dessert

Cooking Time: 25 minutes |Serves: 4 |Per Serving: Calories 380, Carbs 42g, Fat 22g, Protein 8g

Ingredients:
- Split chickpeas – ½ cup.
- Water- 1 cup.
- Thin coconut milk – ½ cup.
- Brown sugar powder - ¾ cup.
- Thick coconut milk – 1 cup.
- Clarified butter - 2 tbsps.
- Cashews – 15.
- Raisins – 1 tbsp.
- Cardamom powder - ½ tsp.

Directions:
Sort and rinse split chickpeas then soak them for 3 hours. Drain the split chickpeas and put it in an insert pressure cooker pan with one cup of water and 1½ cups of water in the pressure cooker. Pressure cook them on medium-high heat for 5 whistles and turn off. You can also pressure cook it directly by removing the insert pressure pan. Allow the pressure to settle naturally and open the cooker. You should not overcook the chickpeas.

Pour the cooked chickpeas in a pan. Add thin coconut milk after mashing the split chickpeas and cook under a medium-low heat. Add brown sugar powder and continuously stir until the brown sugar dissolves. At this point, add thick coconut milk, mix well, and do not overboil it. In another pan, put in clarified butter and fry cashew nuts on a medium-low heat until golden brown and remove from the pan. In the same pan, fry the raisins as well. Transfer the roasted cashew nuts and raisins into creamy dessert. Serve hot or chilled.

Lotus Seed Pudding

Cooking Time: 30 minutes |Serves: 3 |Per Serving: Calories 292, Carbs 41g, Fat 11.2g, Protein 9g

Ingredients:
- Clarified butter – 3 tsps.
- Lotus seed – 1 cup
- Cashew nuts – 12.
- Organic milk – 2 cups.
- Green cardamom – 4, husked and powdered.
- Raisins – 1 tbsp.

- Sugar – 4 tbsps.
- Saffron strands - ⅛ tsp.

Directions:
In a pan, heat clarified butter at a medium-low temperature. When the butter becomes hot, add cashew nuts and lotus seeds until the lotus seeds become crispy. Meantime, the cashews also will become golden in color. Transfer them onto a plate and keep them ready for use.

In a thick saucepan, boil milk by stirring without letting it scorch at the bottom. When the milk starts to boil, add the sugar and stir well to blend. Then, put ⅔ portion of the roasted lotus seeds in the boiling milk. After that, add cardamom powder and the saffron strands. Put the remaining ⅓ of the roasted lotus seeds in the grinder and blitz to powder. Then, add the powdered lotus seeds into the boiling milk and stir well. Reduce the heat to a medium-low and simmer it for about 10 minutes. Scrape the milk solids stuck to the saucepan and keep stirring. Now, add the roasted cashew nuts and raisins. Keep stirring and simmer for 1 minute. Serve it warm or cold.

Carrot Halwa

Cooking Time: 30 minutes |Serves: 4 |Per Serving: Calories 374, Carbs 61g, Fat 12.8g, Protein 7g

Ingredients:
- Carrots – 1¼ lbs.
- Milk – 2 cups.
- Sugar - ¾ cup.
- Cardamom – 4, husked and powdered.
- Clarified butter – 2 tbsps.
- Pistachios – 5.
- Almonds – 5.
- Cashew nuts – 10.
- Raisins – 2 tbsps.

Directions:
Rinse and peel the carrots. Grate the carrots using a hand grinder or food processor. Chop the nuts and roast them under a medium-low heat with a little clarified butter until they become a light golden color. Transfer them to a plate and keep ready to use.

In a heavy bottom deep pan, pour milk and bring to boil at medium-low heat without scorching the milk in the bottom of the pan. Add grated carrots into the boiling milk and keep stirring until the milk evaporates entirely. Now, add sugar and stir to mix well. The sugar will start to melt, and the ingredient will become soft carrot halwa. Continue cooking until the moisture evaporates to a moderate level. Add clarified butter and combine it with the carrot halwa until the moisture evaporates fully. When the carrot halwa starts to thicken, add ground cardamom powder. Stir and continue cooking for a further 3 minutes. Sprinkle with roasted nuts, raisins, and serve warm.

Conclusion

We all love tasty foods, and also, we would like to experiment with different types of foods. When we want to have a choice between vegetarian and non-vegetarian food, people may find it easy to make a selection from non-vegetarian foods. But few know that there enough vegetarian foods that are equally tasty and nutritious like non-vegetarian foods. In fact, vegetarian meals have a lot of health benefits. I have introduced many delectable Asian foods in this book, particularly Indian vegetarian foods, which will be a new experience for many of our readers. The cooking processes are explained in a comprehensive manner with ingredients and measurements/units.

Vegetarians foods are the new world trend, especially among people who are into diet practices. Each recipe shows the calories, fat, protein, and carbs per serve, making people select the dish as per their preference. You will find various vegetable recipe techniques, using the pressure cooker, Instant Pot, non-stick skillet and saucepan, instead of traditional clay and ceramic utensils. I have consciously designed the recipes suitable for the modern kitchen. Your feedback is vital for me, and it will be a catalyst for me to research and write new vegetarian recipes. Please leave your comments and feedback. Thank you for buying the **Indian Veg Recipe** book.

Printed in Great Britain
by Amazon